The Hidden Author

SATHER CLASSICAL LECTURES

Volume Sixty

The Hidden Author

AN INTERPRETATION
OF PETRONIUS' *SATYRICON*

Gian Biagio Conte

Translated by Elaine Fantham

University of California Press

BERKELEY · LOS ANGELES · LONDON

University of California Press
Berkeley and Los Angeles, California

University of California Press, Ltd.
London, England

© 1996 by
The Regents of the University of California

Library of Congress Cataloging-in-Publication Data

Conte, Gian Biagio, 1941—
    The hidden author : an interpretation of Petronius' Satyricon /
Gian Biagio Conte.
        p.   cm.—(Sather classical lectures ; v. 60)
    Includes bibliographical references (p.   ) and index.
    ISBN 0-520-20715-7 (alk. paper)
    1. Petronius Arbiter. Satyricon. 2. Satire, Latin—History and
criticism. 3. Rome—In literature. I. Title. II. Series.
PA6559.C64   1996
873'.01—dc20   96-17101
                                                     CIP

Printed in the United States of America
9 8 7 6 5 4 3 2 1

Contents

Preface

The six chapters of this volume correspond to the six lectures I had the honor of delivering as Sather Professor at the University of California, Berkeley, in the spring of 1995. A few changes have been made to the version given in the Wheeler Auditorium and in Dwinelle Hall. These consist of sporadic additions, some bibliographic updates, and occasional second thoughts. As I have continued my studies, many ideas have become clearer, partly because of discussions I have had with friends and colleagues who were present at the lectures.

Since I am a philologist trained in precise interpretation, I must admit that when I was invited to present the Sather Classical Lectures, I felt apprehension about the nature of my task— to arouse the interest of an audience comprising not only classical philologists but also historians, archeologists, philosophers, anthropologists and scholars of comparative literature. This is why I have tried, so far as possible, to shun overspecialization, at least in the main text: I hope that Latin philologists, and those who may wish to follow me into the minutiae of single problems, will find what they need in the detailed information given in the notes. In any event, if I had decided to confront all the difficulties which I continue to find in reading the *Satyricon,* the corpus of notes would have run to hypertrophy.

The fame of Petronius' novel is mainly due to the episode—certainly possessing great appeal—often called "Trimalchio's Feast." But this episode is only a part of a larger contin-
uum. My interpretation started with the idea that our image of
the *Satyricon* will be a distorted one if Trimalchio is allowed to
lord it over the whole of Petronius' novel in the same way as he
is a tyrant over "the Feast." I would simply like to recall that
the fragmentary nature of the surviving text has conditioned
our perception of Petronius' work by overstressing its realistic
features. Thus modern readers are induced to extend the exceptional mimetic effort localized in the "Cena" to the whole of the
Satyricon simply because it is the only portion of the text to
have come down to us intact. I believe that the *Satyricon*'s impact on its first readers must have been rather different. In my
interpretation I have tried to limit this bias by looking at the
global structure of the text. My starting point is a conviction
that the true targets of Petronius' story were the *scholastici,*
made objects of derision by the ironic strategy adopted by the
"hidden author." In my view this is the only way of retrieving
the overall meaning of the text—the "intentionality" that gov-
erns it. The author is lurking just outside the story, inviting his
readers to chuckle at the mania for grandeur of a declamatory,
scholastic culture. The aim of striking at the vanity of this culture explains why the author hid himself, preferring to hand
over his stage to degraded characters nourished on great literary
models. One can descry in the background, I believe, the out-
lines of the intellectual life of the early Empire.

I may to some extent have been subject to a professional vice.
My many years of studying poetic texts that adopt a high register have convinced me that the literary sublime—even if it is
mediated in this case by the indirect language of parody—is an
important key to an understanding of the *Satyricon*. The outcome has been a book arranged in two sections: the first three
chapters are dedicated to themes attached to the "sublime,"

whereas the other three deal with themes linked to the "anti-sublime." As will become apparent, this volume aims to achieve unity out of opposing forces, since the two aspects are complementary; they are, in fact, held together by a vigorous dialectic that dominates the whole text, supports it and coherently builds it up.

Besides being a great honor, it has also been a great pleasure to spend a semester at Berkeley. I was given an extraordinary welcome by my new colleagues, a phenomenon familiar to all those who have had the good fortune to be invited by that prestigious university. The Head of Department, Donald Mastronarde, has been extremely considerate to me and always eager to help, while Erich Gruen, Anthony Long, Ronald Stroud, Charles Murgia, John Ferrari, Mark Griffith and William Anderson have been good company every day—generous with their time, their cordial hospitality and their advice. I sincerely thank them. My gratitude goes to Thomas Rosenmeyer, a doyen I admire and to whom I owe many precious suggestions. Benjamin Hughes, a young and brilliant philologist, has been an invaluable assistant; on many occasions his intelligence and good will solved my problems as an outsider. I am also grateful to the graduate students who attended my seminar on the *Aeneid* for the privilege of allowing me to guide such a concentration of new talent.

This is an attempt to express my thanks to colleagues and friends at Berkeley. But quite a few friends helped me earlier, in Pisa, while this book was being drafted. As Mario Labate has been preparing an edition and a commentary on the *Satyricon* with me for several years, it was natural that he should be a precious helper: I have repeatedly discussed with him many of my current views on Petronius. The help of Rolando Ferri has been no less decisive, because he followed step by step all the stages this work has passed through. Of the pupils in my Pisan seminar on the *Satyricon,* which has claimed our attention over the last five years, Ernesto Stagni, Sergio Casali, Andrea Cucchiarelli, Marina Di Simone, Michela Mariotti, Lucia Galli and Federica Bessone have been among those who have contributed most.

I began writing this book three years ago when I was a guest of the Department of Classics at Princeton. Elaine Fantham, an accomplished scholar in Imperial Roman culture, has come to my aid on many occasions with her exceptional skills. But I owe her much more than this: I have greatly benefited from her generous offer to translate my Italian into English. From being an occasional *auxiliatrix* this made her the person I owe most to in the preparation of these Sather Lectures. At many points she has helped me to be clearer, sometimes more precise or to the point. Don Fowler, Richard Hunter and Glenn Most read this book in an almost definitive version, and their comments have led to a substantial number of improvements. If my last-minute additions have been given an elegant English form, that is due to an old Pisan friend, my colleague Anthony L. Johnson.

I would like to thank all these friends, even if many of them think they have already been rewarded—at least those who have confessed to me that they experienced great pleasure in being invited to reread with me this or that passage in the *Satyricon*. For this experience, they and I, all together, must feel gratitude to Petronius.

Pisa, September 1995
G. B. C.

CHAPTER ONE

The Mythomaniac Narrator
and the Hidden Author

Let me warn you at once that I am going to adopt a curious critical strategy: I shall be interpreting a complete sequence of the *Satyricon* as if it were part of a text written in a pathetic and elevated style. The reason will make itself clear, I think, as we proceed.

The narrator and protagonist Encolpius relates how the boy he loves, Giton, was carried off by his friend Ascyltus: this offense has bitterly wounded his pride. All alone now, the young man withdraws to the seashore and drowns his humiliation in lament: (81) *locumque secretum et proximum litori maestus conduxi. ibi triduo inclusus redeunte in animum solitudine atque contemptu verberabam aegrum planctibus pectus et inter tot altissimos gemitus frequenter etiam proclamabam* ("Sadly I rented a secluded place near the shore. Shutting myself in there for three days, as a sense of loneliness and humiliation reentered my heart, I beat my weary breast with blows and with groans from the depth of my heart I cried out aloud").

Achilles too had seen Briseis taken from him by the tyranny of Agamemnon and had withdrawn in offense to the seashore to weep and lament:[1] (*Iliad* 1.348–50) αὐτὰρ' Ἀχιλλεὺς /

---

1. Cf. P. G. Walsh, *The Roman Novel* (Cambridge, 1970), 36–37 (in general this book offers the most balanced introduction to the *Satyricon* currently

δακρύσας ἑτάρων ἄφαρ ἕζετο νόσφι λιασθείς, / θῖν ἔφ᾽ ἁλὸς πολιῆς, ὁρόων ἐπ᾽ ἀπείρονα πόντον· ("But Achilles weeping went and sat in sorrow apart from his companions beside the beach of the grey sea looking out on the infinite water"). It is easy for Encolpius, in a situation which has some features in common with that of Achilles, and so appears to be comparable to that hero's fate, to yield to the temptation of the epic-heroic model, and to feel himself not so different from Achilles, even to the extent of repeating his model's behavior. We shall see that this is a typical tendency—even an obsession—of the character who is our narrator.

Young Encolpius is a petty adventurer who gets his living by wandering aimlessly from place to place; but the pace of the action (that is, his adventures) is continually slowed down by the literary reflections of another Encolpius, the *scholasticus,*[2] victim of his own literary experiences, who naively exalts himself by identifying with heroic roles among the great mythical and literary characters of the past. The desire to be avenged on the traitor who took his lover will shortly provoke him to draw his

---

available). Translations of Homer throughout are those of R. Lattimore, *The Iliad of Homer* (Chicago, 1951) and *The Odyssey of Homer* (New York, 1965).

2. Since the designation *scholasticus* will recur frequently in this study, it requires an expanded definition. Properly speaking, *scholastici* were not only the pupils and the teachers of the rhetorical schools (cf. Virg. *Cat.* 5.4, Quint. *Inst.* 12.11.16; cf. also *Satyr.* 61.4), but also "men who spent most of their time in schools or in declamatory display" (M. Winterbottom, trans., *The Elder Seneca, Declamations,* 2 vols., [Loeb Classical Library, Cambridge, Mass., 1974], viii). Thus Encolpius and Agamemnon are called *scholastici* at *Satyr.* 61.4, but the "huge crowd of *scholastici*" who pour into the portico after hearing an extemporary declamation of someone who had heard Agamemnon's *suasoria* are identified as *iuvenes* (*Satyr.* 6.2).

As J. J. Winkler shows in a generically wide-ranging discussion, *Auctor & Actor: A Narratological Reading of Apuleius's The Golden Ass* (Berkeley, 1985), 160–65, the popular conception of such students as absentminded fools (cf. *Satyr.* 46.2: *prae litteras fatuum,* "made silly by education") led to the formation of a comic type, usually an elderly and unworldly buffoon, as early as Plutarch and Lucian in the first half of the second century.

sword—in the manner, naturally, of the heroic paradigm of high epic. Then suddenly, armed and out of his mind, he will take on the traits of Aeneas, raging as he frantically seeks his wife Creusa on the last night of Troy along all the streets of the burning city: (82.1) *mox in publicum prosilio furentisque more omnes circumeo porticus* ("soon I leap out into the open and search all the porticoes like a madman"), a scene to be compared with the whole sequence of *Aeneid* 2.749–73.[3]

Let me warn you also that we shall be talking simply and systematically of the "hidden author" (Petronius) and the "narrating character" or "mythomaniac narrator," that is, Encolpius in his romanticizing infatuation with literary myth. I have not set myself the wearying task of trying to construct tables of correspondence, to find out how Gérard Genette, Mieke Bal or Jaap Litvelt would have expressed the same idea. Naturally, each one would have found a different, and more complex, way of expressing it, and the terminology would have multiplied out of control. I was afraid that even in the attempt to rid myself of what was superfluous, I would be confronting a Lernaean Hydra: every "instance of focalization" amputated might result in two more threatening instances. So no tables, and no attempt to add a new language to the babel of narratological jargon. Narratology has been valuable, and it is essential to assimilate its most important contributions (Genette, and not just Genette; Greimas and his followers, on the other hand, have from the start done more harm than good). It has helped us, or rather taught us, to read a narrative text in a more rational way. Now we are facing a single text, and this is just what we want to do: read it rationally, and do this in a manner that is clear and direct. Narratological studies have been valuable to us: let us thank them and move on.

Let us go back to our analysis. The narrative strategy set

3. Cf. Walsh, 37.

in motion by our author (Petronius) ensures that the narrator (Encolpius) finds himself in a situation that can be interpreted according to an epic-heroic model. The young man *responds* by adapting himself to this model and claiming it as his own, that is, transforming himself into a "rhetorically" determined role. Having received the stimulus, or swallowed the narrative bait, Encolpius continues to live through the episodic sequence according to the restrictions imposed by the literary model. Once activated, the grand narrative model drives Encolpius to identify himself with a great literary role, that of Aeneas, to the point of losing his sense of reality and of the differences between them. In his mind reality itself will inevitably be interpreted within parameters laid down by the famous models. (But Petronius plays a subtle game: he does not force the models upon the reader's attention, but simply hints at them faintly through generic features, like vague suggestions of a direction to follow. Each model that he evokes is close enough to the narrative situation for some sort of comparison to be possible, but at the same time it must not be too near, to make sure the story does not lose its own narrative autonomy.)

In fact the process that swept Encolpius into this heroic self-identification had already begun before this: at the moment of uttering his indignant monologue against the two violators of the pact, Giton and Ascyltus, the model of the Trojan hero had taken possession of him. Thus his decision to be avenged (*sed non impune, nam:* "but they will never escape unscathed, for I . . . ") was inevitably modeled on the gesture of Aeneas, who again in the second book of the *Aeneid* gives way to heroic indignation and utters a tormented soliloquy condemning Helen to death. The guilty woman could not be allowed to return home as a triumphant queen unpunished after having caused the destruction of Troy (cf. *sceleratas sumere poenas:* "to exact punishment for crime" [576], *sumpsisse merentis laudabor poenas:* "I shall be praised for exacting due punishment" [586–

87]). Aeneas finished his soliloquy and rhetorical questions with the resolve of line 583, *non ita, namque* . . . : "Never, for I . . ."[4] Thus Encolpius, by exploiting the few common features of the two passages (in fact by exaggerating the nature of the events he is really experiencing), creates a pathetic melodrama from the banal material of his own daily affairs.

The great literary model provides ready-made a noble and solemn representation, the one dramatized version capable of giving a little meaning to the empty container that is the petty reality of the everyday. Such theatrical treatment is necessary to promote ordinary life in its narrow scope to the level of grandeur. The elevated literary model has been appropriated "melodramatically" by Encolpius in the sense that he is seeking enhanced significance for his own situation, that is, for his words and gestures. It is as though trivial affairs could acquire grandeur and importance purely by being experienced as theater: as though by giving theatrical voice to experience one could actually make sense of the indifference of reality.

It is precisely this literary aesthetic of excess that concerns us. What I have called the melodramatic mode is to be the focus of my analysis in describing the psychological constitution of the narrating character, Encolpius. He is never without a spurious pretense of drama, a misconceived tragicizing of experience. What we have here is simply a pretentious and illegitimate attempt at self-promotion.

If I speak of the melodramatic—and I am resorting deliberately to a metaphorical approximation—it is because this seems to me to describe the pathetic and grandiose manner in which ordinary events are lived and apprehended by Encolpius. What is melodramatic in him is the projection onto reality of exaggerated and theatrical emotional constructions. The narrating

4. See below, p. 4. Cf. F. I. Zeitlin, "Romanus Petronius: A Study of the 'Troiae Halosis' and the 'Bellum Civile,'" *Latomus* 30 (1971) 56–82, esp. 59 n. 1.

character lives his emotions, or rather expresses them, in the histrionic form of dreams. Literature lends him the background scenario with which to give meaning to his own experiences, his adventures (good and bad), his feelings and his passions.

For him great literature becomes a universe inhabited by suggestive myths, indeed it becomes the secularized mythology of a culture determined to seek out intense emotions which would otherwise be denied to it by immediate experience. Thus we have posturing and gesticulation instead of real actions. Indeed actions, when put to the test of fact, are often avoided and simply renounced: only true heroes are allowed to act. The absence of action is in fact guarantee enough of irony whenever the text invokes attitudes drawn from the high heroic literature. The level of representation predominates over the level of meaning. High—indeed the very highest—literary representations are transformed into invasive paradigms that consume every possible event like parasites, imposing themselves upon it and transferring it out of present reality.

It might seem that reality thus gains something, inasmuch as it is transposed to the level of myth. Instead reality in fact loses its real significance, since literary representation, with its own familiar codes, leads to excess and crushes beneath its weight every occurrence of real life. Reality is impersonated by literature; but the significances required by these excessive signifiers claim a sense that they cannot find. Literature, anthologized in overloaded showpieces, simply becomes a "rhetoric of excess."

These pathos-laden and assertive models presented a form of reality that already carried meaning and was capable of interpretation because of the paradigmatic nature of their representation. There is an excess of will in the narrating protagonist, a wistful "wanting to become" that entraps him, molding him to representations that are only mirages. To paraphrase the words of Schopenhauer, I would say that the World does not exist for him except as "Will and Representation." Literary and mythical representations are the superficial and immediate response with which the naive *scholasticus* fills his longing for grandeur and satisfies his need for sublimity.

In fact Encolpius simply listens to himself to gather those "echoes of a mighty soul," to quote the definition which Pseudo-Longinus gave to the literary sublime: ὕψος μεγαλοφροσύνης ἀπήχημα (9.2). It is as if his sensibility propelled him to share the resonance of the grand emotions produced by the sublime literature of the past which he had read and re-read at school. According to Pseudo-Longinus, the Sublime is a form of participation for anyone who experiences its grand effects, but of *passive* participation, since it is composed of *pathos*. And this *pathos* is also the passivity of the reader or listener: anyone who reads such powerful texts is possessed and carried away, since the sublime is like a "transport," *ekstasis*.

In this aesthetic, which privileges the reception of a text over its production, and is thus closer to the aesthetic of Plato than to the more formalist aesthetic of Aristotle, work and reader, text and soul seem two analogous things: but neither of the two has its own form or identity, since every text and every soul has a tendency to blend with other souls and other texts.[5] In Pseudo-Longinus the idea is implicit that the mind of the reader is the true seat of the sublime (1.4: "the sublime does not carry listeners to a state of persuasion but of exaltation"). This aesthetic can easily be understood if the effects of *hypsos* are displaced from the object (the text) onto the subject (the reader). The reader's mind is the place in which the effects of the sublime are manifest. The sublime reader described by Pseudo-Longinus takes himself, that is his own emotions, as text, and literature as a commentary on his own consciousness, on the emotions aroused in the soul and in the memory by reading the great

5. See P. H. Fry, *The Reach of Criticism: Method and Perception in Literary Theory* (New Haven and London, 1983).

artistic texts. The sublime, understood as the "echo of a noble mind" (9.2) is transferred from the text to the voice of its author, and from here to the mind of the reader, who as a result somehow takes the place of the author himself. In fact Pseudo-Longinus writes (7.2): "under the action of true sublimity, our mind is exalted as if by nature and, taking on some kind of noble impulse, is filled with joy and pride as if it had *itself created* what it has just heard."[6]

As a scholastic addict of these great texts, and naively stimulated by the example of the heroes who serve as models for his need for *megalopsychia*, Encolpius is an agglomerate of high-style heroic figures: an offended Achilles and an Aeneas in search of vengeance give shape to the gestures and thoughts of a would-be hero. But the sublime is limited to his presumptions, to the naive over-valuation of reality that he is living. *Phantasia* and the strong pathetic content of *hypsos* are not sufficient to raise his poor daily reality to the sphere of the ideal: suddenly reality takes its easy and frustrating revenge.

Encolpius, as we have said, imagines himself not only as Achilles possessed by *menis* for the theft of Briseis, but also as Aeneas in his quest to avenge the downfall of his people, and so he runs to hunt down the traitor Ascyltus to obtain satisfaction: *in publicum prosilio furentisque more omnes circumeo porticus* (82.1). A few moments before, having modeled his soliloquy on the *rhesis* of Aeneas confronting Helen, he had looked to the pathetic power of rhetorical questions. Virgil had made Aeneas

6. Cf. Quint. *Inst.* 8.2.21: *auditoribus etiam nonnullis grata sunt haec* (i.e., images of strong expressive force) *quae cum intellexerunt, acumine suo delectantur et gaudent, non quasi audierint, sed quasi invenerint.* Cf. also Ps.-Longin. 13.2–14.1: "many are posessed by a spirit that is not their own. It is like what we say of the Pythia at Delphi: she is in contact with the tripod beside the crevice that opens in the earth from which (as men say) a divine vapor is exhaled, and as a result she is impregnated with supernatural power and prophesies as if inspired. Similarly the genius of the ancients acts like a kind of oracular cavern, and emanations from it flow into the minds of their imitators."

say: *scilicet haec Spartam incolumis . . . / aspiciet partoque ibit regina triumpho? . . . occiderit ferro Priamus? . . . Dardanium totiens sudarit sanguine litus?* ("So shall this woman look on Sparta unharmed and move as queen in the triumph won? Shall Priam perish by the sword? Shall the Dardanian shore so often sweat with blood?"). Just so Encolpius finds himself saying: *effugi iudicium . . . ut inter <tot> audaciae nomina mendicus . . . iacerem desertus? et quis hanc mihi solitudinem imposuit? adulescens omni libidine impurus. . . . quid ille alter?* ("Did I escape trial to lie beggared and abandoned after so many instances of shamelessness? And who forced this solitude upon me? A young man polluted by every lust. . . . What of the other man?"). This might suggest the comment "self-interrogation and reply imitate the spontaneous outburst of passion." But this comment is not mine: it belongs to the anonymous author of *On the Sublime,* where he analyzes the effects produced by series of rhetorical questions upon the reader (18.2) and goes on to remark: "the figure of question and answer leads the listener to believe that each of the thoughts deliberately prepared is coming to birth *in the shock of the moment* and so deceives him." In short, in the sublime there is a confusion of art and nature, without one being able to say that art is reduced to nature or nature to art. Thus it is that through the voice of its narrator-protagonist, the *Satyricon* brings its narrative alive with pathetic colors. Representations that carry the aura of the grand epic tradition offer a model for stylized attitudes and gestures which bear the mark of the sublime. But here *hypsos,* because of the sheer incongruity of the situation, is inherently threatened by the risk of collapse. On each occasion only a little is needed to make Icarus in his lofty flight hurtle headlong into the deep sea of bathos.

Even the opening of the second phase of heroic impersonation (82.1: *haec locutus gladio latus cingor,* "thus having spoken I gird on my sword") is marked by a reminiscence of a typical epic formula used to pass from direct speech to action: *sic ore locutus, sic deinde locutus, ὡς εἰπών.*[7] *Gladio latus cingor* too recalls the epic formula used by Aeneas when arming himself in renewed search of a fight at *Aeneid* 2.671: *hic ferro accingor rursus.*

But immediately after this an additional comment puts the reader of the Petronian text on his guard: *et ne infirmitas militiam perderet, largioribus cibis excito vires* ("and so that weakness should not ruin my campaign I stimulate my strength with generous doses of food"). A prudent addition, rich in common sense—appropriate to *biologumena,* to everyday life—which would certainly have been suppressed in an epic or tragic situation. When has the outburst of heroic anger ever left room for sensible precautions of a practical nature, not to mention diet? The high tension of the scene sinks like a falling graph, and the comparative adjective *largioribus* (*cibis* alone is not enough) seems to increase the irony. But this is just a slight hint, a warning to the reader to alert him and to raise the suspicion that Encolpius is constructing his perceptions on a basis of illusion and mirages. The irony of the text here hints at the differentiation of functions coexisting in Encolpius as protagonist and as narrator: there is a tension between the acting and the narrating "I."[8]

Admittedly some suspicion had been aroused even before this, when the protagonist began his monologue of lament as he contemplated the sea. The young man had begun by rejecting his own fate in lofty sounding language: (81.3) *ergo me non ruina terra potuit haurire? non iratum etiam innocentibus mare?* ("So the earth could not sink and engulf me? Nor the sea, so of-

---

7. The formula *haec locutus* is repeated at *Satyr.* 94.12 and 140.13, and marks, as here, the conclusion of a display speech.

8. F. K. Stanzel, *Theorie des Erzählens* (Göttingen, 1982), 109–48, distinguishes successfully between the "experiencing 'I'" ("erlebendes Ich") and the "narrating 'I'" ("erzählendes Ich"). See also J. J. Winkler, *Auctor & Actor,* esp. 135–53.

ten angry even with the innocent?"). Here is the striving for a
fine and glorious death, one of those deaths that heroes and
heroines of myth invoke when they curse their own wretched
misfortune; Homer, Sophocles, Virgil, the *sermo tragicus* of
Seneca make free use of the formula, "may the earth swallow
me up," one that the anonymous *On the Sublime* would have
listed among the ὁμοτικὰ σχήματα (figures of oath).[9] But immediately after the solemn *obsecratio* of the narrator, the reader
discovers that the utterer of this tragic lament is (by his own express admission) only a poor common criminal: *effugi iudicium,
harenae imposui, hospitem occidi* ("I skipped court, cheated the
arena, killed my own host").[10] The gap between model and reality is conspicuous: the "Will and Representation" of grandeur
clash with the character's pettiness of personality. Encolpius'
fall is inevitable once the speech is matched to his real nature
and not to his pretenses: what fits him is *bathos,* not *hypsos.*

After this soliloquy, the narrative is ready to return all over
again to the height of the heroic register, and the stylistic graph
again soars upwards. Encolpius rushes around in a frenzy,
sword in hand: (82.2) *attonito vultu efferatoque nihil aliud
quam caedem et sanguinem cogito frequentiusque manum ad
capulum, quem devoveram, refero* ("with crazed and enraged
countenance I think only of slaughter and bloodshed, constantly

9. See A. S. Pease, *Aeneidos Liber Quartus* (Cambridge, Mass., 1935) on
Aen. 4.24.
10. A grievous catalogue of past misfortunes in cumulative asyndeton
seems a typical feature of the laments of heroes in the Greek novel: cf. Charit.
4.4.9 "I was sold, I was a slave, I was in fetters" (Chaereas' letter to
Callirhoe); 5.5.2 (Callirhoe's words to Dionysius): "only this was lacking to
my woes, to be dragged before a tribunal! I have died, I have been buried, they
violated my tomb, I have been sold, I have been a slave, and look, in the name
of Fortune, now they are dragging me into court!"; Ach. Tat. 5.18 (Leucippe's
letter to Clitophon): "for your sake I left my mother and agreed to entrust myself to chance; for your sake I was shipwrecked and fell into the hands of pirates; for your sake I was offered as an expiatory victim and twice suffered
death; for your sake I have been sold, I have been assaulted with iron fetters, I
have wielded the hoe, have scratched the earth, and endured the lash."

reaching my hand to the hilt I had once cursed"). This is not the representation of a frenzied young lover: it would be too much even for one of the quarrelsome and infatuated figures of elegy. This is nothing short of Achilles, and precisely that Achilles who appears in a showpiece of the Homeric text, at the very outbreak of the *menis* that introduces the story of the *Iliad*. "And the anger came on Peleus' son, and within his shaggy breast the heart was divided two ways, pondering whether to draw from beside his thigh the sharp sword, driving away all those who stood between and kill the son of Atreus, or else to check the spleen within and keep down his anger. Now as he weighed in mind and spirit these two courses and was drawing from its scabbard the great sword (194: ἕλκετο δ' ἐκ κολεοῖο μέγα ξίφος), Athene descended from the sky." Or if you prefer a second line of approach, Encolpius here is also Virgil's Aeneas as he sees Helen in the conflagration of Troy and thinks of killing her. In fact, the scene of the Trojan hero seized by the madness of vengeance is itself modeled on this crucial passage from the *Iliad*.[11] Once again I refer you to the disputed, but in my view authentic, Helen episode in the second book of the *Aeneid* (567–91), the passage noted above in connection with Encolpius' monologue.

Let us take the opportunity to note the complex way in which the extravagant narrator of the *Satyricon* cross-fertilizes and superimposes the different models of the literary sublime:[12]

11. See G. B. Conte, *The Rhetoric of Imitation* (Ithaca and London, 1986), 196–207.

12. The different models of the literary sublime (memorable scenes from the great poetic tradition and also from great oratory) function as behavioral models for the character but also as literary models for the narrator: this empowers the aspects of naïveté and mythomania which govern Encolpius' attitudes. But obviously, from my perspective, we must assume the unity of the character-narrator, the "agent 'I'" and the "narrating 'I'" (even if occasionally one can perceive a slight tension between the two functions filled by Encolpius; these tensions I have not failed to note here and there). In this respect I disagree with R. Beck (see below, n. 28).

anthology pieces, powerful and memorable passages, scenarios and postures of grand effect which come to the memory under the goad of emotion. Often there is a kind of homology of sense which links together these accumulated literary suggestions. But what most of all unites them is their grandiosity of tone.

Encolpius feels himself to be the enraged Achilles, but his come-uppance is already lurking in the text. *Dum attonito vultu efferatoque nihil aliud quam caedem et sanguinem cogito:* this is a blatant exaggeration. The character's expression is what is used on stage to signify heroic fury; the external attitude has all the emphasis of tragic pathos, the gestures and words that represent them are the very same that mark a "mad scene" in theatrical performance. The rhetoric of excess, of which I spoke earlier, has been mobilized to create an expressive intensification of feeling. But now that *hypsos* has met its target, suddenly every prop is pulled away and the *mise en scène* crumbles, exposing to view the wistful world of illusions. No need for the intervention of a god to rescue the hero; much less will do. A passing soldier sees the young man is armed and looks at his feet: Encolpius is wearing civilian *phaecasia,* fancy white shoes such as were in fashion in imperial Rome among Greek philosophers and *scholastici.*[13] Once his improper dress has been spotted, all Encolpius' warlike ardors are quenched: he goes back to being a poor "declaimer," infatuated and betrayed, who can invoke anger, the sword and a heroic vengeance only in self-deception.

That the rhetoric of excess contains the risk of its own collapse is a principle maintained by a critic whose thought we

---

13. *Phaecasia* (cf. *Satyr.* 67.4: *phaecasiae* with a different gender), so called because of their white color, were worn at Alexandria by priests or gymnasiarchs (Appian *Bell. Civ.* 5.11, Plut. *Ant.* 33.7). In the first century of our era they spread to Rome (where they were originally seen as typical of the dress of Greek philosophers: cf. Sen. *Ben.* 7.21, *Epist.* 113.1) and were worn especially by women and young men. Cf. E. Schuppe, *RE* 19.2, 1561–62, s.v. Φαικάσιον.

have followed as a guideline throughout these pages. The anonymous *On the Sublime* remarks (15.8) that "mad scenes" please declaimers who abandon themselves like a persecuted Orestes to visions (φαντασίαι) of Furies and do not understand that Orestes himself has the right to these displays of frenzy because he is truly mad.[14] And Encolpius too finally realizes his own madness, when at the end (after the tension of the sublime has slackened) he gradually comes out of his state of exaltation and thinks with gratitude in his heart of the lucky encounter with the soldier who brought him round to sanity: (82.4) *immo praecisa ultione retro ad deversorium tendo paulatimque temeritate laxata coepi grassatoris audaciae gratias agere* ("Indeed once my revenge was forestalled I made for my lodging and gradually as my rashness wore off I began to give thanks for the fellow's nerve"). Here again we face the contextual tensions I noted above between the "I" of the agent and the narrating "I": with hindsight, the narrator reinterprets the soldier's intervention as what luckily saved him from his ravings.

Once the pretenses of sublimity to which the mythomaniac narrator aspired have collapsed, *bathos* gapes beneath him, and the graph of stylistic levels plunges headlong. But immediately the narrative once again starts to reach for a new elevation of narrative tone. Encolpius comes to a picture gallery full of Greek Old Masters (chapter 83), representations of love scenes painted by Zeuxis, Protogenes, Apelles. Enchanted by the fame of the pictures, he gives himself over to a great transport of emotions. These scenes present examples of the passion which gods and demigods have felt for beautiful young men: Apollo for Hyacinth, Jupiter for Ganymede, the Naiad for the young

14. 15.8: . . . ὡς ἤδη νὴ Δία καὶ οἱ καθ' ἡμᾶς δεινοὶ ῥήτορες, καθάπερ οἱ τραγῳδοί, βλέπουσιν Ἐρινύας καὶ οὐδὲ ἐκεῖνο μαθεῖν οἱ γενναῖοι δύνανται, ὅτι ὁ λέγων Ὀρέστης [. . .] φαντάζεται ταῦθ' ὅτι μαίνεται; see P. Cosci, "Per una ricostruzione della scena iniziale del *Satyricon*," MD 1 (1978) 201–207, esp. 206 and n. 17.

Hylas whom she stole from Heracles. These are paintings of great artistic value, but we barely see them because they are communicated to us by the heart rather than by the gaze of Encolpius. He himself admits to being struck by the *pictura animorum,* "depiction of souls"—the perfect rendering of feelings which he knows how to recognize in the painted characters. What he tells us is above all his reaction of *bouleversement,* typical of the connoisseur set in front of great art, a sort of "sacred shudder" (83.1: *non sine quodam horrore tractavi*) in full harmony with his own state of mind, an exalted empathy that turns into an actual gesture of adoration: *etiam adoravi.*

The narrator claims he has been seized by the vivid reality of the likenesses (*ad similitudinem* and, a little above, *cum ipsius naturae veritate certantia,* "competing with the truth of nature herself"), but the realistic objectivity which he claims is only a cloak behind which he projects himself subjectively into emotions that make him lose his sense of the situation. He thinks back to his own sufferings in love and voices aloud his own lament (*exclamavi*): "then Love affects even the gods!" *ergo Amor etiam deos tangit.* It is at this moment that an imposing figure, an old man with a dignified but distressed appearance, enters the gallery and approaches the excited young man.

The narrative situation belongs to one of the most traditional categories. The words uttered aloud by Encolpius are a signal that lays bare the workings of the textual construct. They are just close enough to remind us of the words of Aeneas hidden in a cloud and deeply moved as he looks upon the scenes represented on the temple of Juno at Carthage. Recognizing himself and his own tragedy as a defeated Trojan among the paintings of the *Troiae Halosis,* he weeps and cries out: *sunt lacrimae rerum et mentem mortalia tangunt,* "there are tears for such events and human fate touches the heart" (*Aen.* 1.462). At this point in the heroic Virgilian model too, while Aeneas was being moved by his own fate, queen Dido entered the scene: *haec dum*

Dardanio Aeneae miranda videntur, / dum stupet obtutuque haeret defixus in uno, / regina ad templum, forma pulcherrima Dido, / incessit . . . , "while these things seemed so marvelous strange to Trojan Aeneas, while he was stunned and held fast in continuing gaze, the queen, Dido most noble in beauty, approached" (*Aen.* 1.494–97).[15] But it is not just the situation as a whole that repeats itself (Petronius tends to use only a few major *structural* elements in order to evoke a famous literary model), there are also *linguistic* elements that serve to reinforce the allusion. In particular the expressions that open the two passages seem noteworthy; compare *Aeneid* 1.455–56: *artificumque manus inter se operumque laborem / miratur*[16] ("he marvels at the hands [styles] of the craftsmen working together, and the toil of the work") with *Satyricon* 83.1: *in pinacothecam veni vario genere tabularum mirabilem. nam et Zeuxidos manus vidi . . .* ("I came into a gallery marvelous with various styles of paintings: for I saw Zeuxis' hands [style] and . . ."). In both passages the admiration of the spectator and the "hand" of the artist (a rare technical use) are equally prominent.

Let us begin with some provisional reflections, which we shall later try to fill out with further details of interpretation. In brief, there is in the tradition of ancient literary rhetoric a narrative structure which presents (first phase) a character viewing an artistic representation, generally a painting. This viewing arouses (second phase) both emotions and reflections. The process of identification set in motion culminates in the arrival of another character who enters into dialogue with the person

15. Cf. Zeitlin, "Romanus Petronius," 60.

16. *Inter se* seems the correct reading: Madwig's conjecture *intra se* (with *miratur*) is probably unhelpful. R. G. Austin, *P. Vergili Maronis Aeneidos Liber Primus* (Oxford, 1971), *ad loc.* is convincing: "The phrase is loosely appended adjectivally to *artificum;* cf. 2.453f. 'pervius usus / tectorum inter se Priami'. There was a common effort on the part of the *artifices,* each doing his best (cf. DServius 'inter se certantium')."

viewing the images (third phase). These are the three constitutive elements of the structure in question. We can treat it as something like a Warburgian *Pathosformel,* a scheme both psychological and narrative, a pathetic stereotype, a representation at once conventional but also endowed with powerful emotional content. Curtius might well have defined it as a *topos,* as he did for many similar constructs, in the sense that it is a clearly categorized unit of discourse.

So, in the *Satyricon,* the narrative bait leads Encolpius to put himself into a set situation with all the familiar characteristics of *déjà vu:* the narrator adopts a role which has been rhetorically programmed. The patterns in which he perceives his situation are those imposed by the famous narrative model. Losing all sense of the differences involved, Encolpius sees himself as Aeneas at Carthage. In the *Aeneid* the situation has the same structural features, in the same three phases. Aeneas views the tragic representations of the temple of Juno, just as Encolpius in the *Satyricon* views the pictures of unrequited love in the gallery (and let us not forget that in the ancient world many collections of paintings were attached, as were libraries, to temples and cult buildings).[17] Moved by the scenes which deal with his own story, Aeneas utters the lament, *mentem mortalia tangunt* (1.462), that is now reworked in Encolpius' words, *amor etiam deos tangit* (the narrator's sufferings in the *Satyricon* are in fact due to love).[18] While Aeneas gazes and gives vent to his emo-

17. Cf. P. Friedländer, *Johannes von Gaza und Paulus Silentiarius, Kunstbeschreibungen Justinianischer Zeit* (Leipzig and Berlin, 1912), 48 n. 1, citing also L. Friedländer, *Darstellungen aus der Sittengeschichte Roms in der Zeit von Augustus bis zum Ausgang der Antonine,* vol. II, Leipzig, 1872–1873³, 163–64, and Cic. *Verr.* 4.55. Note that a few chapters later Eumolpus, stoned by the audience which had been forced to hear his poetic improvisation on the *Troiae Halosis,* is said to flee out of the temple (clearly the place in which he had met Encolpius and recited his verse): (90) *operuit caput extraque templum profugit.*

18. Cf. Ov. *Am.* 3.9.2: *tangunt magnas tristia fata deas.*

tion in lament, the queen Dido appears before him; just so Eumolpus appears before Encolpius, who is lamenting as he identifies himself with the representations.

In short, as an admirer of sublime representations, Encolpius projects himself into the noble model of the Trojan hero. Consequently, and inevitably, the new character who is introduced also takes on noble and grandiose attitudes, to match queen Dido as she appeared before Aeneas intent on viewing the heroic scenes of Juno's temple. This is how Eumolpus, in keeping with Encolpius' expectations, can seem to him a figure full of mysterious fascination and disturbing grandeur: (83.7) *ecce autem . . . intravit pinacothecam senex canus, exercitati vultus et qui videretur nescio quid magnum promittere . . .* ("then lo! a grizzled old man entered the picture gallery, with distressed expression, and a look promising some great mystery").[19]

This rhetorical narrative structure, which we might label "first party gazing at a picture when the arrival of a second party provides its illustration," must have been typical of the expository technique of the novel, as we can reconstruct it from later instances where such scenarios often mark a new phase of the action. Right at the beginning of Achilles Tatius' novel, *Leucippe and Clitophon,* two visitors meet in front of the great picture of Europa carried off by the bull, which stood in the temple of Astarte at Sidon. The first man is still gazing at the representation—a triumph of love that he, like Encolpius, is led to compare with his own fate—when he meets another young man who turns out to be an expert on the subject of the picture: this man will be the narrator of the novel's real story.[20]

19. See below, chapter 2, p. 40.
20. On ecphrasis as pictorial description in general, see (apart from P. Friedländer, 1–103, and E. Norden, *P. Vergilius Maro Aeneis Buch VI* [Leipzig and Berlin, 1957⁴], 120–22), J. Palm, "Bemerkungen zur Ekphrase in der griechischen Literatur," *Kungliga Humanistiska Vetenskapssamfundet i Uppsala* (1965–1966) 108–211, S. Goldhill, "The Naive and Knowing Eye:

A similar function is provided by the same scenario as an opening device in Longus' *Daphnis and Chloe:* the story of Daphnis and Chloe will develop as a transcription *sub specie narrationis* of the subject of a painting. The narrator, finding himself in a grove sacred to the Nymphs, gazes upon a picture representing scenes of happy rustic life—streams, flowering trees and gentle shepherds, sheep and goats suckling newly born babes. He is so charmed by the beauty of the images that he decides to turn them into a story (but there are also pirates and brigands in the picture, as necessary ingredients of the future romance).[21]

We see then that the stereotype which the Greek novel of love and adventure exploits is basically a lively narrative structure that normally serves to advance the narrated action and gather together the new materials of the intrigue. In fact, as we said, this scenario, precisely because of its inherent dramatic qualities, met the requirements of every kind of theater, which could use it as a natural device to bring new characters on stage. The Greek novel (even before Achilles Tatius and Longus) certainly made repeated use of this scenario as a helpful narrative procedure. It was exploited like so many other procedures that properly belonged to the elevated literary genres and were then recycled without scruple by novelistic forms of writing. Such a

---

Ecphrasis and the Culture of Viewing in the Hellenistic World," in S. Goldhill and R. Osborne, edd., *Art and Text in Ancient Greek Culture* (Cambridge, 1994), 197–223. For the use of ecphrases in romances, see O. Schissel von Fleschenberg, "Die Technik des Bildeinsatzes," *Philologus* 72 (1913) 83–114; S. Bartsch, *Decoding the Ancient Novel: The Reader and the Role of Description in Heliodorus and Achilles Tatius* (Princeton, 1989); M. Fusillo, *Il romanzo greco: Polifonia ed eros* (Venezia, 1989), 83–90; A. Billault, *La création romanesque dans la littérature grecque à l'époque impériale* (Paris, 1991), 245–65.

21. Cf. also the temple scene in Philostratus' *Life of Apollonius of Tyana,* discussed by D. P. Fowler, "Even Better than the Real Thing: A Tale of Two Cities," forthcoming in J. Elsner, ed., *Art and Text in the Roman World* (Cambridge).

complex process of reuse and "depreciation" can be seen everywhere in the Greek novel, which may be viewed as the final
catchment basin into which countless different literary streams
were channeled.[22]

But in the context of a novel the "scene of the pictures"
would not have had the full charge of pathos which it carried
in Virgil's treatment, where its function was to introduce the
"tragic" character of Dido. On the other hand, it is just this pathetic tone that Encolpius would like to find in the gallery scene,
as if he had forgotten that the discourse of the novel had most
probably already appropriated it (given the hybrid nature of the
novel which, in its undiscriminating tendency to welcome het-
erogeneous material, greatly favored the *ekphrasis* of epic origin). We can be sure that in Encolpius' case the scenario is not
merely a procedure of narrative technique but one carrying
great emotional power: the young man surrenders himself to
outpourings of intense pathos.

The mere chance of returning to an elevated and heroic situation leads Encolpius to interpret the wretched reality he is experiencing in terms of a noble and pathetic *mise en scène*. Con-
centrating on the surface of events, the narrator becomes
protagonist of an enhanced and emotional drama. The gap between the level of representation and the level of signification is
virtually bridged. The activation of sublime models aims to give
events significance by strengthening the emotions and putting
them on display, no longer as moments and actions of real life
but as rhetorical gestures.

Encolpius is thinking of some of the main stereotypes of high
literature: if reality offers him a detail (or an appearance) of this
kind, it is enough to make him "fall" into the complete stereotype. So his illusions are aroused at once, and become—from
the point of view of the narrative form—expectations of very

22. Fusillo, *Il romanzo greco,* 25–42, 68–83.

familiar patterns of action. But the naive narrator's exaltation is again doomed to disappointment. The stereotype of "the spectator of pathetic pictures at the moment when a great character enters" is discredited by the sequel. Eumolpus, the new arrival, does not match the expectations aroused by his presentation (*ecce autem, ego dum cum ventis litigo, intravit pinacothecam senex canus, exercitati vultus et qui videretur nescioquid magnum promittere*). He begins a highly pretentious speech, posing as a tormented and austere sage (83.7–84.4), but the sample he offers of his experiences reveals the base carnality of his real nature: the anecdote of the "Pergamene boy" destroys any possible illusion of grandeur provoked by his entrance.

And the text itself (as we have been able to see above in similar cases where the text gave advance notice of the deflation of the sublime) offers us signals. This time there are two: *ego dum cum ventis litigo* ("while I was quarreling with the winds") and *qui videretur nescio quid magnum promittere* ("a look promising some great mystery"). The first signal warns the reader that Encolpius is engaged in one of his usual tirades, a false and melodramatic emotionalism:[23] a fall in the graph of values and the absurdity which ensues are just around the corner. The second signal, still more explicitly, takes the reader inside the mind of the narrator who is victim of his own illusions, ready to let his expectations develop on the lines of the elevated model; the *bathos* is going to be as great as the *nescio quid magnum*. (Here is another case in which the text itself prepares the reader for the drop in level by suggesting a tension between the narrating "I" and "I" as agent.)

Behind the protagonist's narrative we meet the "hidden au-

23. "To quarrel with the winds" in the sense of vainly surrendering to passionate laments (of anger, love, grief) is a stereotyped formulation used here with some irony: the wind carries away the outbursts of lovers by scattering their words. Cf. the long list of passages in A. Otto, *Sprichwörter und sprichwörtliche Redensarten der Römer* (Leipzig, 1890 [= Hildesheim, 1962]), 364–65, s.v. *ventus* 2.

thor," who is also listening, along with the reader, to Encolpius'
narration—and, along with the reader, is smiling at it. Behind
the naive narrator who in speaking of "I" exposes himself and
his desires, an agreement is being reached between the author
and the reader of the text. Both are bound in a close complicity. The words of the soldier assailing the armed and raging
Encolpius, at the moment when his heroic illusions and pretenses of literary sublimity are destroyed, provide the reader
with a direct link to the values proposed by the *auctor absconditus*. The reader cannot help adopting the *bona mens,* that
common sense which is so often invoked in the *Satyricon* as the
significant missing element.

I have described as the "hidden author" the implied self-
image that Petronius creates as author of his text. The ideal
reader too, by forming exactly this image of the author, that is
by agreeing to it, takes shape in the text as a set of values in opposition to those of Encolpius and closer to normality. By making faces as it were behind the narration of Encolpius, the author first ensures that the protagonist and narrator reveals
himself and his own naïveté and then leaves him without the
protective illusions that the narrator has constructed for himself: in this way he secures for himself the reader's conniving
response.

In every respect (that is, intelligence, morality, emotion) the
two, author and narrator, are voices in competition. One voice,
exposed, carries the narrative, expressing and interpreting it;
the other, like a counter-voice, reaches us only indirectly: it
functions like an external frame, the only valid code of reference for evaluation. The two voices are kept forcefully apart, if
only because Encolpius is kept far from every kind of normal
behavior and every value that a sensible author could reasonably expect to be shared by his readers. The result of this dis-
tancing is precisely an "unacceptable" narrative. I mean that
the norms proposed and exemplified by the protagonist and

narrator through his words and deeds are in conflict with the norms claimed for himself by the "hidden author," which he expects to be understood by the readers of his work.

It is generally agreed that the rhetoric of narrative develops its effects through the relation set up between the narrator and the story, not to mention between the narrator and his audience or readers. But if the narrative situation is complicated by refractions and ambiguities, this will generate irony. Irony is simply the outcome of a disparity between what is understood and what is known. In every situation in which someone knows or perceives more (or less) than another it is inevitable that irony either lies in wait or openly flaunts itself.

The meaning of a text is functionally bound to the reader's reactions and the reader's reactions are the true object of the whole strategy of signification set in motion by the text.[24] In front of a narrator who tells his tale in the "I" form (even if it is perceived as a *fiction*) the reader must react by accepting the truth of the account just given to him. Indeed we could say that the first person narrative conveys an inherent quality of verisimilitude and the capacity to convince based on the pretense that it offers firsthand experiences and knowledge: the tangible truth of eye-witness testimony.[25]

But on the other hand first person narration, at least potentially—precisely because it is connected to an obviously subjective situation[26]—is open to the risk of not possessing full objectivity, and thus of not being entirely reliable. So Encolpius, the

24. Cf. D. Goldknopf, "The Confessional Increment: A New Look at the I-Narrator," *Journal of Aesthetics and Art Criticism* 28 (1969) 13–21.

25. Compare the observations of A. Scobie, *Aspects of the Ancient Romance and its Heritage: Essays on Apuleius, Petronius and the Greek Romance* (Meisenheim am Glan, 1969), 9–29; *More Essays on the Ancient Romance and its Heritage* (Meisenheim am Glan, 1973), 35–46, 53–63.

26. See J. Lintvelt, *Essai de Typologie Narrative: Le "Point de vue", théorie et analyse* (Paris, 1981), 90–93; but see also G. Genette, *Nouveau Discours du Récit* (Paris, 1983), 52; Fusillo, *Il romanzo greco,* 159–60.

scholastic addict of myth, the naive character obsessed with models of great literature that he uses as parameters of interpretation for the events of daily life, also wants to be a sincere and trustworthy narrator; but he is certainly a "mythomaniac narrator." I mean this in the sense that even if he does not consciously intend to falsify the narrative, he lacks the ability to keep separate in his account the level of mythical fantasy, inspired by literature, and the level of events around him. The rhetorical function of the mythomaniac "I" narrative is not to discredit the whole complex of reality, but only to filter it, to bring it about that reality is perceived through figures that at times disguise it in the unbecoming rhetoric of sublimity, then finally expose it in all its bare invincible materialism.

The mere fact that the reader of the *Satyricon* is set in front of a dramatized narrator distinct from the author (the "hidden author"), a narrator who narrates in the first person and with a responsible voice—and in a fictional situation mimicking real life—automatically entails a divergence in understanding. Hence the possibility of establishing the ironic nature of the narration. The sophisticated narrative form of the Petronian novel plays precisely on the clear distinction between author and narrator. Irony is generated as a function of the disparity between the points of view activated in the narrative. From this disparity the text derives different kinds of effect. The reader is led to identify himself not with the protagonist but with the hidden author; indeed he feels a strong sense of superiority which the ironic author exploits as a narrative strategy precisely in order to make the reader his accomplice.

It is no exaggeration to say that the decisive effect in the Petronian narrative is provided by this first person narration: the fact that the entire account is mediated through the narrating voice of an "I," naive victim of events constructed at his expense, is the product of a rhetorical strategy which in this way substantially distorts the meaning of the narrative. This is the

powerful device that conditions the whole operation of irony in
the *Satyricon*. If I insist so much on this point it is because too
often criticism has treated (and sometimes wants to go on treating) the *Satyricon* as a real satire, failing to keep distinct the
persona of the narrator and that of the author. Thus Encolpius
would become simply an eye borrowed by the author, an eye
that fixed itself with pitiless wit on rich and vicious *heredipetae*.
Admittedly, we have now learned to distinguish between author
and narrator, but without being willing to give up looking here
and there in the text for the direct presence of the author (who
would resurface, voicing himself in occasional comments, in
ironic personal observations). But who decides where to find
the speaking author, and where the author is letting the narrator speak instead?[27]

I know that it seems to all of us that the sun revolves around
the earth, as it seemed to Ptolemy, but to save "the appearances," Ptolemy was forced to construct an ingenious cosmo-
logical theory: epicycles and unusual revolutions were the complicated and artificial remedy which he used to confront the
difficulties of a theory that partly conflicted with observations.
The cosmography of the *Satyricon* can only gain if the narrating
"I" is put at its center; this is the mythomaniac protagonist
Encolpius, the little sun around whom revolves the entire narra-

27. A model case, just because it is extreme, is the notorious lines 132.15
quid me constricta spectatis fronte Catones etc., a passage which on the surface seems fully qualified to be an *apologia ex voce auctoris*. Instead, here too,
there are hints which enable us to restore this statement to the "character" of
the persona who takes the stance of narrator of a *novae simplicitatis opus* and
is now ready to confront his countless detractors (according to the topos of
poetic self-defense). Mythomaniac narrator that he is, he has just compared
himself to figures from mythology (Ulysses and Oedipus), and now, in verse,
he refers to Epicurean doctrine with such vulgar crudity ("Epicurus as enco-
miast of sexual pleasure as the only goal of life") that it is quite impossible to
see a direct intervention of the author Petronius behind these absurd utterances (but cf. below, chapter 6, pp. 187–90). See the useful critical compila-
tion of P. Soverini, "Il problema delle teorie retoriche e poetiche di Petronio,"
in *ANRW* 2.32.3 (1985), 1772–79.

tive system. The Copernican position, so to speak, has the advantage of being simpler and more economical, inasmuch as its explanation of things is single and elementary.

I believe that had he actually wished to, the Almighty could have constructed a universe as complicated as the Ptolemaic one, and probably one even more satisfying for the scholar who had to study it. But this is of no use to the man of scientific knowledge. The scientist must construct the simplest possible cosmology, one which explains data and problems in the most linear and economical fashion. This is true for us too as interpreters of the *Satyricon,* forced to accept in all its force the elementary simplicity of Encolpio-centrism. Everything makes sense if we accept that the narrator and protagonist is the *only* mediator of the narrative.[28] With his naïveté and school-boy enthusiasms he is the distorting filter interposed between the invisible author and the narrative. Consequently the physiognomy of the implicit and ironizing author (whom I call the "hidden author") can only be reconstructed *in reverse,* by working it out indirectly from the manifest forms of discourse, i.e., by applying critical correction each time to the narrator's naïveté. This is the oblique method by which irony and humor operate in the *Satyricon.* As a deliberate strategy, the author refuses to play a direct role in the account, preferring to make himself a de-

28. The nearest position to mine is probably that well maintained by R. Beck, "The *Satyricon*: Satire, Narrator and Antecedents," *MH* 39 (1982) 206–14, even if I believe the differences are not insignificant. Beck also distinguishes between "experiencing 'I'" and "narrating 'I,'" but the difference between the two functions is not, in my opinion, fully comparable to the one set in motion by the irony of Ovid's elegy (cf. esp. 213–14 and n. 20). In Ovid the double register of voices and the consequent effect of the unmasking of fictions is a meta-literary trait (cf. what I have written in *Genres and Readers* [Baltimore, 1993], 45–52); in Petronius the irony is entrusted to the complicity of the hidden author and his ideal reader who watch together (with a strong sense of superiority) the misadventures and disillusionment of the narrator and protagonist. Useful observations can be found in C. A. Knight, "Listening to Encolpius: Modes of Confusion in the *Satyricon*," *University of Toronto Quarterly* 58 (1988–1989) 335–54.

tached external observer, like the reader whose complicity he is
seeking.

Of course we must believe that in terms of narrative tenses,
there is a gap in the *Satyricon* between the narrated Encolpius
and Encolpius as narrator. The man who sees is the "agent I,"
the man who speaks is the "narrating I"; but the man who
speaks tells the story *after* he has experienced it, at a distance in
time, as if he were a repentant narrator, or at least one now
made aware of his own failings as a mythomaniac narrator
through the constant disappointment of his concrete experiences. Situated at the time of formulation, the narrator Encolpius verbalizes what the character Encolpius has seen in the
time of the story; the narrator (even if he speaks *ex post*) has the
same eyes as those of the person in action, but it is still true that
his new point of view often imposes itself upon the old. Thus an
ironic tension is generated when the "deferred" narrator begins
to talk with hindsight about the vicissitudes of the naive character Encolpius prone to illusions. This ironic tension reproduces
on a small scale the detachment with which the hidden author
beholds his narrating character. But the real Master of the
Game is the author: narrator of the narrator, he is also a plain
spectator of events and of Encolpius' ridiculous illusions; by
adapting himself to an external position he loses nothing of the
game he has invented. He is a lazy player, who simply sets his
traps and waits to laugh when his victim falls into them.

The secret of all this narrative architecture lies behind the linear simplicity of a tale in which Encolpius is set up front-stage
as the "homodiegetic" narrator telling his own tale: he tells the
story to which he belongs, he sees everything, and every character moves within his field of vision. He can carry on the surface
of his narrative, with the greatest possible openness, all the
ideas, the judgments, the associations of his own mind. He sees
everything, but he cannot see himself. Only the author, situated
outside the narrative, like his accomplice the reader, can see the

narrator with the eye of a divine (and ironic) spectator. The narrator and protagonist obviously cannot see himself from outside. If he wants to present himself, he must inevitably watch himself in a mirror. That mirror is myth, the series of myths evoked, in which he reflects his image and so shows himself to himself and reveals himself indirectly to the readers.

In short we have a mythomaniac narrator and an ironic author. On one side a narrator who continually falls victim to his desires of heroic self-promotion, on the other an author who feeds him situations that can be elevated to the sublime. Conniving with the author's strategy, the reader feels all the incongruity of these frenzies (inasmuch as the character who indulges in them is quite unworthy). In these preciosities and melodramatic presumptions of Encolpius, Petronius wants to bring to light the constitutive operation of a genre: the novel of love and adventure.[29] Here indeed the tendency to pathetic monologue, the exaltations and extravagant gestures of characters, are at home: it is here that *Tragoedia* becomes synonymous with "declamations, impassioned tirades."[30]

But these elements of the sublime that have already found their way into the romantic novel assume in the *Satyricon* the form of exaggerated stereotypes: significantly, the mouthpieces for these sublime instances are now schoolmen, *scholastici*. (We shall see that this is the period of the spread of rhetorical themes, *zetemata*, practical exercises, and in the *Cena, quaestiones conviviales* as well.)[31] The text of Petronius simply transcribes some *Pathosformeln*, showpieces and memorable moments originating in great epic and tragic texts, anthologized and set side by side so as to produce declamations for effect.

29. All these novels, together with the most important fragments, are translated in B. P. Reardon, ed., *Collected Ancient Greek Novels* (Berkeley, 1989).

30. Cf. Ach. Tat. 6.4.4, 8.1.5, Heliod. 1.3.2, 2.4.1, Xenoph. Ephes. 3.1.4. See on this the fine observations of Fusillo, *Il romanzo greco*, 35.

31. I discuss this aspect particularly in the second and fourth chapter.

The reader of the *Satyricon* could not fail to notice that the very composition of the text as a concentrated anthology of the sublime resembled the kind of construction produced by the pathetic romance. It is precisely the melodramatic excess in the treatment of these situations that forces us to recognize the degradation undergone by these sublime literary archetypes. At one time exemplary realizations, they have now been drained of all their original capacity to represent life.

But while this kind of treatment certainly signified "romance" to the reader of the Petronian text, we have seen what it signified for the romanticizing or mythomaniac narrator. Alerted by Petronius, the reader interprets the text in open conflict with the way in which the narrating character perceives and reports it. The hidden author has chosen, as his own external and invisible form of direction, the model of the novel of love and adventure: upon this he has constructed the narrative action, the episodes and the characters. But only in order to parody this model. For the role of the narrator he has chosen another directorial device: he has made him unaware of the purely romantic cage in which he has enclosed him, and by making him naive has let him live his own chimerical life of heroic illusions.

The author realized (and for this reason invited the active complicity of the reader's critical smile) that, in some respects, there was no great distance between elevated epic or tragic models and the narrative palette of romances, which vulgarized and degraded precisely these models. By this time a very popular literary genre had developed, one perhaps so widely appreciated that it was preferred to the same noble models which it freely rewrote in prose form.[32] This was a *Trivialliteratur,* what

32. According to B. E. Perry, *The Ancient Romances, Sather Classical Lectures,* vol. 37 (Berkeley, 1967), 45–46, Greek novels of love and adventure (even those before the Second Sophistic) presented themselves as the modern descendants of epic and of the pathetic *fabulae* of ancient drama.

Italians call "letteratura di consumo," a literature written with the immediate purpose of escape, and the gratifying effect of consolation.[33] This at least was Petronius' verdict on the genre. A sociological survey of literary forms would easily recognize in these two aspects of escape and consolation the roots of the banal moralizing typical of these romances; indeed, even if we cannot assume that the readership of the novel was distinct from the rest of the reading public, novels are probably "better

33. S. A. Stephens, "Who Read the Ancient Novel?" in J. Tatum, ed., *The Search for the Ancient Novel* (Baltimore and London, 1994), 405–18, has successfully demonstrated, by a statistical examination of papyrus fragments from Roman Egypt, that it is largely a modern misconception that romances of love and adventure were widely diffused among the less cultivated classes of Greco-Roman society. On the contrary, authors like Heliodorus and Achilles Tatius clearly not only enjoyed a high level of culture themselves but addressed a refined public. Indeed the sophisticated stylistic analysis of M. D. Reeve, "Hiatus in the Greek Novelists" *CQ* 21 (1971) 514–39, had already shown (before Stephens' article appeared) that these writers assumed a considerable level of rhetorical education in their readers. Nonetheless we should note that this holds true chiefly for a later period (second to third centuries after Christ), when the genre was already widely known and could count among its authors several rhetoricians of the Second Sophistic (I have in mind particularly works like Longus' *Daphnis and Chloe,* for which one can legitimately expect readers of refined literary culture, according to R. L. Hunter, *A Study of "Daphnis and Chloe"* [Cambridge, 1983]). The Greek novel of love and adventure probably experienced the same transformation as the pantomime, which was originally a vulgar genre, loved by the general public, but was subsequently composed by serious writers (e.g., Lucan and Statius: see below, pp. 184–86). In short, the Greek novel was probably, *in its beginnings,* an inferior form of literature intended for popular consumption: the parody created by Petronius bears witness both to its actual success with the public and to the low esteem felt by the cultivated classes for this literary genre. Petronius attacks it as a cheap deformation of great literature. But this does not mean that educated readers found no interest or amusement in this escapist literature; on the contrary, this seems precisely the aspect that preoccupies a "classicist" like Petronius.

The problem of the Greek novel and its history is skillfully discussed by B. Reardon, *The Form of Greek Romance* (Princeton, 1991), 41–42; 72 n. 47; see also K. Treu, "Der antike Roman und seine Publicum," in H. Kuch, ed., *Der antike Roman: Untersuchungen zur literarischen Kommunikations und Gattungsgeschichte* (Berlin, 1989), 178–97. E. Bowie ("The Readership of Greek Novels in the Ancient World," in J. Tatum, ed., *The Search for the Ancient Novel,* 435–59) well shows that for many Greek novels, especially in

regarded as off-duty amusement for the highly literate than as a product aimed at those with lower grades of taste and education."[34] Yet, whatever may have been the intended readership of these romances, it is evident that Petronius regarded them with a smile of aristocratic condescension. Nostalgic as he was for the great classical authors of the past, he could not but judge the romance of love and adventure to be a modern degradation of the great literature of earlier periods. At the same time this new narrative genre, markedly conventional by nature and stereotyped in its development and structure, must have seemed to Petronius particularly appropriate to his own parodic sense of humor.

A shabby and displaced adventurer, a petty thief without scruples, possibly even a criminal, a would-be *scholasticus* with all the weaknesses of the schoolroom, Encolpius is objectively disqualified as a character (and still more as a narrator).[35] He is the chief instrument of the parodic reversal that Petronius is operating as a challenge to the novel of love and adventure in which he has decided to make Encolpius live and breathe. In the hands of the author of the *Satyricon,* Encolpius becomes the antimodel of the idealized hero of romance: that hero is as chaste as Encolpius is debauched, as morally strong as Encolpius is weak and corrupt enough for every trick.

---

the period from 150 to 250 A.D., we should assume educated readers *(pepaideuménoi)* or at least not believe that the readership of the novel was limited to women and young people or "the poor in spirit," contrary to the claim of Perry, 5. See also C. W. Müller, "Der griechische Roman," in E. Vogt, ed. *Neues Handbuch der Literaturwissenschaft,* Vol. 2: *Griechische Literatur,* (Wiesbaden, 1981), 377–412; B. Wesseling, "The audience of the ancient novel," in *Groningen Colloquia on the Novel,* 1 (Groningen, 1988), 33–79. For one suggestion as to how the novel came to be diffused to a varied public see T. Hägg, *The Novel in Antiquity* (Oxford, 1983), 93.

34. J. R. Morgan, "The Greek Novel: Towards a Sociology of Production and Reception," in A. Powell, ed., *The Greek World* (London, 1995), 143.

35. Cf. M. Coffey, *Roman Satire* (London, 1976), 194–95.

This view would fully reinstate the importance of Richard
Heinze's old thesis—that the *Satyricon* parodies the Greek romance.[36] Over almost a century this theory has been contested
more than once and in more than one quarter, but it stands
firm, even if I am arguing that it should gain its validity from a
rather different perspective.[37] In keeping with the genetic tendencies of "Philology" in his day, and as a consequence of
his dispute with the positivistic studies of the *Quellenforscher*
Erwin Rohde,[38] Heinze asked from what combination of models the *Satyricon* could have been born. We are more concerned
to see how the various models interact in Petronius' text. For
Heinze there is substantial congruence between the structures
underlying the *Satyricon* and the narrative scheme of the Greek
erotic romances: it is this which permits the mechanism of parody to function. In this connection one essential move made by
Heinze was to dismantle the recurrent plot of all these romances
and re-express it as a bare functional sequence—the scheme of
a *fabula:* "a pair of lovers, tossed incessantly from place to
place, are continually persecuted by every kind of misadven-
ture, but above all they have to endure many erotic temptations,
like punishments imposed by an erotic deity." The parodic re-
doubling of the *fabula* achieved by the author of the *Satyricon*
functions only to mark this *difference.*[39]

Heinze's intuition is all the more admirable if we recall that it
was founded on the surviving evidence of a body of novels all

36. R. Heinze, "Petron und der griechische Roman," *Hermes* 34 (1899)
494–519 (reprinted in *Vom Geist des Römertums* [Stuttgart, 1960³], 417ff.).
37. A useful discussion, with bibliography, may be found in N. Horsfall,
"'Generic Composition' and Petronius' *Satyricon*," *Scripta Classica Israelica*
11 (1991–1992) 129–38 (esp. 130–31).
38. E. Rohde, *Der griechische Roman und seine Vorläufer* (Leipzig, 1876,
1914³).
39. Cf. the important article by E. Courtney, "Parody and Literary
Allusion in Menippean Satire," *Philologus* 106 (1962) 86–100 (in particular
concerning the reversal of sexual roles, 93).

later than the *Satyricon*. Nowadays we can rely on several papyrus discoveries that confirm Heinze's hypothesis by bearing
witness to the missing links in a long chain of Greek novels;[40]
these are texts that preceded Petronius and which Heinze reconstructed hypothetically because he thought they were presupposed by the parodic attack contained in the *Satyricon*.[41]

40. According to G. Sandy, "New Pages of Greek Fiction," in J. R.
Morgan and R. Stoneman, edd., *Greek Fiction: The Greek Novel in Context*
(London, 1994), 140–41, the papyri that have been most recently discovered
are unfavorable to Heinze's view rather than supportive of it. In any case, classical fiction nowadays appears much more varied than it used to (but Heinze
himself [p. 518 and n. 3] had suggested that there might have been a tradition
of "comic" novel-writing in Ancient Greece capable of influencing Petronius):
in particular, there are evident traces of what S. A. Stephens and J. J. Winkler,
Ancient Greek Novels: The Fragments (Princeton, 1995), 361–62, define as a
"criminal-satiric" genre, with which the *Satyricon* shows affinity in several respects (cf. chapter 5 below). This does not run counter to the fact that the
idealized novel (especially in its original, rather unsophisticated forms) must
itself have constituted an easily recognizable paradigm, and for that very reason have been easily susceptible to parody, without there being any need for
Petronius to have predecessors to pave the way for him. In other words, the
realistic-comic novel did not stop Petronius from writing *direct* parodies of
other novels—the "serious" ones. It is quite likely that other parallel narrative
strands have been used as a parodic resource (a tradition which could only be
called "comic" or, as Sandy says, "picaresque," with some degree of approximation). What is certain is that novels such as those by Chariton or Xenophon
Ephesius, like any text of high literature (at least any text strongly imbued
with pathos), could be subjected to parody. In fact the narrative attitude of the
Satyricon itself prompted a search for the most conspicuous parallels—the
structural ones—in novels. Sandy believes that Heinze attributed excessive
importance to the theme of homosexuality, since this may have appeared earlier in the idealized novels (but, I would add, only in minor episodes and not
as the linking element within the main plot). Of the features mentioned by
Heinze it is actually another—that of faithfulness between the two protagonists—which Petronius stresses in building his mirroring counter-song. The
real error, I believe, would be to consider the *Satyricon* as merely a parody of
the novel—a parasitic, unimaginative parody—instead of being a novel in its
own right, a work that invites the reader (at least on first acquaintance) to
view it as a coherent narrative. It is this that allows the hidden author's game
to function at its best.

41. "Most of the extant Greek romances of pathos and rhetoric are later
than the time of Petronius but the tradition goes back to the pre-Christian

Although this hypothesis is flawed by the prejudices of positivist evolutionism, it gains considerable power from the literary operation that controls the *Satyricon* even if, again, Heinze did not actually distinguish in the parodistic mode which Petronius employed between models drawn from romance (which are discredited and assaulted polemically) and models drawn from great and sublime literature (which I believe have been left substantially unharmed by hostile assault).

Petronius' technique is one of great literary sophistication: the parody is not an open gesture which monopolizes the meaning of the text as if it were *sic et simpliciter* an antiphrasis of the Greek novel of love and adventure. The parodied Greek romance appears through the *Satyricon* like a barely perceptible shadow of meaning, a phantasm that makes occasional appearances, to vanish later and leave space for the action in its own right. The game of parody is conducted with great delicacy, implicitly rather than by open expression. Petronius is master of the art of evoking stereotypes by exploiting their sheer banality, or of communicating to his descriptions an air of spuriousness sufficient to provoke a double (and humorous) reading, but one discreet enough not to distract the reader's attention from the "story." Thus the *Satyricon* has not turned into a treatise of literary criticism that constructs its own meaning like some allegorical account polemicizing against the conventional and repetitive structures of romantic *Trivialliteratur:* it is in itself a

---

era": Coffey, 183–84. B. P. Reardon, *Courants littéraires grecs des IIe et IIIe siècles après J.-C.* (Paris, 1971), 322–38, discusses chronology in general. There is no doubt that the period of gestation of this narrative genre was rather long and that the first examples of the novel in prose can be traced back indirectly to the end of the second century or at least to the first century B.C. The accidents of transmission have preserved for us the phase of the genre's fullest development, especially that marked by the experience of the Second Sophistic, which strongly modified the very nature of prose narrative; from this point of view E. Rohde's approach was not misconceived.

narrative to read and follow in its own peculiar and complex autonomy of meaning. The parodic tone is always balanced by elements of the context that also make it "lifelike" and adapted to the flow of the story.

The ironic manner employs the genre of the novel but does not exhaust its powers in parodying it. Let us give a better explanation. The generic model of the novel drops the narrator into situations that are ghostly parodies of the romantic form; but the picture is brought to life and made complex whenever the character Encolpius, a victim trapped in the snare of melodramatic banality, reveals himself to be a "mythomaniac or romanticizing narrator," devoid of the very basis of reality, and the passive dreamer of his own illusions as a scholastic consumer of sublime literary texts. Thus a dialogue is set up between author and reader, or better, a sort of exchange, which is the substance of the irony in the *Satyricon*.

The ironic manner (much more than the didactic or fantastic manner) is particularly elitist, inasmuch as irony exists solely in texts that the author wishes programmed in this way, and is realized only through the collaboration of a reader able to satisfy certain requirements: of perspicacity and of adequate literary education. All of this implies a special, not merely a general, competence in the reader—an ideological and evaluative expertise.

Comic irony, of course (like tragic irony), depends on a "misreading": the one ironized is the one who reads erroneously the situation that he is facing; but his erroneous reading is corrected the moment it comes under the gaze of the ironizer. This form of irony is a procedure that the author can set up, but which needs to be completed by the reader. In fact the author is laying the basis for an alternative reading (founded on superior knowledge): the reader accepts the perspective of the author and so reaches this superior level of knowledge. Without a competent

reader the ironic strategy is only set in motion, *not* fully imple-
mented. If it is the duty of every intelligent reader to respond
to the strategy of the author, then the smile of understanding
(which makes the reader into the author's accomplice) will always be the best reward for an ironic reader. Let us too learn to
smile with the author if we want a true reading of the *Satyricon*.

CHAPTER TWO

The Mythomaniac Narrator and the Longing for the Sublime

I hope that the distinction I have proposed between the "mythomaniac narrator" and the "hidden author" has provided some useful clarification. The consequence of this duality is that in the economy of the *Satyricon*'s textual functions, the hidden author exercises an ironic control over the model drawn from the Romance: that is, he constructs the story of Encolpius like a continuous parody of the tale of love and adventure. In turn, it is the function of Encolpius, the mythomaniac narrator, to control relations with high epic and heroic literature and the high oratory studied in school. This means, in effect, that he projects the pettiness of events onto the great models of the sublime literary tradition, thus promoting himself and his own debauched life—yet without in any way damaging the nobility of the great models, which remain unharmed and quite out of reach.

In the quest for clarity, we are bound to make this distinction too definite and schematic, but we know that categorical distinctions, after all, are merely a compromise with chaos. It will thus be wise to show due respect for the free expression of Petronius' text, to forget the absolute categories of our scheme, and to try to resume contact with chaos. In the complex realization of the text, the two functions operating the narrative (author and narrator) cannot be just mechanically opposed. We note that one function, represented by the narrator, is subordinate and exposed to the irony of the author; the narrator is a role, a role with well-defined characteristics, indeed defined in terms of his character. The author, on the other hand, is *in* the text but *outside* the narrative; he is not a role (and so cannot be defined by characteristics). Instead, he is a strategy: he can play freely with the text, imposing limits on himself and then breaking them, making himself felt through the roles, if he chooses, but also making space for his own direct ironic intervention—an intervention not mediated through the mythomaniac narrator. Obviously, the devising of the narrative situations is entirely his, and so is the invention of the names imposed on the characters. This is a strategy rich in implications, through which the developments of the narrative are foreshadowed and motivated. The procedure of naming contributes to the characterization of roles: by sheer etymological (or paretymological) force, the name ultimately contains the hidden author's strategies, his ironic attitude, his general direction of the narrative. The choice of names determines the actions and reactions of the roles: the name, sometimes itself a miniature reproduction of a myth, is like a micro-narrative, the generative cell that contains the model with reference to which the narrated action is constructed, heralding the mythical fiction.[1] Thus the entire narrative of the Croton episode in the *Satyricon* follows the mythical paradigm of the story of Circe and Polyaenus; thus Eumolpus is an expressive name that predetermines the behav-

1. In an article subsequently included in his *Kleine Schriften* (Leipzig, 1915 [= Osnabrück, 1965]), I, 437, F. Bücheler collected a very large number of significant names (allusive or *Redende Namen*), sufficient to include virtually all the major Petronian characters. For previous research, see the treatment of J. A. Gonzalez de Salas, *De Satirici Personarum Nominibus*, in P. Burman, *Titi Petronii Arbitri Satyricon quae supersunt*, Amsterdam, 1743[2] (= Hildesheim and New York, 1974), II, 79–85. Consult also the rich collection of material in A. Collignon, *Étude sur Pétrone* (Paris, 1892), 377–87, Walsh, 75–105, 121, 124, S. Priuli, *Ascyltus. Note di onomastica Petroniana*, Brussels, 1975.

ior of the poet; thus all the irony of the hidden author is revealed in names like Ascyltus ("The Inexhaustible"),[2] Pannychis ("Night Watch"), Trimalchio ("Thrice-Powerful Lord"), Fortunata ("Lucky Lady"), Tryphaena ("Femme de Luxe"), Lichas,[3] and Gorgias.[4] In ironic play the events of daily life are modeled on a destiny predetermined by the names.

Let us take up the thread again from the scene in the picture gallery, at the moment when Encolpius, the emotional spectator of pathetic representations, is presented with the mysterious figure of the ill-dressed but austere old man. The sight of Eumolpus, before the old man reveals his true nature with the tale of the Pergamene boy, arouses the greatest expectations in the young man. We have seen how important a part is played in the narrator's illusions by the heroic model in which Virgil's Dido is presented to Aeneas as he is absorbed in the pictures of the temple of Juno at Carthage.

Encolpius' heroic identification is nothing more than a projection of his desires, but admittedly Eumolpus feeds the illu-

2. That the relationship between name and role is a private matter between hidden author and reader is almost made plain in 92.9: the precise translation of the name *Ascyltus* ("inexhaustible": cf. Priuli, 57–59 with bibliography; but see also 58 n. 205 for a different interpretation) is uttered by Eumolpus (*O iuvenem laboriosum!*) just when it is narratologically essential that Eumolpus himself should not know the name of the ultra-talented youth he is talking about. He is telling Encolpius and Giton, who abandoned both Ascyltus and Eumolpus at the *balneum,* an anecdote about the young man with the huge member who was loudly calling for Giton. Eumolpus does not know that the youth is well known to the other two, but just when the theme is the speaker's ignorance of the man he is talking about he offers the exact translation of his "speaking name." This translation has no meaning for Encolpius or Giton: it is provided for the reader, who can enjoy Eumolpus' report at a still greater level of awareness than that of the other two characters precisely at the moment when they (at least Encolpius: 92.12–13) display their superiority to the awareness of Eumolpus, who is speaking.

3. See A. Barchiesi, "Il Nome di Lica e la poetica dei nomi in Petronio," *MD* 12 (1984) 169–75; see also M. Labate, "Di nuovo sulla poetica dei nomi in Petronio: Corax 'il delatore'?" *MD* 16 (1986) 135–46.

4. See G. B. Conte, "Petronio, *Sat.* 141: Una congettura e un' interpretazione," *RFIC* 120 (1992) 307–12. We will return to this in chapter 4, pp. 135–36.

sion by presenting an aspect that fosters the young man's longing for the sublime: (83.7) *senex canus, exercitati vultus et qui videretur nescioquid magnum promittere, sed cultu non proinde speciosus.* ("A white-haired old man of harassed countenance who seemed to promise some great mystery, but not appropriately distinguished in his dress"). What the narrator and protagonist believes he is experiencing is the typical scheme of the tragic entrance scene in which a character who wears rags but has a noble bearing appears to the spectators. He should have presented himself like Telephus: if not the Telephus of Ennius[5] or Accius, then certainly the Telephus of Euripides, who was fiercely criticized for bringing the king of Mysia on stage dressed like a beggar.[6] In fact, some verses have been preserved from Accius' tragedy that seem to belong to Telephus' entrance scene: (*Trag.* 613–18 R.[3]) *quem ego ubi aspexi, virum memorabilem / intui viderer, ni vestitus taeter, vastitudo, / maestitudo praedicarent hominem esse. . . . / nam etsi opertus squalitate est luctuque horrificabili . . . / profecto hauquaquam est ortus mediocri satu.* ("And when I beheld him I would have thought I was looking upon a great man, if his foul clothing, his wildness and gloom did not declare the man to be. . . . For even if he is burdened with mourning weeds and horrendous grief . . . surely he is scarcely of ordinary birth").

It seems we are reading the very thoughts of the narrator Encolpius. The coincidences comprise both the form of the statement (in first person, *aspexi, intui viderer*) and its content. A character of tragedy reports his meeting with a hero who has suffered misfortune and describes his appearance; despite his pitiable dress, his deportment leads to the suspicion that he is not of ignoble birth. Even the next words of the old poet Eumolpus, who unleashes a resounding tirade against the vices

5. Enn. 281 Joc.: *squalida saeptus stola*, 282: *regnum reliqui saeptus mendici stola.*
6. Cf. Aristoph. *Ach.* 432ff.

of the rich, only seem an amplification of what Telephus probably uttered at his stage entrance, as we can reconstruct from another fragment: (619–20 R.[3]) *nam si a me regnum Fortuna atque opes / eripere quivit, at virtutem nec quiit.* ("For if Fortune was able to rob me of my kingdom and wealth, she could not take my moral strength as well").

Encolpius is victim of his own expectations: he had come into the gallery as a hero and expected to meet other heroes, and so, faced with an old man who is ill-groomed and a bit shabby, he cannot keep himself from thinking that this must be some great, even tragic, figure *incognito*. The illusion springs from the desire to upgrade the reality in which the narrator and his interlocutors find themselves; we might say it springs from an intense yearning for the sublime.

Here perhaps we can try to approach larger problems with wider literary-historical significance. Already towards the end of the great Augustan era the idea that the most important sectors of literature were now "saturated" must have been gathering weight. Whatever could be done to reach the highest levels of great poetry and great oratory had already been done: from now on, the contest was unequal, always with models too lofty, perfect, insuperable. Horace as a literary critic had already stressed this problem: his contemporaries all indulged in writing when they should have been reading the masterworks of the past (especially the noble Greeks). One recognizes a sense of malaise and inadequacy; facing the giants of the past, every new poet ends by creating mere caricatures of masterpieces beyond his grasp. Any attempt to compete seems an unwitting parody. Instead, writers needed to understand that certain heights of achievement were now impossible—as Horace in *Epistles* 2.1 says of the great tragic theater, which can now no longer be recreated. Horace confesses he can only suffer a heartfelt yearning for this kind of sublime poetry: there is no other genre of poetry in which he feels such involvement as in a tragic produc-

tion. This carries him away and sweeps him aloft; it seems
to him that the tragic poet is treading on air like a tightrope
walker (a performance that keeps the spectator's gaze raised
heavenwards); tragedy binds him and torments him with false
terrors, it soothes him and then inflames him with anger; like a
wizard, the poet transports him now to Thebes and now to
Athens (*Epist.* 2.1.210–13).

This is surely the transport, the *ekstasis,* that the sublime can
offer, as we suggested. At bottom, there is a little of our mythomaniac narrator, of the naive *scholasticus* crazed by memories
of great literature, even in Horace. But the satirist Horace
knows the risks of inadequacy and takes to his heels (he knows
how to withdraw to the modesty of his *angulus*). He feels sympathy for the man who yields to the great imagining of the sublime, but he protects himself by telling an instructive anecdote
that raises a bitter smile (*Epist.* 2.2.128–40). At Argos there
was a perfectly sensible man, of good character, polite to his
wife and friends, free from vagaries and full of good sound
understanding.[7] He was to all intents and purposes sane, except
for an innocent obsession. He used to sit for whole days ecstatic
in the empty theater of Argos, imagining that he was watching
wonderful tragedies, and he even applauded. To cure him, his
kinsmen treated him with hellebore. But once cured of his obsessions and restored to his senses, he could only lament: "my
friends, you have destroyed me, not saved me, by taking away
my *voluptas* and my *mentis gratissimus error*" (139–40).

The Argive spectator is in a sense a Petronian character, even
if the hellebore of irony that the *Satyricon* uses against Encolpius' madness attacks the ecstatic representations of its protagonist with more violence. To put it another way, Petronius
does not lack sympathy towards the manias of his character,

7. Horace is particularly anxious to deny that this is a case of the *poeta
vesanus:* cf. the finale of *Ars Poetica* and my discussion of it below
(pp. 58–59).

and these manias deserve sympathy for at least two reasons: because they are basically innocent manias, like those of the Argive spectator, and because they are directed to the great models of sublime literature which Petronius himself admires— it is not these, in fact, that he is parodying. To fall victim to deceptive poetic ardor requires naivety but also some culture. "Indeed the charms of poetry have never enchanted people who are quite stupid and devoid of intelligence," says Plutarch in his little work, "How the poets should be read" (*De audiendis poetis* 15C). He goes on to recall the well-known paradox of Gorgias: "tragedy is a deception in which the deceiver behaves better when he succeeds in deceiving than when he does not, and in which the man deceived shows more intelligence than the man who fails to be deceived."

Petronius' aggression towards the illusory claims to the sublime that characterize Encolpius would probably be better called a skeptical complicity, not too different from that shared at about the same period by the anonymous author of *On the Sublime*.[8] Both know that the Sublime is now a blessing beyond

8. The treatise *On the Sublime* probably dates from the early Empire, perhaps from the end of Augustus' reign (by now there is a fairly strong consensus on this). Composed in response to the short treatise by Caecilius of Calacte, a rhetor of the Analogist School and a contemporary of Dionysius of Halicarnassus, it appears to follow the views of the opposed Anomalist School (one of whose representatives was Theodorus of Gadara); its polemic only makes sense if read in the context of contemporary debate. A slightly later date, in the age of Nero, has recently been proposed again by J. M. Crosset and J. A. Arieti, *The Dating of Longinus* (University Park, 1975); see also D. A. Russell, "Greek Criticism of the Empire," in G. A. Kennedy, ed., *The Cambridge History of Literary Criticism*, I, *Classical Criticism* (Cambridge, 1989), 306–311. A wide-ranging discussion on this problem is given by E. Gabba, *Dionysius and the History of Archaic Rome, Sather Classical Lectures*, vol. 56 (Berkeley, 1991), 42–43 and n. 55. What I wish to stress here is that, in any case, the whole cultural scene of the early Empire seems to be distinguished by a rhetorical-literary debate in which the sublime in oratory and in poetry was a recurrent, highly topical theme. A little earlier, Dionysius of Halicarnassus, although an Atticist, had in his *De compositione verborum* tended to identify what was beautiful within literature with the sublime (in

recall. But Petronius prefers to show this indirectly, inflating the naive illusions of a character who makes one laugh because he thinks he can still live the myths of great literature. Pseudo-Longinus, on the other hand, declares outright that the evil of the age is the lack of true greatness in poetry and oratory: (44) "We must ask ourselves why, in our times, there are persons supremely clever in the art of persuasion and expert in court cases, eloquent and gifted in rhetorical skills, but there are no more truly sublime and extraordinary intellects ὑψηλαὶ δὲ λίαν καὶ ὑπερμεγέθεις . . . φύσεις), except perhaps very rarely. Such is the universal poverty of our age in rhetoric and literature."

Indeed this seems a fundamental theme of the *Satyricon*, to the point that Petronius (or better the hidden author) gives his protagonist powerful words that express all the yearning for that sublime literature which the giants of the past could create. Petronius makes him lament that today's young men do not promise a Sophocles, a Euripides, still less a Homer, a Pindar, or a Plato, Demosthenes or Thucydides. It is the schooling that must be held responsible for the corruption and degradation that has overwhelmed oratory and poetry, maintains Encolpius: (chap.1) *et ideo ego adulescentulos existimo in scholis stultissimos fieri* ("and that is why I think young men are made so utterly stupid in the schools"). Indeed, Encolpius' tirade against

---

particular, with the "severe" style, as opposed to the "refined"/"pleasant" style). On the convergence between the themes discussed by the major rhetors (Dionysius, Ps.-Demetrius, Ps.-Longinus) at the end of the Republic and in the early decades of the Empire, see G. P. Goold, "A Greek Professorial Circle at Rome," *TAPA* 92 (1961) 168–92; another useful contribution is that by A. Michel, "Rhétorique et poétique: La théorie du sublime de Platon aux modernes," *REL* 54 (1976) 278–307. One topic connected with the debate on the sublime (from which contemporary oratory had already decisively distanced itself) was "de corrupta eloquentia": cf. G. A. Kennedy, *The Art of Rhetoric in the Roman World* (Princeton, 1972), 446–64, 494–96, 515–26; cf. also E. Fantham, "Imitation and Decline," *CPh* 73 (1978) 102–16, which cites Tac. *Dial.* 1, Sen. *Contr.* 1 *praef.* 1, Sen. *Epist.* 114.1–2, the lost Quint. *De Causis*, and Plin. *Epist.* 8.14; D. A. Russell, *Criticism in Antiquity* (London, 1981), pp. 58–59, 116.

the scholastic practice of declamations is itself a typical declamation, with all the defects of the type: the familiar arguments,
the violent vocal manner. Here is the "warmed-up cabbage
soup" which Juvenal called the exercises held in the rhetoric
schools (7.154 *crambe repetita*).[9]

The author is playing with the protagonist, turning him into
a paradoxical censor of just the faults of which he is himself the
unwitting victim: that is why he deserves the author's parody.
Impassioned critic of the defects of scholastic culture, he is himself a *scholasticus* totally imprisoned (as the story reveals) in
the artificial schemes he condemns. The school, the kingdom of
declamation, has replaced the sublime of high oratory and poetry with degraded stereotypes of these great literary models.

Petronius sees the two strands as two parallel paths leading
to the degradation of the sublime literature of the past: on one
side, the popular narrative which banalizes the great literary
models by reducing them to melodramatic schemes; on the
other, the practice of *declamationes* which cheapens the noble
tradition of forensic oratory and produces only empty academic
inventions. There is a converging process that blends literature
and rhetoric and contaminates one with the other; *corrupta eloquentia* overflows more and more into literature, and, conversely, literature draws more and more upon the apparatus of
loci communes. The work of Seneca the Elder enables us to reconstruct the lines of this cultural process in perfect detail.
Beginning with the first generation of empire a huge baggage of
topoi weighs down literature, while rhetoric draws from literature an ever more generalized array of clichés destined for can-
onization in the schools.

The school is precisely the *locus* of fusion between this degraded eloquence and stereotyped literature, between the do-

9. Cf. the note of E. Courtney, *A Commentary on the Satires of Juvenal*
(London, 1980), *ad loc.*; cf. also Otto, 96, s.v. *crambe*.

mains of the spoken and the written word. The product of this fusion is ambiguous; it is the *infelix suppellex* (as Quintilian will call it [2.4.29]) composed of materials halfway between literature and oratory, hybrids that wander from one text to another with absolute indifference and can treat chance, happiness or death with detached intensity. Already Ovid, in his last phase, had written a letter to the rhetor Salanus, teacher of the young prince Germanicus, in which he showed himself well aware of the cultural process that was now assimilating poetry and oratory to the point of confusing different manners and skills: (*Ex Ponto.* 2.5.65−72) *distat opus nostrum, sed fontibus exit ab isdem: / artis et ingenuae cultor uterque sumus. / . . . / utque meis numeris tua dat facundia nervos, / sic venit a nobis in tua verba nitor. / Iure igitur studio confinia carmina vestro / et commiliti sacra tuenda putas* ("our work differs, but springs from the same wells of inspiration, and each of us is a worshipper of the gentlemanly art. As your eloquence gives virility to my meters, so charm comes from us to your words. So you rightly believe you should protect poetry which is close to your own pursuit and which is their fellow soldier").[10]

At first sight it might seem peculiar that the parodic game of the *Satyricon* is equally ready to target the declamations of the rhetoricians and the love romance, if only because the academic

10. And yet we can be sure that this process of rapprochement between poetry and rhetoric occurred before Ovid. I mean that, both in Ovid's and Petronius' time, the disappearance of the barriers between the language of rhetorical prose and that of poetry was a current problem. Hence the existence of a lively and urgent debate, capable of producing different and opposing answers. A good witness to the contemporary urgency of this debate is offered by the treatise *De compositione verborum* of Dionysius of Halicarnassus: there the author, supporting the school of rhetoric that Petronius detested, more than once declares that he wants to provide a general theory of literary language, or a series of principles to be used by whoever wants to compose fine poetry or oratory (*Comp. Verb* 4.13−14); he proudly claims that he has overcome for the first time the traditional antithesis between the language of prose and poetry—a clear antithesis that begins with Aristotle and continues in Stoic and Epicurean aesthetics.

culture of the schools was as sophisticated as the novel's adventurous or pathetic narrative was naive and ingenuous.[11] Under Petronius' satiric lens, however, these two realities can reasonably be assimilated inasmuch as both languages are "derivative": exaggerated gestures that have lost their original authenticity. In both cases we are dealing with by-products which favorable cultural circumstances have raised above the principal creations of literature. Current literary production prefers to recycle worthless refuse rather than work with high quality ingredients.[12]

In Petronius' eyes the great myths of literature have become simply patterns, forms of expressions, collections of memorable gestures; analogously, the passionate political conflicts of Demosthenes and Cicero have become mere competitions of performing rhetoricians, implausible *suasoriae* and *controver-*

---

11. Cf. Billault, 304–305: "Ce domaine, un lieu le faisait vivre: l'école de rhétorique. [. . .] à l'école de rhétorique, l'idée que l'on pouvait faire discours de tout fondait le travail de chacun. Les romanciers font roman de tout, y compris de toute littérature antérieure. C'est en termes d'horizon commun, non d'influence mécanique, qu'il faut considérer les rapports de la rhétorique et du roman. L'une et l'autre assignent comme territoire à leur création un domaine public où cohabitent banalités et bizarreries du quotidien, grands hommes et grandes œuvres de l'histoire et de la littérature, lieux, coutumes et êtres exotiques, paysages et usages familiers. Ainsi, la question de la 'naïveté' ou de la 'sophistication' du roman grec qui renvoie à celle de son public, populaire ou savant, ne peut-elle être tranchée de manière exclusive."

12. The satiric lens may deform, but it is taking in a real phenomenon. For moderns who love to pursue hypotheses about the origin of the novel, it can be seductive to believe the novel was born from the trivialization which literary genres and masterpieces suffered when exploited in the exercises of the rhetorical schools. It was Erwin Rohde's hypothesis that specifically connected the genesis of the romance with the reflowering of the schools of rhetoric in the Second Sophistic; but Rohde's chronological scheme is unacceptable today because it is known that the novel of love and adventure is much earlier than the second century of our era. Yet the connection between the novel and the schools of rhetoric (which did blossom in the second century, but had exercized their influence even in earlier centuries) still seems plausible: cf. Q. Cataudella, "Origini e caratteri del romanzo greco," in *Romanzo classico* (Roma, 1957), ix–xliv, now in Q. Cataudella, *Utriusque linguae. Studi e ricerche di letteratura greca e latina* (Messina and Firenze, 1974), I, 357–95.

siae. The school—with its repetitive and codified rituals—is the outer form of a culture grown utterly spurious, or rather, it is the flip side of that contemporary culture which chose to search in the tepid flame of novelettish *Trivialliteratur* for some of the heat needed to warm up a poor and chilly existence. With an eminently moral intention even Seneca the philosopher protests, in a letter to Lucilius, against the growing artificiality that has now detached culture from reality: (106.12) "we suffer from excess in everything; even in literature we suffer from excess: we learn our lessons not for life but for school."[13]

Even the satirical moralizing of Persius confronts the sophisticated disgust which Petronius felt for the repetitive culture of the schools and the grandiloquent inventions of the declaimers: (*Sat.* 3.44–48) *saepe oculos memini tangebam parvus olivo / grandia si nollem morituri verba Catonis / dicere non sano multum laudanda magistro / quae pater adductis sudans audiret amicis* ("I remember I often smeared my eyes with oil as a boy, if I did not want to utter the lofty words of the dying Cato to win the praises of a demented teacher, words that my father would hear when he brought along his friends"). This is a scene of recitation, a *suasoria* in which a small boy (*parvus*) is obliged to get to grips with the grandiose (*grandia . . . verba*) monologue of a republican worthy. The sublime of these *grandia . . . verba* was intended to please a master who cultivated a taste for excess. Here is the frame of reference: the sublime, the schools, lofty sentiments and petty interpreters. Sometimes satire takes a step towards the *Satyricon.*

Rhetoric itself is composed of pathetic schemata, ossified clichés that seek new meaning by resorting to paradox and *peripeteia* (*colores*): foreign themes, situations at the edge of credibility, paraliterary exercises intended to demonstrate fan-

---

13. *Quemadmodum omnium rerum sic litterarum quoque intemperantia laboramus: non vitae sed scholae discimus.*

tastic invention and to rouse the interest and surprise of an auditorium, genuine courtroom novelettes. The blatantly novelistic nature of many favorite *controversiae* in the declamation schools is abundantly displayed in the works of Seneca Rhetor, in the *Dialogus de Oratoribus,* and in the first chapter of the *Satyricon* itself.[14] The imaginary plots of declamations are like little novels, narratives of stupefying artificiality.

Encolpius, the character who focalizes the narrative of the *Satyricon,* has been invented to embody the caricature of these two forms of degraded culture, ready as he is to entangle himself in novelettish or melodramatic situations, not to mention commenting on them with declamatory aplomb. Victim of the school, he sees behind every event the phantasm of readings he has reiterated in class, and he lives for his own pleasure the illusion of finding himself "a character in his own books." For instance, when he indignantly launches into a vehement indictment of the two treacherous lovers who have fled together, Encolpius does not just feel like Aeneas soliloquizing against Helen (we saw this in the previous chapter[15]), he spices his *rhesis* with a dash of Cicero learned at school. His words, *quid ille alter? qui [tamquam] die togae virilis stolam sumpsit* ("what about the other fellow, who put on a woman's robe on the very day of taking the manly toga," 81.5) are an open allusion to the most insulting charge in the invective launched by the great orator against Mark Antony in the second *Philippic:* (18.44) *sumpsisti virilem, quam statim muliebrem togam reddidisti.*[16]

---

14. Cf. *Dial.* 35: *quales, per fidem, et quam incredibiliter compositae! [. . .] sic fit ut tyrannicidarum praemia aut vitiatarum electiones aut pestilentiae remedia aut incesta matrum aut quidquid in schola cotidie agitur, in foro vel raro vel numquam, ingentibus verbis prosequantur.* See also the comment of A. Gudeman, ed., *P. Cornelii Taciti Dialogus de Oratoribus* (Leipzig and Berlin, 1914²), 462–64.

15. Cf. pp. 8–9, 12.

16. The parallel was noted by N. Heinsius: cf. the comment of Burman *ad loc.*

Among Cicero's speeches the *Philippics* were the favorite of
the professors of rhetoric: the very Demosthenic passion with
which they were written guaranteed the fourteen speeches a
continuous scholastic career from the Augustan age at least until the sixth century.[17] The second *Philippic,* in particular, ended
up as an anthology piece. Juvenal, who did not fail to mock
Cicero's vanity elsewhere, voices his admiration for the "divine
second Philippic, famous beyond all others" (10.124–26). Its
fame was certainly due to the schools: more than a century later
Dio Cassius (46.1–28) could give a report of a fictitious scene
in which Cicero recited a condensed reelaboration of the second
Philippic and an adversary replied, reproducing the arguments
of the Pseudo-Sallustian *Invective.* Here we see staged an imaginary encounter of giants (Cicero against Sallust!) capable of
unleashing the inventive powers of professors of rhetoric who
yearned for the long-lost heroic battles of past oratory.

In this case, as in others, the reader is invited to recognize
and recall more than one model behind a Petronian scene. The
reason for this is that underlying the narrative there is—like a
basso continuo—the parody activated by the author against his
naive character; but on the surface of the narrative, these situations take the imaginary form of fascinating literary experiences
lived through in bookish fashion by the same character. And
the imagination of the *scholasticus* who narrates is full of anthology passages, purple patches that the school has usurped
for its own use, stripping them from the texts where they belonged to turn them into raw material for exercises. This is why
the situation into which the narrating character is dropped is always like an empty frame waiting to be filled, by his melodramatic imagination, with mythical and heroic illusions.

Every situation is a narrative bait waiting for developments

17. Cf. Fr. Schöll, ed., M. *Tulli Ciceronis scripta quae manserunt omnia,*
vol. VIII, *Orationes in M. Antonium Philippicae* (Leipzig, 1918), praef. xvi.

that the scholastic memory hastens to interpret in accordance with sublime literary models. There is thus a plurality of models because the same situation (whether from the novel or declamation) permitted different treatments: either the grandeur of epic, or the dramatic treatment of tragedy, or the magniloquent development of high public oratory. These glorious memories can also converge and combine because fundamentally they have ceased to be distinct single texts: they all belong without differentiation to the great composite text of the schoolroom. If we reconsider from this point of view the complex of models for the scene in which Encolpius interprets his own heroic frenzy, we cannot miss the convergence, and indeed the superimposition, of strong (indeed the strongest) models: the explosion of Achilles' anger, his lament by the seashore, the frenzy of Aeneas on the last night of Troy, the sad meditations of Aeneas as he gazes upon his own story represented in pictures while waiting for the coming of Dido, the "entry scene" of mysterious and tragic roles, the impassioned tirade of Cicero in the last act of his political career. All these are schoolroom pieces, passages from anthologies whose manifestly scholastic status we can confirm from ancient evidence;[18] it is as if one of our own students with a little knowledge of literature reduced all Dante to the episode of Paolo and Francesca in the fifth canto of the *Inferno* or the entire theater of Shakespeare to "for Brutus is an honorable man" or Hamlet's "To be or not to be."

The schools treat literature like a mine from which to extract isolated precious stones: their fixed setting in anthologies which include certain passages and exclude others is another aspect of

18. Virgil rapidly became a classic and was read and studied at school, but obviously in excerpts. It seems likely that above all the first part of the *Aeneid* was a scholastic text (especially Books 1, 2 and 4): from R. Cavenaile, *Corpus Papyrorum Latinarum* (Wiesbaden, 1958), 7–70, it is clear that of twenty Virgil papyri a third are fragments from the first book, a quarter from the second. See also below, n. 20.

the unthinking repetition of pedagogy. It is always the same passages that are read. This is how literature loses status: from being a continuous text it becomes a collection of fine examples, a mere subject for exercise. Some ancient poets had begun to lament this: Horace did not conceal his fear that the schools would take over his poetic output to make it into student anthologies and teaching aids.[19]

Perhaps it is worth noting as a comment on Encolpius' obsessions that it is the first book of the *Iliad*, particularly the quarrel of Agamemnon and Achilles, which is better represented in our surviving papyri than any other scene. This is no coincidence, but rather indicates a greater use in schools.[20] Plutarch too, in

19. Cf. *Sat.* 1.10.74–75: *an tua demens / vilibus in ludis dictari carmina malis?*, *Epist.* 1.20.17–18 and R. Mayer, ed., *Horace: Epistles Book I* (Cambridge, 1994), *ad loc.*

20. This is the claim of H. I. Marrou, *Histoire de l'éducation dans l'antiquité* (Paris, 1965⁶), 246–47. In his opinion the schools gave priority to the study of the first books of the *Iliad* and other well-known books like 22 and 24. It is supported by the evidence of R. A. Pack, *The Greek and Latin Literary Texts from Graeco-Roman Egypt* (Ann Arbor, 1965²) (465 papyri of the *Iliad*, of which 68 come from the first book alone), not to mention the observations of Collart in P. Mazon, P. Chantraine, and P. Collart, *Introduction à l'Iliade* (Paris, 1948), 59–60, where scholastic papyri are given specific attention (these are often elementary exercises). Cf. also G. Zalateo, "Papiri scolastici," *Aegyptus* 41 (1961) 160–235. Marrou is actually referring to the Hellenistic world but there are no serious reasons to think that Rome was different: cf. S. F. Bonner, *Education in Ancient Rome* (Berkeley, 1977), 213. Even among the papyri of *scholia*, glosses of passages from the first book of the *Iliad* are by far the most numerous (approximately one third of the total come from this book); see L. M. Raffaelli, "Repertorio dei papiri contenenti 'Scholia minora in Homerum,'" in *Ricerche di Filologia Classica II: Filologia e critica letteraria della grecità* (Pisa, 1984), 148–153, 158–59; there are excellent comments on the study of Homer in the ancient school in F. Montanari, "Gli 'Homerica' su papiro: Per una distinzione di generi," in *Ricerche di Filologia Classica II*, 125–38 (Montanari distinguishes between different scholastic products: *hypomnemata* or commentaries, alphabetized lexica, anthologies, mythographic *historiae*); cf. also idem, "Filologia omerica antica nei papiri," *Proceedings of the XVIII International Congress of Papyrology, Athens 25–31 Mai 1986* (Athens, 1988), I. 337–44. It is still useful to consult C. H. Oldfather, *The Greek Literary Texts from Graeco-Roman Egypt* (Madison, 1923). Cf. Stephens, "Who Read the Ancient Novel?" 411.

"How young men should read the poets" (*Mor.* 15–18), offers a moralizing comment on just this quarrel scene in the *Iliad,* and the declamations attributed to Quintilian include a reference to this scene.[21]

In the formation of Encolpius as a student there were *exempla* of heroic action and furious anger, and we have seen them. Another category of scholastic *exempla* was that of famous recognition scenes, whether dramatic or epic—Electra's recognition of Orestes or Euryclea's recognition of Odysseus by his scar. In contrast, Petronius' narrative can only present farcical recognitions like that of Lichas who, by casting a glance at the genitals of Encolpius, rediscovers an old acquaintance. Now Encolpius, even in this embarrassing situation—and it seems as if his thoughts were instantaneous, as he stands trembling with fear in front of the terrible "pirate"—is prompted to recall the famous episode of Euryclea: "how can anyone be surprised that Ulysses' nurse recognized his scar after twenty years?" If his reaction is justified, we cannot avoid smiling with pleasure to see how the young *scholasticus,* even at the moment of danger, cannot rid himself of the oppressive burden of how he has read the great works of literature: he remembers not just the canonical texts but also their annotations.[22]

The schools must have known of a question, a *zetema,* discussed by Aristotle; Eustathius attests that the philosopher (probably in his *Homeric Problems*) used to criticize Homer because the scar seemed too general a sign to guarantee Euryclea's

21. Ps-Quint. *Decl.* 306.12. See M. Winterbottom, ed. and comm., *The Minor Declamations Ascribed to Quintilian* (Berlin and New York, 1984), 442. One infers from Augustine that in late antiquity the schools prescribed the reading from Virgil of the last night of Troy and the whole story of Dido (*Conf.* 1.13): cf. D. Comparetti, *Virgilio nel Medioevo* (Firenze, 1937 [reprint of 1896²]), I, 17, 76 n. 3, 86, 188–89.

22. Admittedly the distance between the ironic author and the narrating "I" may be reduced here, since the narrator observes himself with a detached eye, as if he were someone else (one more instance of the "erlebendes Ich" and the "erzählendes Ich") See chapter 1, p. 12, n. 12 and p. 25 with n. 27.

recognition.[23] This was also a topos of the recognition scene in drama, to the extent that Euripides in his *Electra* could implicitly attack the *Choephoroi* of Aeschylus over the "signs" that allowed the sister to rediscover her brother.[24] Perhaps Menelaus' recognition of Telemachus as his father's son in *Odyssey* 4.149–50 was also a regular text: "for Odysseus' feet were like this man's, his hands were like this, and the glances of his eyes and his head and the hair growing."

The terms of the canonical recognition are presupposed by the very different scene we get in the *Satyricon*: 105.9 *Lichas, qui me optime noverat . . . nec manus nec faciem meam consideravit, sed continuo ad inguina mea luminibus deflexis movit officiosam manum et "salve" inquit "Encolpi"*[25] ("Lichas, who knew me perfectly, did not pause over my hands or face, but at once, lowering his eyes stretched out an attentive hand to my loins and said, 'So it's you, Encolpius!'"). Encolpius notices that Lichas is not following the heroic code of etiquette, since he ignores the noble signs—the hands and features of the face. Encolpius, who has studied at school the rules for recognition between great characters of myth, cannot help being disappointed. Lichas, unaware of the etiquette, shows himself *prudentissimus* just by not knowing it. The surprise of the ancient philologist scandalized by the implausibility of Homer's narrative (*miretur nunc aliquis Ulixis nutricem post vicesimum*

23. Cf. N. J. Richardson, "Recognition Scenes in the *Odyssey* and Ancient Literary Criticism," *Papers of the Liverpool Latin Seminar* 4 (1983) 219–35, esp. 230. For the Ἀπορήματα Ὁμηρικά see *Aristotelis Opera*, III, *librorum deperditorum frr. collegit et annotationibus instruxit* O. Gigon (Berlin and New York, 1987), 526–39. On the *zetemata* see *Reallex. f. Ant. u. Christ.* 6, 342–47, s.v. *Erotapokriseis* (H. Dörrie); *RE* 13.2, 2511–29, s.v. Λύσεις (A. Gudeman).

24. See J. D. Denniston, ed. and comm., Euripides *Electra* (Oxford, 1939) on 520–84; F. Solmsen, *Electra and Orestes: Three Recognitions in Greek Tragedy* (Amsterdam, 1967). Aristoph. *Nub.* 534–36 may be a parody.

25. See the excellent note on p. 187 of M. Labate, "Note petroniane," *MD* 25 (1990) 181–91.

annum cicatricem invenisse . . .) is reversed in the surprise of the narrator forced to recognize in Lichas' maneuver the parody of his own imagination and desire for the sublime. As elsewhere in the *Satyricon,* here too the irony comes from the tension between the voice of the protagonist and the voice of the narrator, between the agent "I" and the narrating "I."[26]

But Encolpius never learns; he never abandons his obsessive desire to cloak the events of his personal life in literature. Put him on a pirate's ship and he will be ready to impersonate the shipwrecked sailor who escapes miraculously from the "epic storm."[27] The hidden author plays with the exquisitely novelistic model of the hurricane and ensuing shipwreck, the unforeseen catastrophe that overturns the action of the narrative.[28] This is an epic and tragic topos so common and so stylized that in the novel-like narrative of the *Historia Apollonii regis Tyrii* (Ch. 11) it can without further ado take the form of a composition in heroic hexameters placed in the middle of the prose discourse.

Hurled into the tempest, the narrator of the *Satyricon* is ready to interpret it according to the "rules of the art" (*Satyr.* 114). I mean that all the topical apparatus of the literary tradi-

26. See above, n. 22.

27. The knave Encolpius, faced by the terror of his companions, had already invoked a meteorological *deus ex machina* in the *consilium salutis* of chapters 100–101: (101.7) *fingite, inquit, nos antrum Cyclopis intrasse. Quaerendum est aliquod effugium, nisi naufragium ponimus et omni nos periculo liberamus* ("unless we imagine a fine tempest and free ourselves from all danger"). We must read *ponimus* with Bücheler: Müller[2] accepts the correction of H. Fuchs, "Zum Petrontext," *Philologus* 93 (1938) 157–75, who conjectured *patimur* for *ponimus.* But *ponere* is good here as a technical term for the *exemplum fictum,* the imaginary "theme" begotten by the fantasy of the poet-declaimer Eumolpus; it also fits well his exordium: *fingite.* Cf. Quint. *Inst.* 1.10.33: *est etiam non inerudite ad declamandum ficta materia in qua ponitur tibicen . . . accusari.* Cf. W. Kissel, ed., comm. and trans., A. Persius Flaccus *Satiren* (Heidelberg, 1990), ad 1.70 (*nec ponere lucum*), p. 202.

28. Cf. e.g. Charit. 3.10, Xenoph. 2.11.10, Heliod. 5.27.1, Ach. Tat. 3.1–2. Cf. H. Whitehouse, "Shipwreck on the Nile: A Greek Novel on a 'Lost' Roman mosaic?," *AJA* 89 (1985) 129–34; Billault, 195–98.

tion is unfurled; no element is missing to make it conventional. The introductory *inhorruit mare* is a metaphor deriving from the celebrated storm of Pacuvius, which is recommended by Cicero as a model (*De Or.* 3.157).[29] Then follows the mêlée of the winds in mutual conflict and coming from all points of the compass, based on the unrealistic model of the epic storm which goes back to the fifth book of the *Odyssey* (331–32) and is recalled by Virgil at the opening of the *Aeneid* (1.84–86). The impossible simultaneous onset of all the opposing winds provoked the scientific criticisms of Seneca (*Nat. quaest.* 5.16.2): the winds of poets, he comments, all band together whenever a tempest breaks out, *quod fieri nullo modo potest.* Virgil too meets a condescending smile: *una Eurusque Notusque ruunt creberque procellis / Africus . . .* [*Aen.* 1.85–86] *et qui locum in illa rixa non habuit, Aquilo* ("The East and South winds rush together and the African blast thick with hurricanes . . . and the North wind too, which had no business in that storm"). But Seneca too, when he puts on his poetic cloak, must inevitably, like Encolpius, follow the poetic rules and adopt the implausibility of literary convention: the great tempest of *Agamemnon* 466–578 ignores rationalist ironies, as the winds turn and confront each other from all directions (476 . . . *adversus Euro Zephyrus et Boreae Notus*).[30] The same familiarity with the exaggerating tendencies of poetic storm scenes provides Juvenal with a satiric opportunity in the twelfth Satire, when he admits seeing his own verses run the risk of this second-hand sublimity: (22–24) *omnia fiunt talia tam graviter, si quando poetica surgit tempestas* ("Things always happen as badly as this when a poetic storm rises").

29. For other testimonia from ancient *grammatici* see the apparatus of O. Ribbeck, ed., *Scaenicae Romanorum Poesis Fragmenta*, vol. I, *Tragicorum Fragmenta* (Leipzig, 1897³), Pac. *Inc.* 45.

30. Cf. R. J. Tarrant, ed., *Seneca Agamemnon* (Cambridge, 1976), *ad loc.*, p. 265.

Encolpius could have learned to narrate a *poetica tempestas* either from poetry at school or in the halls of the declaimers. Seneca Rhetor remembers that descriptions of storms were *de rigueur* in the schools of declamation,[31] while Cestius Pius, one of the most famous rhetors (*Suas.* 3.2) put into one of his "themes" as a note to be developed, *describe nunc tempestatem*. In short, the storm is so stereotyped that the title is enough to suggest a whole bouquet of commonplaces. For Seneca Rhetor it is precisely these storm scenes which are typical of the poetry of excess beloved by the declaimers: his collection of memorable *flosculi* and *sententiae* also records comments and criticisms on the subject damning the insanity of many declaimers, more like characters in a satire than in an oratorical treatise.[32]

If Encolpius the mythomaniac narrator yields to the temptation of showing his skill in treating the topos of the storm according to all the rules of poetry and rhetoric, he is probably not the only victim of this source of inspiration among those on board with the "pirate" Lichas. I suspect that his friend, the *scholasticus* and poet Eumolpus, had shut himself below deck while the storm raged to write a poem about the storm itself. (What else can a professional poet do, when inspired fury seizes him, except set down verses, whatever his circumstances, including deadly peril?) Nothing in the text says outright that Eumolpus is busy producing a fine mannerist piece on the storm, but the sound of his verses is certainly lofty and

31. Cf. S. F. Bonner, *Roman Declamation in the Late Republic and Early Empire* (Liverpool, 1949), 59; M. P. O. Morford, *The Poet Lucan: Studies in Rhetorical Epic* (Oxford, 1967), 32–36; further bibliography in M. Labate, in F. Della Corte, ed., *Enciclopedia Virgiliana* (Roma, 1984), vol. V, esp. pp. 494–95, s.v. *venti*.

32. Cf. Sen. *Suas.* 1.13 Wint.: *efficit haec sententia ut ignoscam Musae (?) qui dixit ipsis Charybdi et Scylla maius portentum "Charybdis ipsius maris naufragium" et ne in una re semel insaniret "quid ibi potest esse salvi, ubi ipsum mare perit?"*

booming.[33] In fact the only sign that the other victims of ship-wreck have of his presence is a savage and fierce rumbling coming from the pilot's cabin: shut in there Eumolpus is reciting aloud the verses he has just composed on an enormous parchment (so this is a big poem of vast scope and effort). His companions try to bring him to his senses: *extrahimus clamantem iubemusque bonam habere mentem* (115.3), but to no avail; his frenzy reaches new heights.

This entire vignette presupposes the finale of the *Ars Poetica,* those verses (455–56) that Horace devoted to the *poeta vesanus,* personification of *error* and caricature of poetic possession.[34] Here Horace's satirical manner takes a few steps towards satiric narrative of a Petronian kind: *vesanum tetigisse timent fugiuntque poetam / qui sapiunt: agitant pueri incautique sequuntur* ("men of sense fear to touch a crazed poet and flee from him: little boys harass him and rashly pursue him"). Horace knows that *dum sublimis versus ructatur* ("while he belches out sublime poetry," 457) the possessed poet is incurably frenzied like a ferocious animal eager to escape its cage: (472–74) *certe furit ac velut ursus / obiectos caveae valuit si frangere clatros / indoctum doctumque fugat recitator acerbus* ("he is raging and like a bear, if it succeeds in breaking the bars of its cage, the relentless reciter puts to flight the unschooled and the schooled alike"). This is just how Petronius represents Eumolpus when he yields to the delirium of his poetic genius: (115.1) *audimur murmus insolitum et sub diaeta magistri quasi cupientis exire beluae gemitum* ("We hear a strange murmur

33. M. Labate, "Il Cadavere di Lica. Modelli letterari e istanza narrativa nel Satyricon di Petronio," *Taccuini* 8 (1988) 83–89, compares Eumolpus' situation on board ship in the storm with Ov. *Tr.* 1.11.7, where the poet depicts himself "bent on writing poetry amid the unleashed fury of the elements."

34. Cf. M. Labate, "Eumolpo e gli altri, ovvero lo spazio della poesia," *MD* 34 (1995), 153–75, but also Collignon, 253–54.

and a growl like that of a wild beast in the captain's cabin, frantic to get out").

Petronius has in mind Horace, poet of balanced judgment: the whole *Ars Poetica* had tried to blend *ingenium* and *ars* in a dialectic that would not mortify the creative genius by reducing it to poetic technique, but at the same time would heal the excesses of imaginative fervor with the antidote of classically defined form. In his ironic attack upon fashionable excesses perpetrated in the name of the sublime, the hidden author of the *Satyricon* set alongside his enthusiastic and mythomaniac narrator the extraordinary figure of a poet possessed—a *recitator acerbus.*[35] Eumolpus is the perfect complement of Encolpius, since both are inadequate interpreters of a shallow poetics of the sublime which calls down on itself all the arrows of an implacable irony. Even in this episode we can glimpse behind the mask of a continuous and easy narrative the serious ideology that directs the *Satyricon;* I mean by this the polemic to reaffirm the great literary values, which have been reduced to serve as everyday material for figures that are degraded and stultified by the schools of declamation and the fashion for *recitationes.* Great Literature and Great Poets are now far in the past.

The very idea of a novel about *scholastici* might in fact be a witty elaboration of materials drawn from the dossier of "scenes from academic life" which Seneca the Elder had already exploited. It is his *Memoirs* that give us lively evidence of the satiric possibilities of *reportage* on the schools and the principal

---

35. That Eumolpus can simultaneously be a *poeta vesanus* and a *recitator acerbus* goes back to Horace, especially *Ars* 453–54. Eumolpus reveals himself from his first appearance as an insatiable promoter of his own verses. In 90.3 Encolpius is forced to threaten him in order to interrupt his continuous recitation: *quid tibi vis cum isto morbo? minus quam duabus horis mecum moraris, et saepius poetice quam humane locutus es.* The adverb *humane* contrasted with *poetice* should be compared with Hor. *Ars* 468–69: *nec si retractus erit iam / fiet homo.* We might say against Eumolpus what Martial says to an equally insistent poet (3.44.4) *nimis poeta es.*

tendencies of rhetoric. *Furor, insania, mania, tumiditas* are recurring charges:[36] in short, excess, theatricality, exaggerated postures. But see how Petronius, as if in retribution, carries the *scholastici* out of the halls of recitation and thereby makes the disproportion between word and action even more comically paradoxical. Petronian satire transforms into continuous narrative some of the caricatured details already popularized in the works of Seneca Rhetor.

For example, one day the celebrated rhetor Porcius Latro, the most talented man of the time, agreed to leave the enclosed space of the classroom to help a kinsman and defend a real case in the forum (*Contr.* 9 *Praef.* 3). What happened to him was just what Encolpius and Agamemnon unanimously denounce in the opening chapter of the Petronian novel: he seemed to have been carried into another world (cf. *Satyr.* 1.2: *cum in forum venerint, putent se in alium orbem terrarum delatos*). As soon as he began to speak he made a mistake of Latinity, then had a nervous collapse and could not resume until the magistrate, out of respect for the famous orator, transferred the case inside the four walls of a nearby basilica.[37] The fact is that these *scholastici* and *umbratici* were exceptionally smart at making speeches which were like experiments *in vitro*, but they could not do anything except juggle rhetorical showpieces and tours de force. Everything was easy for them so long as it was not the real life[38] of the law courts. Like their pupils they are ripe for satire.

The storm is the umpteenth trap in which that implacable tormentor Petronius has ensnared his protagonist. The set piece on the storm and ensuing shipwreck give birth to the following

36. See the general index of J. Fairweather, *Seneca the Elder* (Cambridge, 1981).

37. Cf. Quint. *Inst.* 10.5.20.

38. Sen. *Contr.* 9 *praef.* 5: *usque eo ingenia in scholasticis exercitationibus delicate nutriuntur ut clamorem silentium risum caelum denique pati nesciant [. . .] in foro partem accipiunt, in schola eligunt;* cf. A. Gwynn, *Roman Education from Cicero to Quintilian* (Oxford, 1926) 166–67.

rhesis on the hollow ambitions of men, the *planctus* on the misery of human existence. All over again the *auctor absconditus* lays a new pathos-laden bait for his narrating character. The sea regurgitates a drowned corpse (115.7), the ideal opportunity for a long and resounding declamation. The unknown is revealed as the "pirate" Lichas, the fierce enemy who so recently had inspired such terror. But the memory of past fear produces in Encolpius only disconsolate thoughts on the infinite mutability of the human lot, on the absolute dominion of death. The young devotee of rhetoric finds in the baggage of his own experience a series of topoi worthy of a preacher of diatribe. It is a great theme, of course, perhaps the greatest possible theme for a declaimer, and Encolpius shapes from it a real repertory performance.[39] Ready for artificial emotions and sentiments, the naive *scholasticus* falls into the ironic author's snare. Even the scenario—an inspired monologue uttered on the shore before a corpse thrown up by the sea—seems one of those situations of high emotional content which the school loved to appropriate, if we are to judge from the sixth major declamation of Pseudo-Quintilian, entitled "the cast-up corpse."[40]

What may look like a parody of a showpiece declamation ac-

39. In developing the motif of human frailty the tyrant is the type selected to represent the whole *genus mortale*. The *magnae cogitationes* of the tyrant (or whoever arrogantly abuses force, like the *terribilis* and *implacabilis* pirate here) are cancelled as he faces the spectre of the *necessitas exeundi* and the constitutional weakness of the human body. Cf. 115.12–13: *ubi nunc est . . . iracundia tua, ubi impotentia tua? nempe piscibus beluisque expositus es, et qui paulo ante iactabas vires imperii tui [. . .] ite nunc . . .* Compare also Plin. *Nat.* 7.43–44: *quam sit frivola animalium superbissimi origo [. . .] his principiis nascuntur tyranni, his carnifex animus! Tu qui corporis viribus fidis, [. . .] tu cuius imperatoria est mens [. . .] tanti perire potuisti!* The motif had passed into the school exercises, as we see from the older section of Voss. Q 86: *A.L.* 437 Riese and especially 438: *iunxit magnorum casus Fortuna virorum: / hic parvo, nullo conditus ille loco est. / Ite, novas toto terras conquirite mundo, / nempe manet magnos parvula terra duces.*

40. Collignon, 265–66, had already recognized that the Petronian passage is influenced by the highly pathetic episode of Ceyx and Alcyone in Ovid's

tually takes the form here of pastiche. There is a real difference between the methods of parody and pastiche. Properly speaking parodic intertextuality aims to bring out the differences between texts; pastiche aims to exaggerate their similarities. In setting out to reproduce faithfully a style of writing, pastiche hides its aggression behind the appearance of servile imitation, only to reveal itself in the end for what it really is: a deforming caricature in which all the structural elements of the mannered declamation are accumulated.[41] This wholesale appropriation of distinctive traits produces not so much an intertext as an "interstyle," if I may call it that. In this sense the destructive irony of pastiche is more radical than that of parody: it undermines the very foundation of the model, instead of seeking to correct it. Its rejection is total.

Thus a sermon of unbelievable banality emerges from Encolpius' words, a sermon that seeks to reinforce the poverty of its arguments by loading them with magnificent gestures. Rhetorical questions in anaphora, apostrophes at the highest end of the emotional register, sententiae for grand effect—this is the traditional armament recommended by any manual of declamatory rhetoric. The technique of a good declamation controls the articulation of the speech in such a way that every individual situation can blaze up into wholly general reflections. Each event, each story, must be also capable of losing its uniqueness to become an *exemplum* (*factum aut dictum memorabile,* as Valerius Maximus' collection names it, a collection intended to simplify the orator's task). From this paradigmatic status we should be

---

Metamorphoses (cf. especially 11.715–22). Alcyone sights from a distance a corpse cast up by the sea and weeps for the fate of the stranger until the waves thrust it nearer and reveal her husband Ceyx; the heroine abandons herself to renewed grief. There is a fine analysis in Labate, "Il Cadavere di Lica," 83–89; cf. also Courtney, "Parody and Literary Allusion," 98.

41. Collignon, 298–99, compares Petronius 115.16 with Sen. *Contr.* 7.1.9, a declamation of Cestius Pius in which a series of examples illustrates the sententia, *nascimur uno modo, multis morimur.*

able to derive moral instruction or edification. What is more important in this type of literature is the art of creating "transitions," that is of returning a particular instance to a topical constellation, reducing it to a familiar category of motif.[42] Facts find meaning and value only if they are interpreted within a receptive framework of preestablished categories. If the theme is obligatory, the speech ultimately only recommends itself by its reassuring lack of originality.

In the preface to the first book of *Controversiae*, Seneca the Elder recalls that Latro, the professional rhetor he so admired, had the habit of spending entire days writing nothing but *epiphonemata* or *enthymemata*, or developing only those conventional passages (*translaticias . . . sententias*) which "are not intimately rooted in the controversy but can be transferred from one speech to another, concerning for example fortune, cruelty, modern times, riches" (*hoc genus sententiarum suppellectilem vocabat* [*Contr.* 1 *Praef.* 23]). In short, a speech is like an empty house; the rhetorician is its interior decorator. Encolpius too furnishes his tirade with thoughts that strike him as powerful: (115.16) *si bene calculum ponas, ubique naufragium est* ("if you sum things up correctly, there is shipwreck everywhere"), (115.18) *quicquid feceris omnia haec eodem ventura sunt* ("whatever you do, all things will come to the same end"). But what is important is that the death of Lichas can become the *exemplum* of a theme that we can call *de mutabilitate fortunae* or *de humana fragilitate*. In fact Encolpius in his anxiety to be a

---

42. The *corpus humanum circumactum levi vortice* (115.7) is the pathetic bait that brings on the *humana condicio mortalitatis*. The association is almost obligatory for a *scholasticus* like Encolpius, since the image of the *naufragus in litore eiectus* has become in the mannerist thesaurus an emblem of human fragility and subjection to the blows of fortune. To refute the idea of a kind and providential nature, Lucretius had compared the condition of man at birth to that of a castaway: . . . *ut saevis proiectus ab undis navita* (5.222–23). Equally pessimistic and stylized representations of the human condition can be found in Plin. *Nat.* 7.2–3, Sen. 6.10.6

declaimer has taken on several themes at once, and the various parts of his speech are stitched together without even an attempt at the logical coherence of argumentation.[43]

Encolpius devotes himself so earnestly to his heartfelt meditation that some critics have even believed (in order to find some meaning behind such solemnity) that they can hear the voice of the author behind his words. Thus the author would be introducing into his narrative the tragic awareness of death.[44] It is easy to pass from this to an existentialist interpretation of the whole *Satyricon:* the face that weeps behind the mask that laughs. I do not want to set before you the image of a thoughtless and hedonist Petronius, lacking any gloominess or sense of anguish;[45] if I say that Petronius speaks and thinks in terms of literature, it is because he is talking about a world where literature invades life and claims to substitute itself for life. But this

43. The entire monologue of Encolpius is an "incorrect" mixture of topoi of the funeral lament and consolatory topoi traditionally adopted to reject the use of the lament. The declamation is recited *lamentoso* (cf. 115.8: *tristis . . . umentibus oculis,* 115.11: *deflebam,* 115.12: *non tenui igitur diutius lacrimas, immo percussi semel iterumque manibus pectus*). The *loci communes* of lament are frequent (115.9), as is the motif of death which takes away the good things of life, attested in funerary epigraphy (e.g. *CIL* 10.2483) and scholastic exercises (cf. Cornelius Severus on the death of Cicero in Sen. *Suas.* 6.26). It is clear that the whole speech is an application of topoi, since the elements of argumentation are common to different philosophical schools (cf. e.g. Lucr. 3.894–96 and 879–93, Cic. *Tusc.* 1.83 and 106); Encolpius even employs two different types of argumentation without realizing the distinction. He assembles the diatribic topoi on the constitutional frailty of man to show the unconquerable dominion of death, but precisely these motifs formed part of the exercise on *cogitatio mortis* for consolatory purposes (cf. Philodemus *De morte* 4.37.26–27). The drift of his declamation leads Encolpius to orient the consolatory topoi in the sole direction of the pathetic lament: rhetorical exaggeration and the taste for excess annul any argumentative rigor.

44. Cf. V. Ciaffi, *La Struttura del Satyricon* (Turin, 1955) 98–99; Perry, 199–200.

45. O. Raith, *Petronius. Ein Epikureer* (Nürnberg, 1963), 15, sees a mark of Epicurean doctrine in the attitude of Encolpius when he first asserts that it would be a matter of indifference to him whether, after death, a corpse were

very "existentialist" attitude, which is found in the declamation *de fragilitate humanae vitae* put into Encolpius' mouth, belongs with those schoolroom posturings which the text condemns.

If we want to hear the author's real voice, surely we will have to look for it in the implicit ironic counterpoint which the text provides immediately after, in the ensuing development of the narrative. For in this case the author follows the highly colored words of the naive narrator with one of the most humorous scenes of the entire work. Eumolpus too participates in the ritual, devoting himself to composing a funeral epigram for poor Lichas (probably in the style of those collected in Book 7 of the *Anthologia Palatina*): he casts his gaze far over the sea (the gesture of any good professional poet) in the search for inspiration.[46]

If there was still any doubt about the authenticity of Encolpius' tirade, and the author's possible support for these emotional words, the caricature of the poet Eumolpus demystifies Encolpius' claim to move us. The author's irony is centered in the parallel treatment of the two characters who form the pair of discredited adventurers: one who thinks himself exalted by a spontaneous transport of sublime emotions, the other more overtly exploiting the opportunity to keep his own professional skill well honed. So Encolpius' discourse is revealed by the juxtaposition to be an artificial production, simply a

---

burned or devoured by wild animals, but then makes provision for the burning of Lichas' body. I would, however, exclude the possibility that this scene is meant to be taken seriously or raises major philosophical issues. The entire scene—as I attempt to demonstrate—has an ironic function. The author smiles as he watches his naive hero Encolpius again falling victim to his own scholastic rhetoric. Encolpius is intent above all on fabricating a quasi-philosophical lamentation on the uncertainty of mortal life, stuffing it with reflections drawn from the most banal repertoire and reciting it in a sententious, high-sounding style.

46. *Satyr.* 115.20: *Eumolpus autem dum epigramma mortuo facit oculos ad arcessendos sensus longius mittit.*

second-hand sermon. It is as if the young man was ever ready to profit by the accidents of life to display the great and elevated conceits which he has long kept in reserve. Similarly Eumolpus, another *scholasticus* at heart but a poet by profession, uses every possible circumstance as raw material for poetic compositions. Although each occasion fits a different literary genre (tragic, epic, elegiac, iambic), each occasion without differentiation has to be turned to profit in versification: life is just the obverse of poetry.[47]

The longing for the sublime that obsesses Encolpius lacks the chief feature of the true sublime, as Pseudo-Longinus would claim, namely the miraculous fusion of talent and art which enables art to become nature: heated "*ma non troppo*," spontaneous "*ma non troppo*." Encolpius is schoolroom and nothing but schoolroom: he has no talent. He tries to compensate for his deficiencies by exaggerating pathos, but he forgets that the excess of pathos is the real enemy of the sublime. Pseudo-Longinus also talks of "inflation" (οἰδοῦν, 3.1–3), which consists in oversaturating the colors in relation to the real contents in order to achieve surprising effects.[48] He seems to have in mind the cultural setting offered by Asianic reciters and declaimers when he inveighs against those who confuse the sublime with an excess of pathos: theirs is a false inspiration (ἐνθουσιᾶν), not bacchic possession but a childish pretense or game (οὐ βακχεύουσιν ἀλλὰ παίζουσιν).[49] When the attempt

---

47. A hilarious example is the episode in which, during the great fight in the *deversorium*, the *procurator insulae* Bargates (96.6–7) intercedes to save Eumolpus and after having recognized and greeted him as a great poet (*O poetarum disertissime . . . tu eras?*), uses the opportunity to request a few lines against his partner who is treating him with proud disdain (obviously he is asking for an iambic invective: *maledic illam versibus, ut habeat pudorem*).

48. Excessively pathetic diction is not tragic but paratragic: ibid. 3.1: οὐ τραγικὰ ἔτι ταῦτα ἀλλὰ παρατράγῳδα.

49. The polemic against pathetic excess runs right through the treatise up to 15.8 where Pseudo-Longinus takes a stance against the absurd mania of

at exaltation fails, the inevitable lapse produces the exact opposite of grandeur—puerility (τὸ δὲ μειρακιῶδες, 3.4).

But the real fault of anyone who falls short of the sublime, of Encolpius in fact, is a misuse of the pathetic: false enthusiasm, exaggerated emotion, τὸ παρένθυρσον.[50] It is an inopportune and hollow pathos, appearing where there is no need for pathos, or sounding unrestrained where restraint is needed (3.5: πάθος ἄκαιρον καὶ κενὸν ἔνθα μὴ δεῖ πάθους, ἢ ἄμετρον ἔνθα μετρίου δεῖ); it is the same emotional excess shown by drunks who wallow in emotions quite uncalled-for by the real circumstances, a peculiar pathos "suggesting the schoolroom," a hysterical and even academic kind of pathos (ἴδια ἑαυτῶν καὶ σχολικὰ παραφέρονται πάθη). They confuse their exaltation with divine inspiration and behave like sophomores full of enthusiasm but short on talent. And Pseudo-Longinus adds, "they have lost their senses but address themselves to an audience that has not." This is just what happens in the *Satyricon* to the *scholasticus* Encolpius, laid bare before the sane and ironic gaze of the hidden author.

It would seem that at least on one matter the hidden author agrees with his discredited characters, the narrator Encolpius and the rogue-poet Eumolpus: they share a profound feeling of longing for the great literature of the past. But while Encolpius and Eumolpus always think their enthusiasm will be enough to reach the sublime, Petronius uses them (or rather their aspirations) to show just how irredeemably it is now beyond reach. It is only irony that makes him choose them as his "seekers in the quest for the sublime": if it is up to them to find it, he seems to be saying, then it is well and truly lost.

---

contemporary orators for seeming to be possessed by Furies ("like Orestes pursued by the Erinyes"). Compare the earlier discussion in chapter 1, p. 14.

50. In fact the term comes from Theodorus: see the comment of D. A. Russell, ed., *"Longinus" On the Sublime.* (Oxford, 1964), *ad loc.*, p. 75.

There is another passage of the *Satyricon* in which we might find the critical ambiguity which blurs the words of the character and the thought of the author: I refer to the so-called poetic manifesto of Eumolpus, at the point of transition between the adventure on board ship and the new adventure at Croton. Here Eumolpus adumbrates an *Ars Poetica* containing sound principles which the author might well share, particularly the polemic against the predominance of rhetoric, and even more the predominance of the schools of rhetoric with all their faults (so often attacked, as we have seen, in the *Satyricon*).

Even the eulogy of great poets of the past—Homer, the lyricists, Virgil and Horace—might seem to be spoken *ex voce auctoris*. Instead, the range of agreement is relatively small. Eumolpus urges us to take up the great classics, which combined *ingenium* and *ars,* passion and practice, enthusiasm and imitation, but his invitation to a poetics based on models lacks the essential balance between the elements; he focuses entirely on the enthusiasm with which the new poet must submerge himself in the stream of his models. Indeed the models must flood over the poet, who is now no longer master of himself: (118.3) *mens . . . ingenti flumine litterarum inundata* ("a mind flooded by the mighty stream of literature").

Eumolpus tries to reformulate the old Horatian dichotomy, but the distinctions are blurred beneath the pressure of the sublime driven to excess; the *furor* of *enthousiasmos* gets the upper hand. In Eumolpus' *Ars Poetica* the two components of the Horatian prescription can still be recognized: *neque generosior spiritus sanitatem amat* (this is *ingenium*) *neque concipere aut edere partum mens potest nisi ingenti flumine litterarum inundata* ("a truly noble inspiration shuns sanity, nor can the mind conceive or give birth to its offspring unless it is flooded by a mighty stream of literature"). This ought to be *ars*, except that, as we have just seen, the technical component retains nothing of the "cool" characteristics that rightly belong to it but is assimilated to the excesses of possession. It is indeed Horace's *Ars Poetica* which offers just the control we need.

Eumolpus' declaration, *neque generosior spiritus sanitatem amat,* unwittingly shapes itself to the caricature that Horace sketched of the *poeta vesanus,* or better, of those who, in order to feel themselves truly inspired, took on the pose of the *poeta vesanus.* Horace says: (295–96) *ingenium misera quia fortunatius arte / credit et excludit sanos Helicone poetas / Democritus bona pars non ungues ponere curat / non barbam, secreta petit loca, balnea vitat* ("because Democritus believes inspiration is more blessed than unlucky art and excludes sane poets from Helicon, a great number choose not to trim their nails or beard and seek seclusion, shunning public baths"). Eumolpus too, like Democritus, dislikes *sanitas* in poets: his model is that of Platonic *mania.*[51] Even in the physical portrait of these poets we have no trouble recognizing our Eumolpus: neglectful in grooming, tormented in expression, a true poet of high inspiration.

Petronius the hidden author sides ironically with Horace against Eumolpus. He too is not happy with the predominance of the sublime in literature, if it is understood as the predominance of inspiration. But perhaps even so the problem should not be put in strictly theoretical terms: what Petronius really cannot stand is contemporary fashion, the vogue for "passion" which turns poetry-making into an uncontrolled *raptus* and confuses the sublimity of the great authors of the past with frigid magniloquence, with *parenthurson.* In this, at least, he does not seem too far from the preoccupations of Pseudo-Longinus. His act of hiding, his oblique and ironic discourse,

---

51. Fraenkel (followed by Müller[1]) does not notice the parodic irony turned against Eumolpus, the overkeen supporter of poetic possession; he makes the poet more sane than he is by deleting the first *neque* of 118.3: *[neque] generosior spiritus sanitatem amat neque,* etc. But the deletion destroys the correlation *neque . . . neque* and removes the sting from the phrase; in subsequent editions Müller returns to the paradosis.

has a polemical ring in relation to the theatricality of Neronian culture, in which literature becomes exhibition, speech becomes declamation, artistic emotion becomes the desire to gratify the audience.[52] Behind this position of Petronius there is an aristocratic, even conservative, attitude. Paradoxically, his polemical gesture is not entrusted to a manifesto, or a satiric scream of protest, but is embodied in the sobriety of a bare and economical Atticist style, a style against the current, quite the opposite, in short, of the style which Eumolpus recommends to the future poet. Eumolpus uses strong words: imagination should have free rein, rushing headlong (118.6: *praecipitandus est liber spiritus*). These are passionate expressions, but we should not miss the fact that they all have equivalents in the technical vocabulary of the theory of style. Quintilian is quite severe with those who resort to a corrupt style (*Inst.* 12.10.73: *vitiosum et corruptum dicendi genus*) in quest of easy acclaim, straining for sudden leaps as if they were sublime (*praecipitia pro sublimibus habet*) and acting as if going crazy were a mark of free expression (*specie libertatis insanit*). This is in fact the false sublime, which Quintilian will complain is so fashionable that it now seems a kind of excellence: (7.1.44) *in hac quaerentur sententiae, si fieri poterit, praecipites vel obscurae (nam ea nunc virtus est)*. This refers to the tormented and distorted style which Horace defined as *praeceps* and compared to the utterance of an oracle: (*Ars* 216–18) *facundia praeceps . . . et divina futuri / sortilegis non discrepuit sententia Delphis* ("this headlong eloquence and prophetic utterance is little different from oracular Delphi").[53]

Indeed Eumolpus too wants the poet's voice to sound like a

52. Some hints in S. Bartsch, *Actors in the Audience: Theatricality and Doublespeak from Nero to Hadrian* (Cambridge, Mass., 1994), 10–12 and *passim*.

53. Cf. C. O. Brink, *Horace on Poetry: The "Ars Poetica"* (Cambridge, 1971), *ad loc.*, p. 272, and O. Immisch, *Horazens Epistel über die Dichtkunst, Philologus Suppl.* 24.3 (1932) 136–37.

prophecy; the paradigm of the poet possessed by the god takes on the features that Pseudo-Longinus attributes to the Pythia inspired by Apollo: (13.2) "many writers are enthused by the spirit of other writers, as men say of the Pythian priestess when she draws near to the tripod: there is a chasm in the earth from which the spirit of the god is said to emanate (ἀτμὸν ἔνθεον). It impregnates the priestess with a supernatural power and makes her instantly utter inspired oracles (χρησμῳδεῖν)."

In Eumolpus' literary reminiscences, the Pythia is clearly transformed into Virgil's Sibyl: *per ambages . . . praecipitandus est liber spiritus* recalls *Aeneid* 6.98–100, *Cumaea Sibylla / horrendas canit ambages . . . / obscuris vera involvens* ("the Sibyl of Cumae sings dread riddles . . . wrapping true things in darkness"). In a sense even the words of the Sibyl are an "inspired song" like the poetic song which Eumolpus is recommending to the poets of historical epic, a song that adorns real events with the dress of fantastic invention; his *specimen* of the *Bellum Civile* will be entirely conceived like the vision of one possessed.

I suspect that the entire Petronian sequence *per ambages deorumque ministeria et fabulosum sententiarum tormentum* has been influenced by Virgil's *mise en scène*. Prophetic *furor* (*Aen.* 6.102) causes a terrible suffering in the Sibyl (as it should in the possessed poet of Eumolpus' fancy); consider 6.77–80: *at Phoebi nondum patiens immanis in antro / bacchatur vates, magnum si pectore possit / excussisse deum; tanto magis ille fatigat / os rabidum, fera corda domans, fingitque premendo* ("But the priestess, not yet submissive to Phoebus, rages in the cavern, trying to shake the mighty god from her breast; he all the more harasses her frenzied mouth, taming her fierce heart, and shapes her speech by his pressure"). I am inclined to believe that we should keep the reading, *fabulosum sententiarum tormentum,* in Petronius' text: with an original turn of phrase, it indicates the tortuous elaboration with which the prophetic poet (like the Sibyl) marks his discourse, the effort necessitated by the struggle to "expel" the spirit of divine inspiration (cf. *ex-cussisse deum*). The verbal violence contained in *tormentum* seems to match the violence contained in Virgil's text: *rabidum, premendo* and above all the verb *fatigare,* which is a virtual synonym of *torquere.*[54]

The long composition that follows Eumolpus' *ars* is a real outburst of the sublime, or rather of the false but fashionable sublime that is both grotesque and revolting. But the entire *ars* finally reveals itself as a deception played on the demented poet: the brilliant originality with which he preaches is much less brilliant and original than he would like us to think. Sharing the faults of many poets and rhetoricians of his age, expert in the poetics of *furor,* Eumolpus is just one among many. Unlike Encolpius in his gift for insinuating himself into the most varied narrative situations, he shares with him the passion for tumid and pretentious literature. The lurking author turns the same ironic smile upon them both.

In short the great models from the literature of the past entice the mythomaniac narrator into exaggerated poses and gestures: yet put to the test of action his longing for the sublime is exposed as pure declamatory artifice, a scholastic kind of exaltation. This allows the hidden author to demolish the drama of the narrative situations. To expose them as inauthentic or illusory he need only pull out from under the narrator's inopportune imaginings the props of his pathetic and pretentious utterances. But for all that the author works on demolishing the drama, he too is not immune from an intense longing for the sublime. But his longing is unlike that of his protagonist: it is the full awareness of regret. He knows that the sublime is now a lost blessing, past and irretrievable. No polemical irony can cancel this bitter truth.

54. Cf. Pacuv. 159 R²: *fatigans artus torto distraham* (with Nonius' comment, 179.14, *"torto" pro tormento*); cf. also Porph. on Hor. *Epist.* 2.2.124: (the poet in stylistic labor) *torquebitur et fatigabitur ut pantomimus.*

CHAPTER THREE

The Deceptiveness of Myth

It is now clear that whereas declamation gives the mythomaniac narrator his pretext for mannered outbursts of eloquence, it is always the popular novel whose narrative model drives the protagonist into the snare of stereotyped situations. Once he has fallen into them he is impelled to dramatize them. This is the world of shock, of sensationalism, a disturbing and a tormenting world. In this sense the Greek novel can be considered as a "popular" melodrama which has reduced the great literature of pathos to stereotypes and so trivialized it.

As we saw, it is the hidden author's responsibility to generate the situations in which the protagonist Encolpius finds himself. The young *scholasticus* becomes the unconscious victim of narrative schemata which eventuate in parodic reverses of the most typical scenarios of the idealized Greek romance. It should also be clear that the parody of the Greek romance is not just an episodic stylistic device in the *Satyricon:* it is the structural foundation of Petronius' narrative form. The unfolding of the narrated action develops as a kind of echo, a parallel discourse that depends for its meaning upon the reader's understanding. In fact it is just because the reader *can* recognize the fixed schemata of the popular novel behind the narrated action that he enters into the parodic game and assumes for himself the ironizing attitude of the author. The reader's smile as he turns into an accomplice makes explicit the author's implicit voice, a voice that would otherwise be bound to silence in a text in which the narrator's "I" ostensibly conducts the entire narration.

To parody the hackneyed conventions of the Greek popular novel the *auctor absconditus* uses the approach of exaggeration or inversion, but even when he inverts (for example, by transforming the heterosexual pair of chaste and faithful lovers into a debauched and fickle homosexual couple), Petronius likes to signal very clearly to his readers. The very title of the work indicates the literary operation which determines the formation of the text. *Satyrica* (*Satyricon libri*) is an expressive formation based on a parodic contamination; its suffix *-i(a)ca* is the counterpart of Greek novels whose titles were like the examples we know, *Ephesiaka, Milesiaka, Babyloniaka, Aethiopika, Kypriaka, Phoinikika,* while the category "satura" points to the parodic manner maintained by the narrative. (I do not see how one can decide whether this refers to the literary genre of satire or to the disruptive intervention of *Satyroi,* who regularly attack the conventions of high literature in drama.)[1]

It is really in the construction of themes that this parodic mimicry of the adventure novel becomes more transparent. If adventures at sea are a recurring theme of this genre, inevitably followed by kidnapping on a pirate ship, well then all of a sudden the respectable bourgeois Lichas engaging in a trading voy-

---

1. It is more than likely that the Latin linguistic consciousness associated *satura* with *satyroi;* see C. A. Van Rooy, *Studies in Classical Satire and Related Literary Theory* (Leiden, 1965), esp. 155 (for evidence, see R. Maltby, *A Lexicon of Ancient Latin Etymologies* [Leeds, 1991], 547, s.vv. *satyricus, satyrus*). See also E. Courtney, "Parody and Literary Allusion," 93; Coffey, 181. It will become more obvious in chapter 4 that many of the themes employed by the *Satyricon* in the construction of the narrative follow the pattern indicated by the satiric repertoire. Cf. N. Holzberg, *The Ancient Novel,* trans. C. Jackson-Holzberg (London and New York, 1995), 63–64, who finds an analogy between Petronius' parodistic attack on the idealized Greek romance and the way in which satyresque drama degrades tragedy.

age takes on the role of pirate, indeed of Pirate Chief[2]—the pure essence of the romantic theme.[3] This equation arises only because Encolpius has a holy dread of him based on the old relationship between the two, compounded of troubled and incurable resentments (amongst other offenses, Encolpius seduced Lichas' wife Hedyle).

If the shipwreck is another fixed ingredient of the adventure novel, Encolpius and his companions, as we saw, will end up in a fully fledged storm which follows all the rules of the genre. And the ship will also serve as courtroom, with Eumolpus as the defense lawyer (*Satyr.* 107), so that we do not miss the parody of another basic ingredient of the novel, the legal trial.[4] In short, *normality* in the novel is a series of *extraordinary* incidents, like piracy and shipwrecks and trials—adventures that enliven the novel's race towards the required *happy end,* so much so that each one of the peripeties serves as a metaphor for romance. These are situations that aim to be extraordinary but by their sheer repetition become totally predictable. In the *Satyricon* it is enough to combine them with weak characters always ready to lapse into the comic register, and all the advantages of parody can be extracted. There is a preamble in Chari-

2. Cf. *Satyr.* 101.5. It is worth noting that the significant description of Lichas as *archipirata* is employed by Eumolpus to bring the melodramatically desperate Encolpius and Giton down to earth: "Lichas of Tarentum, an honest merchant: *hic est Cyclops ille et archipirata, cui vecturam debemus* ("here is your Cyclops and pirate chief to whom we owe our passage"). This is one of the key passages in reading the *Satyricon* as a representation of a confrontation between different perceptions of reality. When he learns Lichas' story, Eumolpus' reaction, *fingite nos antrum Cyclopis intrasse,* openly contradicts his original "commonsense" reaction. The hidden author marks his characters' melodramatic delirium through the comment of another character who seems sensible only because he is uninformed; then he too is immediately swept into the hallucinatory logic of the others.

3. Cf. Billault, 197–99 (in the chapter entitled "Pirates et brigands").

4. See F. Létoublon, *Les lieux communs du roman: Stéréotypes grecs d'aventure et d'amour* (Leiden, 1993), 177–79, 221.

ton (to the eighth and last book of the novel, the one that must bring about the happy end of the intrigue) which is worth some careful consideration: "I think this last book will be the most pleasing to my readers, because they will find in it the purging (καθάρσιον) of the tragic elements (σκυθρωπῶν) in the preceding books. No more piracy and enslavement and trials and battles and attempts at suicide and wars and captures, but lawful love and legitimate marriages" (8.1.4). Chariton says "tragic elements," meaning "misadventures and sorrows," but he could as well have said "melodramatic elements." To the idealizing narrator of the Greek romance his own material is a tragedy with a happy end. He imagines that the pleasure lies in leading his reader to the soothing spectacle of virtue rewarded (as if his aim was merely to edify) and he hides the fact that all the pleasure of the narrative lies in the torment of the catastrophes which the characters experience. What the reader of the popular novel wants are just these things: pirates, trials, storms, attempted suicides. All the more, in fact, since the happy ending is guaranteed.[5]

The rhetoric of the idealistic love romance requires that the narrator feign horror at the misfortunes that destroy the protagonists' initial happiness and expose them to uninterrupted persecution. Among so many idealizing fictions of the novel, this too is a fiction that Petronius will unmask, showing that we are dealing with rhetoric and with a conventional scheme that can

---

5. I. Stark, "Strukturen des griechischen Abenteuer- und Liebesromans," in H. Kuch, ed., *Der Antike Roman: Untersuchungen zur literarischen Kommunikations und Gattungsgeschichte* (Berlin, 1989), 82–83, shows the principal theme of the novels to be actually that of eternal love and incorruptible fidelity. "But if love and fidelity are to be confirmed as unchanging, then they must necessarily be subjected to trials. The result is a continual sequence of trial situations." For this reason the plot consists of a more or less conventionalized sequence of misfortunes. Cf. D. Konstan, *Sexual Symmetry: Love in the Ancient Novel and Related Genres* (Princeton, 1993), 14, with much up-to-date bibliography; cf. also Holzberg, 9–10.

be parodied. Often it is the catastrophes that provide material for the satiric narrative of Petronius. They are the sources of the parodic reversals set in motion by the ironic awareness of the hidden author, but conversely they are the bait which each time hooks the mythomania of the hero, ever ready to raise to mythical heights the degraded stereotypes of romantic *Triviallitteratur*.

In the basic "morphology" of the adventure novel which Chariton articulates, we must include suicide attempts, those powerful scenes of melodramatic pathos in which the despairing protagonists (in order to defend unswerving loyalty in love) choose the ultimate solution of death by their own hand. This is a stereotype particularly exposed to the ironic attack of the *Satyricon,* inasmuch as a would-be suicide never really dies in the Greek romantic novel; as often as the protagonists attempt it, they survive.[6]

In chapter 94 Encolpius enacts a first comic version of the suicide for love. Left alone with his jealousy (Eumolpus is lying in ambush for his beloved Giton), he plans to take his own life by hanging himself from the bedstead set upright against the wall of his hotel room. But Eumolpus and Giton arrive unexpectedly to defuse the danger (according to the standard model of last-minute rescue); so Giton, protesting that he is ready to die first as proof of his own love for Encolpius, snatches a razor from Eumolpus' attendant and strikes a blow at his throat.

6. One of my students, Lucia Galli, has clearly established in her thesis ("Petronio e il romanzo greco," Pisa, 1992) that there is a stereotype of "aborted suicide": one of the two lovers chooses to die by his or her own hand, either in order to remain faithful or because he or she misguidedly believes that the beloved is dead. The attempt always fails (in order to guarantee the "happy ending"). Cf. especially the series of attempted suicides by Chaerea in Char. 1.5.2, 1.6.1–2, 3.3.1, 3.5.6, 5.10.6–10, 6.2.8–11, 7.1.5–11; but see also Xenoph. Ephes. 2.7.1, 3.5–8, 5.8.8–9. The motif appears less commonly in novels of "the second phase"; cf. Ach. Tat. 3.16.5–17.1, 7.6.3–4, Hel. 2.2.1, 2.4.4–5.1.

Now the romantic action challenges Encolpius to a noble
and heroic act of sacrifice, and he cannot fail it. The boy falls
at his feet and Encolpius lets out a cry and throws himself on
top of him, striking with the same weapon (94.12–13: *semel
iterumque cervice percussa ante pedes collabitur nostros. Exclamo ego attonitus, secutusque labentem eodem ferramento ad
mortem viam quaero*).

The mythical scene into which the hero projects himself is
nothing less than the death of Nisus over the body of Euryalus
in the ninth book of the *Aeneid:* (444–45) *tum super exanimum
sese proiecit amicum / confossus, placidaque ibi demum morte
quievit* ("then he hurled himself onto his lifeless friend and at
last rested in the calm of death"). The two loving friends of
heroic Virgilian epic have found their physical union in death:
first a cry of terror before the death of his friend (compare
exclamo ego attonitus with *Aen.* 9.424–25: *tum vero exterri-
tus . . . / conclamat Nisus*), then the embrace and the comfort of
a shared death. The mythic-heroic paradigm has created its illusion. Among school reminiscences Virgil provides a fine example of a sublime scenario.

But Encolpius is not Nisus, nor is Giton Euryalus: the other
characters in the episode have no doubt about this. The razor
has no edge, it is the training instrument of a barber's appren-
tice. That is why Eumolpus and his slave are not particularly
alarmed and can stand by enjoying the scenario of the lovers'
death (*nec Eumolpus interpellaverat mimicam mortem*, 94.15).
It is a farcical death, a show by actors playing a part. Even the
narrator finally realizes this, although he began by deceiving
himself that he was living through a moment of great and heroic
emotion, and now he explicitly defines as "play-acting" the
feigned death which he unwittingly began to perform.

Here too the text seems to divide itself between the two separate functions that coexist in the voice of Encolpius, both narra-

tor and protagonist: this is the tension between the "agent I"
and the "narrating I."[7] As if it was not enough, the delusion of
the protagonist-narrator is further ironized by the meta-diegetic
instruction that follows: (95.1) *dum haec fabula inter amantes
luditur* ("while this play was being performed by the lovers").
The two lovers are merely *actors,* characters of a myth, or
worse, characters of a mime that burlesques the myth.

But the moving scene of Nisus sacrificing himself to save
Euryalus has a longer life in our text. It had been partly foreshadowed a few chapters earlier when Giton thrust himself between the dueling Ascyltus and Encolpius. There the boy offered
himself as a victim of the anger he himself had provoked: (80.4)
*quod si utique . . . facinore opus est, nudo ecce iugulum, con-
vertite huc manus, imprimite mucrones. Ego mori debeo, qui
amicitiae sacramentum delevi* ("but if there must be a crime, see
I bare my throat, turn your hands against me and pierce me
with your blades. It is I who should die, since I destroyed the
oath of friendship"). Nisus too cried out: (*Aen.* 9.427–30) *me,
me, adsum qui feci, in me convertite ferrum / o Rutuli! mea
fraus omnis . . . / tantum infelicem nimium dilexit amicum.*[8]

In fact the primary scenario here is quite different. It is a
famous tragic model (one in fact reshaped in Latin close in time
to the *Satyricon*), namely the scene of Jocasta thrusting herself between Eteocles and Polynices. Giton explicitly refers to
the myth with the words (80.3), *ne Thebanum par humilis
taberna spectaret* ("lest the humble inn should witness another
Theban duel"). The sight of Encolpius and Ascyltus dueling
would be a degrading repetition of the fratricide of the sons of
Oedipus. The part of the mythical heroes is assigned to unlikely
characters; the model is sublime, but the scene that interprets it

---

7. Cf. chapter 1, p. 12 n. 12, p. 25 n. 27, chapter 2, p. 53 n. 22.
8. Collignon had noticed this allusion: cf. 120; cf. also Zeitlin, 58–59 n. 3.

is low.[9] Once he has recognized the Theban pair in the *fratres pugnantes,* Giton is bound to play Jocasta, the queen and mother from the tragedies of Euripides and Seneca. It is precisely the Roman theater, more inclined than the Greek to spectacular dramatic effects, that highlights the figure of Jocasta, placed between the opposing ranks. Compare Seneca *Phoenissae* 443ff. *in me arma et ignes vertite, in me omnis ruat / unam iuventus . . . ;* (447–49) *hunc petite ventrem, qui dedit fratres viro, / haec membra passim spargite ac divellite: / ego utrumque peperi . . . ;* (456–57) *si placuit scelus / maius paratum est: / media se opponit parens* ("Turn your weapons and your fires on me, let all the youth charge against me. . . . Aim at this belly, which gave brothers to her husband, scatter these limbs and tear them this way and that: I gave birth to both. . . . If you are resolved on crime, here is a greater crime, your mother stands exposed between you").[10]

9. Compare K. Preston, "Some Sources of Comic Effect in Petronius," *CPh* 10 (1915) 260–69, esp. 261 and n. 1, who mentions the dramatic genre of the *tabernaria.*

10. Another model may also appear behind the construction of the melodramatic scene: the celebrated myth of the Sabine women who put themselves between husbands and fathers to separate them and prevent mutual slaughter. Cf. Liv. 1.13.2–3: *hinc patres, hinc viros orantes ne sanguine nefando soceri generique respergerent, ne parricidio macularent partus suos . . . "si adfinitatis inter vos, si conubii piget, in nos vertite iras; nos causa belli, nos volnerum et caedium viris ac parentibus sumus: melius peribimus quam sine alteris vestrum viduae aut orbae vivemus."* Livy is here clearly indebted to models provided by dramatic historiography (one important model is Phylarchus' description of the taking of Mantinea: cf. F. W. Walbank, *A Historical Commentary on Polybius,* I [Oxford, 1957], on Polyb. 2.56; and C. Ampolo, *Le vite di Teseo e di Romolo* [Milano, 1988], on Plut. *Rom.* 19.3). It has also been hypothesized, however, that Livy is borrowing from Ennius' *Annales* (F. Bömer, *Ovidius Die Fasten,* I-II [Heidelberg, 1957–1958], on 3.206). This heroic model may have been revived by the mythical fantasies of the young *scholasticus.* We may compare *Satyr.* 80.3–4: *neve sanguine pollueremus familiaritatis clarissimae sacra* (if *clarissimae* is not corrupt, it must be interpreted as a pretentious attempt to elevate the friendship of Encolpius and Ascyltus to the mythic level of heroic friendships like those of Orestes and Pylades or Theseus and Pirithous). On the other hand, it is quite likely that Livy's narration, in view of the pathetic elaboration of the text, was itself

Giton is well aware that he is putting on the mask of Jocasta's tragic role without being worthy of the role he is interpreting. But the sublime model reactivated by Giton-Jocasta still finds its usual victim, Encolpius. The poor *scholasticus* falls prey to the scenario prepared by Giton, and he stays deceived when the boy suddenly abandons the role of the tragic mother as impartial arbiter between the two sons and follows Ascyltus. Encolpius really believes in the values and models of high literature which they are impersonating. Giton mocks them both.

The form of prosimetrum allows the hidden author to deflate the frustrated illusions of the mythomaniac narrator; the verses that follow straight after the scene of the *discidium* contain all the protagonist Encolpius' disillusionment. He too finally realizes that he is dealing with a fiction, a recital in which each man has a role to play (cf. 80.9: *grex agit in scaena mimum*). Encolpius is only deceived because he naively tried to clothe the banal reality of his life with the vestments of a revered mythological scenario.

---

influenced by tragic models; the idea of fratricidal war and the specific motif of a character intervening to divide the combatants would suggest Jocasta in the *Phoenissae*: cf. A. Barchiesi, "Tracce di narrativa greca e romanzo latino: Una rassegna," in *Semiotica della novella latina*, "Atti del Seminario interdisciplinare 'La novella latina,' Perugia 11–13 aprile 1985" (Roma, 1986), 225. A. La Penna has just re-examined all these passages: "*Me, me adsum qui feci, in me convertite ferrum . . . !* Per la storia di una scena tipica dell'epos e della tragedia," *Maia* 46 (1994) 123–34. Among other things, he rightly stresses the frequent appearance in Etruscan-Roman iconography of the theme of Jocasta between her two sons on the battlefield. Note also Prop. 2.9.49–50, already quoted by Gonzalez de Salas *ad Satyr.* 80 (in Burman II, 129). See also M. Labate, "Petronio, *Satyricon* 80–81," *MD* 34 (1995), 165–75, nn. 3–4, who remarks, in this connection, that earlier evidence of interference between mythical paradigms such as that of Thebes and that of the Romans and Sabines (which share the theme of civil strife) occurs in the only surviving fragment of Ennius' *Sabinae* (*scen.* 370–71 V², to be compared with Eur. *Phoen.* 571–76; interesting views on this fragment can be found in H. D. Jocelyn, "Ennius as a Dramatic Poet," in *Ennius, Entretiens Hardt*, vol. 17 [Vandoeuvres and Genève, 1972], 82–88; see also A. Barchiesi, "L'incesto e il regno," in A. Barchiesi, ed., Seneca *Le Fenicie*, [Venezia, 1988], 19–20).

The strong link that binds these verses to the narrative context lies in their capacity to interpret and comment on the text freed from the sublime travesty of the tragic model. Encolpius takes the pose of a cynic philosopher (the metaphor of the world as fiction and theater belongs to the repertory of the diatribe and Lucianic satire)[11] in order to say that the values of men are all poses and fictions, masks and stage costume. Deserted by his lover, Encolpius has learned this to his cost. Even friendship is just a name, a cloak ready to be shed once it is no longer useful.[12] This is the logical thread that should be traced in the text and which guarantees (against any possible suspicion of a lacuna)[13] the substantial unity and continuity of the metri-

11. On the widely used topos of life as a stage (a topos whose ultimate source may be the Socratic school; it became important in the Stoic and Cynic diatribe), see R. Helm, *Lucian und Menipp* (Leipzig, 1906), 44–53; O. Gigon, *Kommentar zum 2. Buch von Xenoph. Mem.* (Basel, 1956), 98; M. Kokolakis, *The Dramatic Simile of Life* (Athens, 1960); E. R. Dodds, *Pagan and Christian in an Age of Anxiety* (Cambridge, 1965), 8–12; on the recourse to this topos in Medieval and Post-medieval culture, see E. R. Curtius, *Europäische Literatur und lateinisches Mittelalter* (Bern, 1954²), 148ff. This metaphor sometimes takes on a negative sense, e.g., Hippocr. *De victu* 24.8–11; Lucian *Icaromenipp.* 29; on this too, see Helm, 52–53. In any case, there was in philosophically inclined Latin literature a clear awareness of the opposition between stage presentation and reality, e.g., Lucr. 3.58; Sen. *epist.* 76.31, cf. 24.13. Lastly, the verses of 80.9 are discussed as part of C. Panayotakis' general analysis of the *Satyricon* in terms of theatrical structures (the mime), *Theatrum Arbitri: Theatrical Elements in the Satyrica of Petronius* (Leiden, New York and Köln, 1995), 114–16.

12. Note that Mario Labate, "Petronio, *Satyricon* 80–81," 173–75, emended *nomen amicitia est* on the model of Ov. *Ars* 1.740: "friendship is only a word."

13. The lacuna seems to have been conjectured by P. Pithou in the second of his editions of the *Satyricon* (1587). In modern times, Bücheler has defended its plausibility, voicing the suspicion that the second pair of distichs was inserted into chapter 80 by an interpolator. The tradition of the verses and the section of the text where they are inserted does not offer a safe basis for endorsing Pithou's hypothesis; indeed in correspondences of metrical sequence one must evaluate information about lacunae, whether transmitted or not, with great caution. Some centuries before Pithou, John of Salisbury offers a paraphrase of the verses of chapter 80 arguing for the connection between friendship betrayed and life as a dramatic fiction. His paraphrase does not

cal passage. The two tetrastichs—the first on the precarious nature of all friendship, the second on the hypocrisy of men—follow a single line of thought: friendship is one of many roles that the theater of life assigns to men (v. 1: *nomen amicitia est,* v. 6: *nomen divitis ille tenet*), and this is why a friend can turn his back on you as quickly and as carelessly as an actor takes off his mask.

These verses, which might seem to express the protagonist's new disillusionment, also serve to throw light on the nostalgia for another epic theme, that of heroic friendship. This was suggested by Encolpius, witnessing Giton's ostensibly noble gesture when he offered himself as a victim (as we saw above in our analysis). Euryalus and Nisus make a fine example of the theme, "sacrifice in the name of friendship"; in his exile poetry, which is dominated by the theme of friendship, Ovid had inserted Euryalus and Nisus alongside the traditional pairs of Theseus and Pirithous, Orestes and Pylades (*Trist.* 1.5.23–24). But in Ovid the Virgilian model of Euryalus and Nisus remains but one example among many, and has not yet been exploited in all its possibilities for emotional expression. Encolpius, on the other hand, relives this moving episode very faithfully: in his imaginary poetics the mythomaniac narrator relishes, along with the grandiose suggestions of sublime literature, the sentimental heroism of the great melodramatic models. Thus Euryalus and Nisus, as we saw, enter the text as a powerful idea, a theme rich in possible narrative developments; the scene of the double suicide in chapter 94 is still entirely constructed on this paradigm.

---

presuppose a break in continuity between the two pairs of distichs and confirms the homogeneity and coherence of the Petronian text. John of Salisbury's position seems to me acceptable: progression by sententious generalization is a typical trait of so many metrical sections of the *Satyricon*. Starting from the motif of friendship betrayed, the verses incorporate the motif of the fictionality of life, recalling one of Petronius' favorite themes, the mime (see Coffey, 186; see also Panayotakis, 112–15 and 191–96).

Once again the noble narrative model has driven the naive protagonist to identify himself with the characters of myth. But even if analysis has brought up from beneath the surface of the text the models which determine the pattern of the narrated action, I do not want to suggest that the sense of the *Satyricon* is to be found at a textual level beneath that of the actual narrative. Petronius wants above all to tell a story with all its actions, but these actions have a glorious prehistory in the body of great literature. And every one of them recalls a great mythical model. By a sort of paradox, the great myths of literary tradition emerge as the illustrious antecedents of the impoverished actions of the present day, which seem to keep repeating their great ancestors.

So far, Petronius and his Encolpius have not been too distinct. The longing for the sublime seems a kind of infection. It is not absurd to want to recover the emotions of the great adventures of the past, but it is absurd not to realize the difference between the possibilities of present-day literature and the great achievements of the past. The author of the *Satyricon* shows great sensitivity to all the aspects of literary stylization; he knows how to differentiate between various languages, registers and codes of style. Indeed it is just this taste for the differences and boundaries between forms that suggests to him the amusement, often at the expense of his protagonist, of making different worlds and cultural models collide: tragedy, the *taberna,* the tender heroism of Virgil. Whole episodes of great poetry are often recalled by the figurative index of a single *Pathosformel* or condensed emblematically in a significant gesture.

In short, Petronius introduces into the text a character who is like himself in longing for great literature, but who is essentially different because he lacks the necessary critical awareness. The error that makes Encolpius absurd is that of not seeing the distance—or rather the inaccessibility—of the great literary models. These may seem near, or even easy to imitate, just because they are well known, but any imitation of them can only produce a caricature. The schools believed that by anthologizing and repeating these great models, they could appropriate them; similarly, the popular novel believed it could harvest a glorious inheritance. The error of the idealized Greek novel is that of Encolpius: it wants to reduce the whole great literary tradition to its own level. It wanted to be the τραγῳδία of the present day, the δρᾶμα of its time:[14] so Encolpius is the kind of protagonist it deserves.

This must be how the mythomaniac narrator came to birth: instead of living his real present existence, he prefers to deceive himself and live the past of his sanctified models. The irony of the hidden author consists entirely in his apparent condescension towards his protagonist. He lets him promote himself to a great mythical figure, but only in order to frustrate at once his pretenses and illusions. Schooling—this what the author of the *Satyricon* is telling us—should not be carried too far. The adventures of his degraded characters, miserable *scholastici,* are also the adventures of a culture that has been dragged from the declamation and recitation halls and carried into the open air.

This critical awareness does not prevent the text from being a true narrative. The parodic game does not destroy the legibility of the story in its own right, the horizontal direction of the narrative. These models which proliferate in the space of the narrative are not components of a technique of allusion, since the author is not aiming to embellish his narrative with a series of "tributes" and erudite references, as if wishing to give it status or obliged to gratify the recipients of his tributes. The models enter the text only when they have been stripped of their au-

14. See N. Marini, "Δρᾶμα: Possibile denominazione per il romanzo greco d'amore," *SIFC* ser. 3.9 (1991) 232–43.

thentic "poetic" value, when they have been reduced to pathetic schemata. It is important for Petronius' strategy, in short, that they retain their own literariness which is their hallmark; the hidden author does not want to attack the essential nobility of these models, only the improper use that has been made of them.

It is the scholastic gaze of the naive and unworthy narrator that transforms events into models and novelettish situations into famous scenarios, into stereotyped *Pathosformeln*. This is a process of transformation that absorbs and assimilates its models by reducing them to theatrical poses and fixing them in exaggerated gestures. Thus the wrath of Achilles becomes a hand that furiously tugs at the haft of a sword; the fury of Aeneas running amok on Troy's last night is summarized in Encolpius' posture as he runs to find Giton with sword in hand; Giton thrusting himself between the rival brothers offers his throat like Jocasta on the stage of the *Phoenissae;* a desperate cry and two bodies that collapse on the ground function as signifiers for the whole pathetic episode of Euryalus and Nisus. It is the same visual rhetoric as that of the pantomime, which knew its greatest success at this time; the pantomime too made a spectacle of sentiment and exaggerated poses.[15]

The same spectacular tableaux are presented more than once, as though in this way the process of banalization which the great models of pathos were undergoing would be better revealed. For example, the theatrical gesture of Jocasta rushing in to separate the duelists will return in Tryphaena's address on the ship when she averts a miniature civil war and hints at a Civil War epic of Lucanian scale: (108.12–14) *stante ergo utraque acie . . . praetendit ramum oleae . . . atque . . . "quis furor" exclamat "pacem convertit in arma?"* ("so when each

15. See P. Cunningham, "The Novelty of Ovid's *Heroides,*" CP 44 (1949) 100f. More on this theme in chapter 6.

battle line was at arms she held out an olive branch and cried out: 'what madness has turned peace into battle?'"). Here is another fragment of the scholastic iconography which seems to dominate the *Satyricon*. The images of literature are transformed into repertory, they become the examples of a recitation manual to be consulted for arguments. Do you need a sensational suicide? Here is the answer: you can cast yourself from a cliff, cut your throat, hang yourself from a bedstead.[16] Not only can these pathetic stereotypes be serially repeated but they can be accumulated as possible melodramatic options.

This line of argument might provide a further way in which to confront the problem of the models employed in the *Satyricon*. Let us start again from chapter 80, where we saw Giton assume the poses of Nisus, the voluntary sacrifice, and simultaneously of Jocasta, the arbiter between the combatants (not to mention, if you like, each and every Sabine woman thrusting herself between husband and father).[17] Here we have a convergence of famous models. In reality, the expression of pathos in the *Satyricon* needs to be multiplied, to be said in many ways; the echoes must be heaped up in order to recall powerful moments of the literary universe. The course of the narrative creates generic situations which purely by their generic nature can

16. Cf. *Satyr.* 94.8–11: *Inclusus ego suspendio vitam finire constitui. Et iam semicinctio <lecti> stantis ad parietem spondam vinxeram cervicesque nodo condebam, cum reseratis foribus intrat Eumolpus cum Gitone meque a fatali iam meta revocat ad lucem. Giton praecipue ex dolore in rabiem efferatus tollit clamorem, me utraque manu impulsum praecipitat super lectum <et> "erras" inquit "Encolpi, si putas contingere posse ut ante moriaris. Prior coepi; in Ascylti hospitio gladium quaesivi. Ego si te non invenissem, periturus <per> praecipitia fui* (but see E. Stagni, "Petronio, *Satyricon* 94, 11," *MD* 20–21 [1988] 317–21, who convincingly defends the *petiturus praecipitia* reading of the *lr* manuscripts). The hesitation of the would-be suicide between different forms of death (three possibilities are often mentioned) seems to be rooted in folklore; many instances are found in literary texts that appeal to pathos: see S. Trenkner, *The Greek Novella in the Classical Period* (Cambridge, 1958), 62–63.

17. See above, n. 10.

evoke more than one similar and famous situation. The "demon of analogy" that possesses the minds of the *scholastici* provokes an overload of associations, which results in the discharge of a whole series of models. The models advance to retrieve the situation, that is to interpret it in noble terms. Then, somehow, one comes to predominate and the others remain subsidiary, as associated possibilities merely hinted at. The sources of sublime inspiration are collected as if they were under so many rubrics like "see s.v." If, for instance, the novelettish situation needs a lemma, "self-sacrifice by putting oneself at risk," the repertory will refer you to the mother Jocasta, the friend Nisus, or the Sabine wives. In the scholastic mentality, literature is reduced to memorable citations. Rhetoric has classified all the precious material by association: impromptu recitalists can readily draw on a large and well-organized dictionary.

But the handling of models in the *Satyricon* is not uniform. Certain models are ironized while others are left unharmed, if not actually revered. There are models that belong to the author's strategy and others that belong to the narrator's fantasy. The series of romantic models has an architectonic function and is under the author's control. The author employs them to throw his characters into adventures and situations that are particularly typical of the idealized Greek narrative; parody cuts into the substance of these narratives. The narrating protagonist and his fellow players in the *fabula Petroniana* use this romantic structure imagining themselves living in texts of a higher kind of literature: high epic, tragedy, deliberative oratory. I must insist on the point that this separation of functions makes Petronius' procedure very different from the knockabout joke that simply constructs caricatures for playful purposes. Any philological recovery of the models and interpretation of their textual functions must take account of this distinction if we want to use it to reconstruct a chapter of history and literary culture.

The discovery of the parodic dimension of the *Satyricon* runs the risk of becoming a deceptive filter for criticism unless we learn to distinguish between the different voices and functions of the narrative. The portrait of a cynical and iconoclastic Petronius was begotten out of this misunderstanding. All the models that can be recognized behind the surface of the text are treated without differentiation as targets of a sacrilegious irony; in the end the text offers mere skepticism without positive purpose. Perhaps also under the influence of Collignon's work, *Étude sur Pétrone,* now a century old, criticism has continued to catalogue the models parodied, and all alike end up among the victims: Homer, Virgil, Sophocles, Euripides, Cicero, Ovid, Lucan, Roman national history. Already in Collignon there was this philological tendency, which has persisted ever since, to accumulate parallels without questioning their relevance or their meaning—that congenital (and perhaps incurable) vice of the philologist's inferential procedure which I have called "*conferrismo*" ("comparisonitis").[18] We forget that the use of models is not just an act of imitation but rather an act of communication, an indirect means of signifying; discourse agrees to speak with a voice that is doubled, making us see how something has already been said and how the author would like to say it differently, with a different emphasis and a different intention. In the *Satyricon* it is often a question of establishing stratification and conflict between different literary codes. That is how they superimpose themselves one on the other, creating weird hippogriffs of mixed language.

But what I want to underline is the fact that the author's real victims are Encolpius and his scholastic companions, unworthy employers of the sublime models. With Encolpius a whole literary culture is under fire, the culture that transformed these

18. Conte, *The Rhetoric of Imitation*, 23.

great moments into spectacular and melodramatic themes. The works that inspire his *illusions de grandeur* are not the objects of Petronius' satire, nor are they subject to ironic degradation. All the great literary episodes pass unharmed through the hands of the poor *scholastici*. Great texts are handled and ransacked by them but not defiled; they keep their prestige untarnished.

So Encolpius can deceive himself that he lives inside the framework of myth. The sequence of events narrated in the *Satyricon* will be enough to mortify his illusions and restore him to the miseries of his reality. This continuous disillusionment even fuels Petronius' narrative. Now we understand clearly the meaning of a scene like that of the picture gallery (from which we began): it is a typical representation of the ways in which the character Encolpius is constructed, a character always in need of examples in which to see reflected his own wishful emotions of heroism. It seems that the goal of his literary knowledge is his own self-promotion into myth, an illusory way to dispel the poverty of his own degraded condition. Myth is exploited as a high horizon of reference and an interpretative pattern to apply to his own vicissitudes.

Scholars such as Collignon and his followers, good as they were, missed the division of functions characteristic of Petronian narrative, in which there is both the irony of the hidden author beneath the surface of the text and, at ground level, the obsessions of the mythomaniac narrator. As a result, scholars came to believe that the *Satyricon* could be interpreted as a direct parody of the *Odyssey,* and that Petronius had burlesqued the adventures of Ulysses by transforming them in a farcical rewriting. Such readers experienced the deception of another "reader," himself deceived, namely Encolpius. He is the first to have read his own experiences as an incarnation of the Ulysses myth and to have interpreted his adventures as episodes of an *Odyssey*—an *Odyssey,* of course, which was not for him farcical but rather dramatic, or at least melodramatic. Petronius is not Encolpius, and above all Encolpius is not Petronius.

The crucial moment at which the recognition is triggered—the self-identification by the mythomaniac narrator with the archetypal hero Ulysses—comes when Encolpius, under the Odyssean pseudonym of Polyaenus (useful for the deceit agreed upon with Eumolpus at Croton), welcomes the enticements of the enchanting Circe (127) and enters the world of myth. Circe's beauty, as required by the conventions of the novel, is more than human: (126.14) *nulla vox est quae formam eius possit comprehendere, nam quicquid dixero minus erit* ("no words could encompass her beauty: whatever I say will fall short"). The description is a showpiece, and its many details are the very features the Greek novels use to portray their various heroines, Callirrhoe, Anthea, Chariclea. The formula of the topos, as always in these cases,[19] is "lovely as a goddess": *et osculum quale Praxiteles habere Dianam credidit* (126.16). Encolpius' words add an extra note to the stereotype: beauty needs the extraordinary art of a Praxiteles, the sculptor famed for the sensual charm of his works. The stereotype falls short, and he reaches for the superlative of a superlative: the work of art is like literature, it is a mythical superlative.

We are in the midst of an idealizing romance. The mannered description of beauty is only one example of the kitsch typical of the popular novel, in which all the successful scenarios taken from great poetry are recycled. But what would have been a spectacular page in the novel, with all the readers falling in love with the heroine, is used by the ironic author of the *Satyricon* to prepare a scheme characteristic of his parodic game. The scheme ensnares Encolpius by leading him to believe he might really love a goddess (127.5: *libuit deae nomen quaerere*). What

19. See Létoublon, 122–24.

was just a hyperbolic simile in the Greek love romance becomes
a pretty illusion ready for his use. She speaks and her voice is so
seductive and harmonious that the mythomaniac narrator feels
like Ulysses hearing the Sirens: *ut putares inter auras canere
Sirenum concordiam* ("so that you would think the harmony of
the Sirens sang on the breezes"). The deception is complete
when she identifies herself to the stranger: "Don't you know my
name is Circe? . . . it is not without reason that Circe loves
Polyaenus: always between such names some fire of passion
springs up" (*non sine causa Polyaenon Circe amat: semper inter
haec nomina magna fax surgit*). The mythical illusion goes
further. When Circe makes Encolpius lie down in the flowery
meadow, this natural bed transforms itself into the spring of
flowers that miraculously accompanied the *hieros gamos* of
Hera and Zeus in the *Iliad*.[20] The metrical interlude is constructed as an explicit simile between the mythical past (*quales . . . flores . . . cum se concesso iuxit amori / Iuppiter*) and
Encolpius' present moment (*talis humus*). The verses express all
the illusion of the mythomaniac narrator who feels himself to
be a Jove seduced by Juno.

But the narrator's mythical memory has calculated without
the irony that the author brings against him. In the *Iliad,* the
sudden flowering of nature veils but also euphemistically signifies the union of the divine pair. By way of contrast, Encolpius
has already abandoned himself to the description of the flowery
meadow when he is only just at the stage of amorous foreplay;
he does not yet realize that the hidden author intends to deny
him any satisfaction. The fact that his *locus amoenus* recalls
that of the *Iliad* is not enough to guarantee his success. The
irony of the situation is recognizable in the contrast between the
voice of the "agent I" enchanted by his mythical illusion, and

20. Cf. 14.347–49: τοῖσι δ' ὑπὸ χθὼν δῖα φύειν νεοθηλέα ποίην, / λωτόν
θ' ἑρσήεντα ἰδὲ κρόκον ἠδ' ὑάκινθον / πυκνὸν καὶ μαλακόν, ὃς ἀπὸ χθονὸς
ὑψόσ' ἔεργε.

that of the "narrating I" who warns the reader: (127.10) "we were amusing ourselves with a thousand kisses, as foretaste of a more strenuous pleasure" *(mille osculis lusimus quaerentes voluptatem robustam).*

The scene of erotic passion, prepared with such excitement, is doomed to the disappointment of impotence. Yet the mythomaniac narrator does not abandon his fantasies. In an adventurous life full of woes like that of Encolpius some banal accident which is hardly worthy of much attention is always possible. But *nothing* befalls Encolpius which is not worthy of a full comparison with some illustrious model. He has put on the role of Ulysses and is trying to relate everything that happens to him to the paradigm of the myth. To explain his misfortune, i.e., his poor performance as a lover, he can only resort to the hostility of a god: Priapus, god of sex. So it is that a routine sexual disappointment stands in for the storms and monsters that Neptune stirred up to hinder the return of the Ithacan hero. But it is not enough to have just Ulysses in the catalogue of persecuted heroes. Many others must have suffered at the will of a hostile god: (139.2) *non solum me numen et implacabile fatum persequitur* ("the deity and merciless fate does not persecute me alone"). So after the *défaillance* repeats itself, humiliating him even more intensely, Encolpius seeks the consolation of a little poem in which he reviews a parade of persecuted heroes.[21]

---

21. Encolpius' argument (rhetorically definable in the terms of T. Krischer, "Der logischen Formen der Priamel," *Grazer Beiträge* 2 [1974] 79–91, as a generalizing Priamel) relies on the *non tibi soli* motif typical of *consolationes.* Cf. R. Kassel, *Untersuchungen zur Griechischen und Römischen Konsolationsliteratur* (Munich, 1958), 70–72; H. T. Johann, *Trauer und Trost* (Munich, 1968), 70–73; M. G. Ciani, "La Consolatio nei tragici greci. Elementi di un topos," *Boll. Ist. Fil. Gr. Univ. Padova* 2 (1975) 89–129, esp. 91, 96, 105 and n. 40, 120f. Naturally Encolpius has his own form of self-validation, transferring himself into the deceptive world of epic and myth, and even his "I am not the only man to have been persecuted by a god" (with his list of heroes) aspires to match the celebrated *consolatio* of Dione to Aphrodite after she is wounded in the fifth book of the *Iliad:* (382–404) "many of us who have our

We said that in the imagination of the protagonist's scholastic culture the sublime models of myth are registered as if in an ideal dictionary classified by types. Under the entry "hero persecuted by a god" should figure Hercules as victim of Juno, Ulysses dogged by Neptune, and a few other less familiar unfortunates. Encolpius lists them all: Hercules, Pelias, Laomedon, Telephus, Ulysses, all his idealized predecessors. He had begun by choosing the Odyssean pseudonym of Polyaenus for his new adventure; now this name loses any element of pure chance and becomes the true name of someone enduring another *Odyssey*. Significantly, the paradigm of Ulysses as suffering hero rounds off the catalogue of great victims of persecution: *et regnum Neptuni pavit Ulixes*. Then there follows the memory of his own lot, uttered with an inspired solemnity which aims to elevate him to the level of the Ithacan hero: *me quoque per terras, per cani Nereos aequor / Hellespontiaci sequitur gravis ira Priapi* ("me too over land and the water of hoary Nereus the wrath of the Hellespontine god pursues"). The reference to his own misfortunes is transfigured by a style that takes as model the very proem of the *Odyssey* (πολλῶν δ' ἀνθρώπων ἴδεν ἄστεα . . . πολλὰ δ' ὅ γ' ἐν πόντῳ πάθεν) and also the allusive imitation that Virgil presents in the *Aeneid* when Anchises greets Aeneas after his wanderings imposed by the wrath of Juno: (6.692) *quas ego te terras et quanta per aequora vectum.*[22]

As Neptune is to Ulysses, so is Priapus to Encolpius. Encolpius seems quite unaware of the distance between a terrible god like Neptune and Priapus, the obscene guardian of gardens. He is quite unconscious of the comic gap that is opened up. There is even a strong effect of *aprosdoketon:* after the lament so ex-

---

homes on Olympos endure things from men," followed by a list of injured gods (a passage with a future in the epic tradition; cf., from the *Heraclea,* Panyass. F. 16 Davies).

22. Conte, *The Rhetoric of Imitation,* 33–34.

aggeratedly prolonged over eight verses, every pretense of nobility falls as soon as the name of the persecuting god Priapus is uttered, *gravis ira Priapi*.[23] Indeed Encolpius must be equipped with an extraordinary power of self-delusion in order to transform this routine (and absurd) misfortune into a terrible persecution. We cannot escape the suspicion that Priapus is just one of the mythomaniac narrator's many unwarranted flights of fancy, preoccupied as he is to construct the blazon of a tragic hero even in the most unworthy situations.

Perhaps it all began on the night of the *Pervigilium Priapi,* when Encolpius disrupted Quartilla's rituals dedicated to the god of sex. He only had to find himself impotent some time later in front of a lovely woman like Circe to be convinced that he had committed a serious offense that night and so had incurred, like Ulysses after the blinding of Polyphemus, the persecution of the offended deity. Moreover, on the ship before the shipwreck, he happened to overhear a conversation between Lichas and Tryphaena in which Lichas revealed that the god Priapus had appeared to him in a dream. "Encolpius is on your ship, the god said, and it was I who made him embark." So Priapus was persecuting him and handing him over to the vengeance of his enemies. Tryphaena too had dreamed that Encolpius was on board ship, but it was the statue of Neptune that revealed this to her.[24] In short, we have all the signs that Priapus' anger is an obsession of Encolpius, begotten by his scholastic tendency to live in constant imitation of models

23. *Gravis ira Priapi* is a parodic variation on the repeated expression which Virgil had used to indicate the intensity with which Juno persecuted the hero Aeneas: cf. *Aen.* 5.781: *Iunonis gravis ira* (cf. also 1.4: *saevae . . . Iunonis ob iram*). Once again this is an Encolpius like Aeneas, but one that makes Priapus correspond to Juno!

24. It seems that here already we meet the possibility that Encolpius is the incarnation of Ulysses, with Priapus functioning as Neptune's counterpart. I mean that the interchangeable hostilities of Priapus and Neptune suggest an early comparison between Encolpius and Ulysses.

drawn from great heroic literature. Thus the last part of the
Satyricon, what we may call the "mime of Croton," contains
in itself a second story that could be called "the persecution of
Priapus." In the mime of Croton, Eumolpus provides the new
momentum of the narrative action, since he designs the trick
(117.4: *mimum componere*) against the *heredipetae* (fortune-
hunters) of Croton. In contrast, Encolpius' participation in
these rascally inventions seems marginal; the atmosphere of
Croton does not change him, and he remains the usual naive
prisoner of his own scholastic myths.

This part of the Petronian narrative clearly offers the strongest indications of a structure derived from farce. The typical
roles of Atellane farce can be reduced essentially to two: the
knave and the fool. Here, more than anywhere else, Petronius
seems to have wanted to display this clear division of functions;
here, the naive Encolpius finds his complementary type in full
action, and so he is even more closely bound to his role as
mythomaniac narrator (even if Encolpius is not the real victim
of Eumolpus' rascally tricks, and thus the relationship between
the two roles is not the typical one that structures the mimic
form in which the trickster properly uses the fool as his butt).

Encolpius' obsession with myth never leaves him, and it
makes him act as if he is forever waiting for his life to fulfill
some legendary paradigm. Ulysses was persecuted by Neptune
but Minerva came to his aid; so if Priapus pursues Encolpius,
damning him to impotence, some other god must intervene to
help him. We see now that his restored virility is credited to
Mercury, the divine benefactor who has power to cancel the
pernicious behavior of the persecuting deity. The cure becomes
a true miracle: (140.12) *Dii maiores sunt qui me restituerunt in
integrum. Mercurius enim, qui animas ducere et reducere solet,
suis beneficiis reddidit mihi quod manus irata praeciderat,
ut scias me gratiosiorem esse quam Protesilaum aut quemquam*

alium antiquorum ("the gods are greater, who have restored me
to my full self. For Mercury, who conducts souls to and from
Hades, by his kindness gave back to me what an angry hand
had cut off, so be sure that I am more lucky than Protesilaus or
any other of the ancients").[25] Encolpius' delirious identification
with a heroic role continues to impose upon him the pattern
of the persecuted character of myth. Ideally we should read
these lines alongside the verses of chapter 139, *me quoque per
terras,* etc.

As a comment on Encolpius' habit of mythologizing his own
experience, we can cite some famous verses of Ovid, who re-
counted in the *Tristia* (with similar melodramatic exaggeration)
his own tormented voyage towards the Black Sea, no less persecuted by an angry god, Caesar. Amidst the full onset of a terrible tempest, Ovid too turns to the misfortunes of Ulysses:
(1.2.9–12) *saepe ferox cautum petiit Neptunus Ulixem. / eri-
puit patruo saepe Minerva suo. / et nobis aliquod, quamvis distamus ab illis, / quis vetat irato numen adesse deo?* ("Often savage Neptune attacked wary Ulysses, and often Minerva saved
him from her uncle. For us too, although we are so different,
who forbids some deity to be at hand when the god is angry?").
But Ovid is only composing a rhetorical exemplum, and he
keeps his sense of the difference (*quamvis distamus ab illis*).
Certainly he too wants to believe that a hostile god must inevitably be accompanied by a savior god, *saepe premente deo
fert deus alter opem* (ibid. 4). Analogously, Encolpius can tri-
umphantly boast of the successful intervention of Mercury, one
of the *maiores,* before whom the anger of a lesser god like Priapus must needs yield.[26]

25. See G. W. Bowersock, *Fiction as History: Nero to Julian,* Sather Clas-
sical Lectures, vol. 58 (Berkeley, 1994), 112–13, with bibliography.
26. The distinction between greater and lesser gods is a common one (cf.,
e.g., Plaut. *Cist.* 522: *di me omnes magni minutique et etiam patellarii / fax-*

In his power to defeat an angry and vengeful Priapus, Mercury is not the thieves' god (as critics usually believe),[27] but a phallic god, more phallic indeed than even Priapus, the rustic *cultor horti*. In the theology of Mercury, a connection with sex and fertility was maintained by the iconography of Hermes,[28] and Cicero records the tale of an ithyphallic Mercury aroused by the sight of Proserpina, a scene which the scandalized Christian apologist Arnobius, a fierce denouncer of pagan theology,

---

int . . .). Priapus is a *divus minor* and he actually describes himself as such: *nos vappae sumus et pusilla culti ruris numina* (*Priap* 4.16); *inter cunctos ultimum deos numen* (ibid. 63.11); cf. H. Herter, *De Priapo* (Giessen, 1932), 240. As a *divus minor* he is opposed to the *dei maiores* in *Priap.* 53.5 (*tu quoque, dive minor, maiorum exempla secutus / quamvis pauca damus consule poma boni*) and many other times in the *Priapea* (37.3, 39.9, etc.).

27. E. Klebs, "Zur Composition von Petronius' Satirae," *Philologus* 47 (1889) 623–35, claims an exact correspondence between the triad Odysseus-Poseidon-Athena and the Petronian Encolpius-Priapus-Mercury. The role of divine benefactor in the *Satyricon* would be performed by Mercury by virtue of his function as protector of thieves, a motivation more or less explicitly accepted by those who support the thesis of a real persecution of the protagonist by a *numen inimicum*. It is not entirely surprising that such a significant aspect of the cult of Mercury as his phallic nature should have been ignored, since no one has started from the analysis of the text, but rather from an *a priori* notion of the relationship between the persecuted hero and the protecting god. There is an isolated hint of an ithyphallic Mercury in a note of Walsh, 79 n. 2, where however the aspect of fertility is underlined at the expense of genuine sexual power, and this alongside the traditional interpretation which is the only one considered in the author's discussion (cf. 79). We must not pass over the fact that Hermes-Mercury can appear as a succoring deity to Encolpius' heroic and literary memory as he lies entwined with the lovely Circe only because it was Hermes and no other who came to save Ulysses from the real Circe with his gift of *moly*. Furthermore, a famous Priapean poem reread Homer in parodic terms and gave an anti-heroic version of the whole *Odyssey*: the plant *moly* given by the god had to be (with word play) the hero's *mentula*; cf. *Priap.* 68.21–22: *hic legitur radix, de qua flos aureus exit / quem cum "moly" vocat, mentula "moly" fuit.* Cf. Barchiesi, "Il Nome di Lica," 172 n. 12; V. Buchheit, *Studien zum Corpus Priapeorum* (München, 1962), 99–105, which surveys the passages that are pertinent to a "Priapic" reading of Homeric poetry.

28. Cf. W. H. Roscher, *Ausf. Lex. d. griech. u. röm. Myth.*, 1.2, 2391–94, s.v. *Hermes*; *RE* 8.1, s.v. *Hermes*, 15.1, s.v. *Mercurius*; R. Lullies, *Die Typen der Griechen* (Königsberg, 1931). On the connection Mercury-Priapus, cf. Herter, 309.

reported in these terms: *Mercurius . . . qui in Proserpinam dicitur genitalibus adhinnivisse subrectis* (*Ad Nat.* 4.14).[29]

On the other hand, the expression with which Encolpius refers to his own impotence (*quod manus irata praeciderat*) is certainly a strong one; indeed, the phrase properly denotes castration.[30] Before the final miracle that restored the hero's virility, the field of metaphorical reference with which the text had indicated his impotence was that of death: (129.1) *funerata est illa pars corporis qua quondam Achilles eram;* (129.6–7) (Circe is speaking) *medius iam peristi . . . licet ad tubicines mittas.* This is the usual metaphor if we think back to the famous Ovidian elegy *Amores* 3.7.15–16: *truncus iners iacui, species et inutile pondus / et non exactum, corpus an umbra forem,* 60: *neque tum vixi nec vir ut ante fui,* 65: *nostra tamen iacuere velut praemortua membra.* Here the image is quite different, namely that of a mutilated herm, i.e., an ithyphallic Hermes damaged by the *manus irata* of a *hermokopides.*[31] Encolpius, as usual, is dramatizing. In his imagination the young man, once

29. Cf. Serv. Dan. *Aen.* 4.577; cf. also A. S. Pease, *M. Tulli Ciceronis De natura deorum,* vols. 1–2 (Cambridge, Mass., 1955, 1958 [= New York, 1979]), *ad* 3.56. The phallic element was essential to the figure of Hermes from its earliest origins; on herms there is a rich bibliography and a catalogue in G. Siebert, *LIMC* 5.1, 295–306; on the rare representations of an ithyphallic Hermes, apart from herms, cf. K. Schauenburg, "Hermes Ithyphallikos," *Meded. Rome* 44–45 (1983) 45–53, esp. 48 and n. 62. From the classical age on, Hermes was depicted as a beardless youth. Alongside Heracles and Eros, he became the protector of athletes and gymnasia. In any case, it seems clear that the phallic and homoerotic element never disappeared: W. Burkert, *Griechische Religion der archaischen und klassischen Epoche* (Stuttgart, Berlin, Köln and Mainz, 1977). This god was appealed to in amorous adventures (see Wilamowitz's hypothesis on *Inschr. von Priene* n. 320), and is named in magic papyri as the lord of love (S. Eitrem, *RE* 8.1, esp. 775.1–19).

30. Cf. 131.11: *Ecquid hodie totus venisti?* It may be noted that *praecido* is a technical term for castration: cf. Lucil. 281; *Priap.* 26.2; Mart. 2.45.1.

31. The historic episode of the mutilation of the hermae, of which Alcibiades was accused on the eve of the expedition against Syracuse, had already been travestied by comedy in Aristoph. *Lys.* 1093–94: the coryphaeus tells the men to put their cloaks on lest the *hermokopidae* see them (ὅπως τῶν Ἑρμακοπιδῶν μή τις ὑμᾶς ὄψεται).

struck with impotence, feels like a mutilated Herm, until Mercury restores his body to its full functioning.

At the moment of the miracle, Eumolpus, invited to watch, will rub his eyes before the generosity of the gods. Encolpius has been transformed into a genuine ithyphallic deity, an ithyphallic Hermes of flesh and blood: *at ille [Eumolpus] primo exhorruit, deinde ut plurimum crederet, utraque manu deorum beneficia tractat* (140.13).[32] The vocabulary continues to exude the religious exaltation with which the protagonist experienced both his impotence and its marvelous healing. Eumolpus too seems impressed by the miracle and like a new Saint Thomas confirms his faith by grasping what has been resuscitated. But one suspects that here too Encolpius' naïveté is deceived. The mysterious sacrality doesn't seem to overwhelm old Eumolpus; his religious *horror* is not contemplative but resolves itself in the comic bathos of an earthy gesture, *tractare utraque manu:* to verify so great a miracle both hands are needed, one is not enough.

With the transformation of Encolpius into the living embodiment of an ithyphallic Mercury the story of the persecution of Priapus comes to an end. The intervention of the savior god— Mercury here corresponds to Athena in the *Odyssey*—is a crucial feature of the process of identification that leads the mythomaniac narrator to feel himself a rival of the Homeric Ulysses. The idea that Priapus is pursuing him, as Neptune had pursued the Ithacan hero, came to Encolpius as an illusory interpretation of some events of the narrative; Encolpius has violated the *Pervigilium Priapi* and has heard Lichas and Tryphaena speaking of Priapus' anger. Mercury, on the other hand, is brought into the narrative only by the heroicizing imagination of the

32. On the cultic rituals of adorning or touching the phallus of a *herma,* see H. Herter, *RE* 19.2, 1690.18–43, s.v. *Phallos,* with references and bibliography.

protagonist *scholasticus;* the promotion of Priapus to merciless persecutor needs an adequate counterpart, and Mercury's intervention is necessary to complete the parallel to the mythical triangle of Ulysses-Neptune-Minerva.

But Encolpius does not suspect that along with the persecuted hero, the persecuting god, and the succoring god, there is hidden behind the mythical scenario in which he likes to imagine himself a structure which romance literature had already desacralized. Here too, in fact, mythomania does not even have the merit of originality, but ends by reverting to the stereotype. The intervention of the savior god (here Mercury) must have been already trivialized as a narrative scheme, since it is later found as a cliché in Chariton (where the *deus ex machina* is Aphrodite), in Xenophon of Ephesus (Isis), in Longus (Pan), and in Apuleius (Isis).[33] So here too we see a regular procedure of the parodic game of the *Satyricon.* Everything that seems to aspire to the height of myth and great literature is brought down by the hidden author to the degraded level of popular literature, where the discoveries are always the same and the same showpieces are always plundered by scholastic imitation. The mythomaniac narrator falls into the trap held out for him by the author's irony and projects himself into nostalgic impersonations. Petronian satiric discourse shapes itself as a representation of representations, a complex discourse in which the satirist's targets are the obsessions of a rhetorical and repetitious culture.

We have seen that impotence takes on for Encolpius the connotations of either death or castration, and so Mercury the healer can act on both, being called upon by the text in his double prerogative of psychopomp and ithyphallic god. As psychopomp he brings back to life the dead member of Encolpius,

33. Cf. Walsh, 79.

and in his ithyphallic manifestation he has the power to restore its virility. In Encolpius' exalted praises of the divine benefactor both qualifications are brought into play: *qui animas ducere et reducere solet* and *quod manus irata praeciderat.* The scholastic memory functions cumulatively: in the protagonist's mind all the traditions that he has learned press forward to be inter-woven and superimposed on one another. Now he feels like a real ancient hero, one of those who enjoyed the good will of the gods. But it is not enough to be just any Homeric hero: he feels like Protesilaus, the hero who best incarnated the myth of melo-dramatic love. First of the Greeks to fall at Troy, Protesilaus be-came the hero of love *par excellence* when Hermes restored him to life so that he could embrace his wife Laodamia for a first and last time. Even now that his woes—at least the sexual ones—are at an end, the mythomaniac narrator does not re-nounce his ambitions to heroic excellence. He has passed un-scathed through a degrading adventure, resisting all attempts to reduce his pretenses and illusions, and now he is looking for a new paradigm of sublimity. He has been the angry Achilles, the furious Aeneas, he has relived the generous heroism of Nisus, he has suffered with Ulysses the persecutions of a god, and now he seems ready to embrace a new role of tragic or elegiac love, the very emblem of love poetry. Mythomania functions as an inex-haustible narrative energy. Encolpius is never content to have found one point of reference; he must seek out others to satu-rate all the possibilities of scholastic comparison, all the associ-ated possibilities registered in an ideal mythological dictionary arranged on analogical principles.

As a fanatic for literature and a rival of his models, Encolpius passes through all the great lives of the most famous characters. Born to incarnate a poetics which, were it only noble, we might even call mannerist, he would like to imitate on equal terms the great men, but he lacks *decorum.* The slightest analogies are enough for him to associate the inspired grandeur of sublime models with his trivial dramas. Ultimately, at the root of his mythomaniac character, Petronius seems to have wanted to suggest a faith that the same things would return, that the great moments of literature were figures of a single and always accessible sublime inspiration. But this is the heart of the deception, the author's parodic game. It seems to me that this deception is well defined in a famous idea of Hegel to which Marx gave epigrammatic formulation: "History repeats itself; all the great events and great personalities of world history reappear in one form or another. But the first time it is tragedy; the second it is farce."

CHAPTER FOUR

Sex, Food, and Money

Low Themes versus High Scenarios

There is a story that when a certain lady of Ephesus, a woman of exemplary chastity, was widowed, she was not content with weeping for her husband in the usual manner, beating her breast at the funeral or further shutting herself away in inconsolable mourning; she went so far as to bury herself with her husband in an underground tomb. Here the model approaches myth, as the faithful wife treads the ground of the great heroines devoted to their husbands and condemned to grief beyond all consolation. This is the world of Evadne, Laodamia, Alcestis, Andromache, Dido. The grief of the widow of Ephesus, like that of certain heroines of the romantic novel, found satisfaction only in the longing for death, in the love-suicide that would unite the two partners.[1] So the lady showed signs of wanting to starve herself to death: *sic adflictantem se ac mortem inedia*

---

1. Cf. O. Pecere, *Petronio: La novella della Matrona di Efeso* (Padova, 1975), 54–56 (with bibliography), a study of unusual richness and critical complexity. See C. W. Müller, "Die Witwe von Ephesus: Petrons Novelle und die 'Milesiaka' des Aristeides," *A&A* 26 (1980) 103–21; P. Fedeli, "La matrona di Efeso: Strutture narrative e tecnica dell'inversione," in *Semiotica della novella latina. Atti del seminario interdisciplinare "La novella latina"* (Roma, 1986), 9–35; and, most recently, G. Huber, *Das Motiv der "Witwe von Ephesus" in lateinischen Texten der Antike und des Mittelalters,* Mannheimer Beiträge zur Sprach- und Literaturwissenschaft 18 (Tübingen, 1990).

persequentem (111.3). The language evokes great scenes of sublime poetry (and there are Virgilian echoes and phrases of epic pathos). The scenario is that of pathetic melodrama, marked with a strong theatricality.

But the frame which surrounds this picture of tragic intensity does not belong to a sublime text. We are in the *Satyricon,* and the voice that tells the story is that of Eumolpus. The short story of the widow of Ephesus opens a window directly onto the function played by realism in the narrative. We should note an important feature here, namely that the narrative is no longer mediated by the words of the mythomaniac protagonist. It is entrusted to a character closer (*scholasticus* though he be) to the incurable cynicism of the hidden author. For once, the text can free itself of the deforming perspective created by the rhetoric of a narrating "I" who relates everything to himself, to his false imaginings and his crazy hallucinations. With its cover removed, the *Satyricon* can look at its own laboratory from the outside. The Milesian tale told by Eumolpus doubles the ironic strategy activated by the hidden author, for it reproduces in miniature the parodic crests and dips of the satiric narrative, first the rise and then the fall, *bathos* following *hypsos.* The same forces are active here which my analysis has tried to bring to light in the construction of the *Satyricon.* Here too there is that tendency to exalt reality, a tendency to which Petronius constantly opposes the unconquerable energy of a "low" world that knows only physical desires. We shall see that the body, food, sex and money are the forces that Petronius musters to demystify the pretenses of the false sublime in the *Satyricon.*

There is a close correspondence between the ironic cynicism of the majority of Milesian tales and the Petronian taste for irreverence, so much so that criticism has often thought it should include "Milesian tales" among the literary genres of Greek origin which converged to form the satirical narrative of Petronius.[2] There is no need to linger over genetic hypotheses (I do not in fact believe that genetics is the critical method best suited to interpreting the *Satyricon*), yet it is true that many of the strange and licentious adventures of the Milesian tradition bear a certain resemblance to the Petronian narrative, which is constructed by the degrading and inverting of the idealized narrative of love.

In a sense, the widow of Ephesus parodies chaste romantic heroines. But it is the structural mechanism of the narrative that is like the undulation of values (from high to low) which characterizes the whole *Satyricon*. There is a complete inversion, from the bonds of *pudicitia* displayed in exemplary fashion to the absolute license of sexual pleasure. Working on a traditional theme of anecdote (the story of the unfaithful widow is also present in the corpus of Phaedrus and of Romulus),[3] Petronius' ironic art transforms the secular tale into a very sophisticated narrative whose ultimate meaning is "all appearances are deceptive"; indeed, the very appearance of moral perfection must be taken as sure evidence of fraud.

The process of degradation can be set out in four stages. (a) The *matrona* initially behaves like a *spectaculum* of moral perfection and fidelity, the object of admiration, almost a myth, for the whole *civitas* (111.5: "it was the talk of the town," *una igitur in tota civitate fabula erat*). (b) With the help of the maid the soldier begins to besiege the faithful widow's virtue (111.10: *expugnare dominae pertinaciam coepit*); his most effective weapons are wine and food. (c) Once she has given up starving herself to death, and taken food and drink, the widow also yields

---

2. An excellent discussion is supplied by Walsh, 10–18.

3. For a full discussion see Pecere, 3–14, and also M. Massaro, "La redazione fedriana della 'Matrona di Efeso,'" in *Atti del convegno internazionale "Letterature classiche e narratologia," Materiali e contributi per la storia della narrativa greco-latina* 3 (1981) 217–37; Huber, 57–91.

to the soldier's sexual advances (112.2: *ne hanc quidem partem corporis . . . abstinuit, victorque miles utrumque persuasit*): first food, then sex. (d) It seems that the process of degradation is now complete, but not so: there is an added surprise, a cynical turn of the screw whereby this former model of fidelity actually takes the initiative and sacrifices her husband's corpse to save her lover (112.7–8). In short, the graph of values plunges under the pressure of the vital forces of food and sex, and after dropping to zero it finds a new low to reach.

The Milesian interlude, ostensibly a quick, almost anecdotal sketch, about anonymous people whose characterization is very schematic, seems designed to be used as a reagent in the analysis of the *Satyricon,* as a microstructure inside which some of the fundamental narrative procedures of the entire novel are reproduced. If the critic uses it as a paradigm demonstrating how powerfully bodily needs, the needs for food and sex, challenge the ennobling pretenses of the sublime, he discovers that it behaves like a miniature narrative reflecting the hidden author's ideology and his hostility to the false sublime.

One example will do. After the repeated sexual disappointments with Circe, Encolpius-Polyaenus, afflicted with impotence, resorts to the remedies of Oenothea, the priestess of Priapus who is supposed to help him recover his virility. During her brief absence to get fire for the purification ceremony, Encolpius is attacked by three geese sacred to Priapus. One of them assaults him and bites him so furiously that he is wounded. Armed with a table leg as a club, Encolpius then kills the sacred bird. This is the prologue. When Oenothea returns she is thrown into despair by the accident. Giving way to a scene of fury she accuses Encolpius of having committed sacrilege since he has killed the favorite of Priapus, a goose beloved of all matrons (137.2: *occidisti Priapi delicias, anserem omnibus matronis acceptissimum*). Oenothea's indignation is the first stage (a) which elevates the narrative register. Another assault on the idealizing claims of the sublime is thus opened, or rather, we are entitled to expect that we have just reached the rising phase which will be followed (inevitably) by the fall.

The next stage (b) is Encolpius' proposal of compensation for the inexcusable sacrilege with a couple of gold coins: *ecce duos aureos pono* (137.6). Here money is the weapon of persuasion. Immediately the money wins him pardon (c), though one laced with a good dose of hypocrisy: *"ignosce" inquit "adulescens, sollicita sum tua causa.... Itaque dabimus operam ne quis hoc sciat. Tu modo deos roga ut illi facto tuo ignoscant."* Now that the pardon has been bought from the priestess and the gods, the parodic reversal of the opening situation seems complete: from the horror of sacrilege we have sunk to friendly bargaining. But the process of degradation continues. Here too, as in the widow of Ephesus, there is a turn of the screw, a *surenchère* (d): the priestess herself cuts up the sacred animal and, to hide all traces of the offense, cooks it on the spit, thus preparing a nice little dinner which is accompanied by many glasses of wine. The *sacrilegium* has been transformed into a *sacrificium*. Indeed, so as not to waste the occasion, the utilitarian Oenothea avails herself of the poor goose's carcass to take auspices from its innards. Religion has come through unscathed: there is an *extispicium*, and thus Encolpius can also discover his own future.[4]

The story of the goose reveals features that increasingly resemble those of the widow of Ephesus. In this farce the goose is the analog of the poor dead husband, while the indignant priestess plays the part of the chaste wife, sublimely absorbed in her role of one shattered by grief. The correspondences of func-

---

4. The suspicion lingers—admittedly it is a sin to be suspicious, but Petronius is so malicious that perhaps we shall not go wrong—that even the *fortissimum iecur* of the goose has a particular gastronomic interest: cf. Hor. *Sat.* 2.8.88. But there is no need to accept the emendation *fartissimum iecur* proposed by Heinsius (see Burman *ad loc.*) and accepted by Bücheler.

tion are obvious; the widow is a paradigm of chastity, Priapus' priestess of religious *pietas*. The matron has reshaped the role of Dido as faithful wife of Sychaeus, and there are many explicit signs in the text that mark the widow's self-promotion to a heroic or epic role.[5] When she sees herself forced to sacrifice her husband's corpse for love of the soldier, she is described by the narrative voice as *non minus misericors quam pudica* (112.7). The compassion motivating her decision is simply the desire to save the soldier from the punishment that awaits him: "I would rather crucify the dead that let the living die." A sound logic, "utilitarian" if you like (indeed the text is careful to call the lady *prudentissima* [112.8]), but above all a logic far from any idealizing and melodramatic posturing. It is the same logic as that of the priestess Oenothea, who excuses herself with the specious claim that she wants to save Encolpius from the terrible punishment awaiting the sacrilegious: *sollicita sum tua causa. Amoris est hoc argumentum, non malignitatis. Itaque dabimus operam ne quis hoc sciat* (137.7–8). Repeating the same formula that Petronius had employed for the matron of Ephesus, we might say of Oenothea that she is now "no less ready to show mercy than previously she was pious towards the sacred goose."[6]

The parallelism that we have set up between these two passages clearly shows that sex and food, food and money, are mutually equivalent and are drawn from the same field of operation; they are three interchangeable elements of the same

5. Cf. Pecere, 22ff., 115ff.; also P. Fedeli, "La Matrona di Efeso," 27–30.

6. The transformation of Oenothea, from her great affectation of the sublime to the ensuing opportunism, is explicitly remarked by the narrating "I" in 137.12: [Oenothea] *epulas . . . lautas paulo ante, ut ipsa dicebat, perituro paravit.* The phrase *paulo ante* refers to the first phase (i.e., the moment of religious indignation a little before, when Encolpius was worthy of death for committing the unpardonable sacrilege); *ut ipsa dicebat* ironically implies quotation, bringing to mind the words of fierce condemnation she had uttered (137.1–3).

realistic pressure which is brought to bear against the sublime. Whether kept apart and clearly distinct or brought together in various combinations, they always appear in time to return the false idealism of the sublime to the harsh law of the way things are.

As there is a scenario of the sublime, composed of *Pathosformeln* and melodramatic gestures, so there is an opposing scenario of realism, compounded of food, sex and money, as if these too were typical and conventional factors that could be combined in a similar structure to the one we have described: rise, fall, final twist (*surenchère*). To make this reality effective and recognizable, Petronius builds it from exaggerated structures: reality is not neutral, it must be comic to challenge the sublime. Sex, food and money become elements of a counternarrative; they are the stage properties which make it possible to represent reality, the scenery which enables real life to become entertainment.

The little group of *scholastici* lives on the border of two conflicting codes which ancient literature kept well apart. The "low" of material themes attracts them, but their education draws them towards the "high," towards the example of mythical heroes. Prepared for the torments of tragedy, they are ill adapted to face reality: they struggle to descend to the low level of Petronius' realism. Now reality, precisely because it cannot be reduced to one of their familiar *schemata*, becomes a mechanism of constant challenge. This is a process we have already seen: first reality assumes the purple robes of high literature, and then those magnificent images are shown to be mere illusion, nothing but hollow projections of great aspirations. As unsophisticated addicts of grandiose stereotypes, the *scholastici* become easy prey to a reality disguised in the form of melodrama.

The fact is that the literature of scholastic stereotypes, Petronius seems to be saying, is not difficult to fake. In the *Satyricon*, victory falls to the man who knows how to impersonate these stereotypes with the most skill. Thus in a long episode in the first part of the novel, Quartilla holds the stage. She is the rich matron who takes a fancy to the *scholastici* and who knows how to make them behave as she desires by staging a clever little scene (16–26.6). The atmosphere is alarming from the start. According to the allegations of Quartilla's maid, the young men have disturbed the sacred mysteries of Priapus (*vos sacrum ante cryptam turbastis*); they have committed sacrilege, if only involuntarily, and are thus exposed to the risk of punishment. This is when Quartilla appears. For the three terrified young men it is as if a tragic character has come on stage: the woman throws herself down on the bed and abandons herself to convulsive sobs. The matron's gestures are based on theatrical models: first the lament with covered head; then her mantle falls to reveal a stately figure; she wrings her hands to show her tension and anguish.[7] Finally she speaks, first in a tone of harsh accusation, and then in supplication: the young men themselves must help her to expiate the serious profanation of Priapus which they have caused.

The young men can only react with fear: they are paralyzed by the thought of sacrilege (18.2: *ego eodem tempore et misericordia turbatus et metu*). Obviously we cannot expect the religiosity of a Vestal from a character like Quartilla. What is more, the young men must have guessed what kind of cult is in question if they have somehow succeeded in penetrating into the

7. On the pathos of the gesture of clenching the hands see Sen. *De Ira* 3.4.2 (in fact as a manifestation of anger): *adice articulorum crepitum, cum se ipsae manus frangunt, et pulsatum saepius pectus, anhelitus crebros tractosque latius gemitus*; cf. ibid. 1.1.3–4. More significant is Quint. *Inst.* 11.3.158 (where these attitudes are categorized in the language of theatrical gesture): *in hac cunctatione sunt quaedam non indecentes, ut appellant scaenici, morae: caput mulcere, manum intueri, infringere articulos, simulare conatum, suspiratione sollicitudinem fateri.* Cf. Alciphron *Epist.* 4.19.5: τοὺς δακτύλους ἐμαυτῆς πιέζουσα καὶ τρέμουσα (Glycera is writing to Menander).

shrine of Priapus: *ne . . . quod in sacello Priapi vidistis vulgetis* (17.8). At the same time, the poses assumed by the offended matron are so dramatic that they arouse awe and shame in Encolpius and his companions. Quartilla's speech spares no theatrical effects of *indignatio* and *deprecatio* (17.2–3: *attoniti expectavimus lacrimas ad ostentationem doloris paratas. ut ergo tam ambitiosus detonuit imber*).[8]

Encolpius is inevitably deeply impressed by the tragic poses of Quartilla, and his own naive tendency to pathetic gesture drives him into the trap. With great ceremony, he declares himself ready to put right the error and satisfy the lady's demands. Now, all of a sudden, when we have reached the melodramatic peak, tragic tumidity deflates and, following the regular narrative pattern, the level of representation plummets to the depths. A theatrical laugh, but one from the crudest form of theater, the mime, marks the transition to the "low," leaving the young men dumbfounded (18.7: [Quartilla] *complosis deinde manibus in tantum repente risum effusa est ut timeremus*[9] *. . . omnia mimico risu exsonuerant*). Here the mechanisms of Petronian reality are exposed: the "low" is revealed as a construction inimical to the "high"; it is a symmetrical but subversive strategy. Now Quartilla will get what she wanted, namely the best antidote for the burning fevers of an initiate of the mysteries of Priapus. The *pervigilium Priapi* will celebrate the triumph of the most unbridled sex.

---

8. I have accepted *detonuit* instead of *detumuit,* proposed by Gruter and adopted by Müller. *Detonare* is a Virgilian coinage and here in the Petronian text *detonuit imber* is without doubt a neat reminiscence of *Aen.* 10.809–10, *Aeneas nubem belli dum detonet omnis / sustinet:* Encolpius and company wait for the storm to pass, i.e., the shower of tears shed so ostentatiously by Quartilla (*ambitiosus . . . imber*), a real epic downpour like that of the Virgilian simile (803–808). *Detumesco,* in any case, would be inappropriate here in reference to rain falling from heaven: it is the *vox propria* for the swollen floods of sea and river.

9. With good reason M. Labate, "Note petroniane," 181 supplements *ut <etiam> timeremus.*

The lapse into *bathos* is as sudden as it is disproportionate: sex will turn into violence, indeed into real sexual torture. The degradation engulfs all the characters, without distinction and without limits. The sexual orgy has an intermezzo during which a banquet is set out (and a very luxurious banquet it is, with hors d'oeuvres and costly wines) because food refreshes the victims of sexual aggression (21.5–7). But food, which might seem momentarily to act in defense of the young men by giving them a break in their torture, becomes one more ally of the destructive power of sex, since after the meal the young men are forced to submit to new assaults. The materializing powers of food combine with that of sex to destroy every appearance of *decorum* and sacrality, by confronting all the earlier noble fictions of Quartilla. Even so, her orgiastic fury surpasses every limit. The *pervigilium Priapi* will culminate in the defloration of Pannuchis, the little girl who will give herself to Giton.

Here too the scenario of realistic degradation is repeated. As in the Oenothea episode and in the tale of the widow, sex and food are privileged means of attacking our characters' display of respectability.[10] The narrative is composed and orchestrated on the usual principle. It begins by staging a display of exaggerated seriousness—the grandiose opening gestures provoke great expectations—then allows everything to sink towards the "low." But the fall is unbroken; the graph of values continues to drop until it sinks even lower. After degradation comes the final twist, the addition of insult to injury. As the narrative had apparently soared towards the sublime, so must it now descend. Even in the more expansive narrative segments, like Quartilla's vigil and the *Cena Trimalchionis*, the same narrative structure recurs, the same forces are mobilized to demolish the false sub-

---

10. There are analogies between Quartilla and Oenothea, both based on the satirical type of the "hypocritical woman who masks sexuality beneath the guise of religion," as already noted by J. P. Sullivan, *The Satyricon of Petronius: A Literary Study* (London, 1968), 122–23.

lime. Sex, food and money produce both an alternative scenario and two major antagonists: Quartilla and Trimalchio.

The parodic inversion challenges the fictitious distinction between high and low, and the hierarchy of values is shattered. Reality is no longer subordinated to sublime ideals but opposed to them; high and low are forced together, leveled, put on equal terms. The two divergent visions of the world are set in parataxis by the materializing energy of the satiric narrative: once the order that segregated them is overthrown, the two complete systems of interpreting life turn out to be simply two different rhetorics. The Petronian narrative reduces the spiritual and the abstract to the same level as the physical and material, and it concentrates on the body's natural functions to make this happen. By describing the processes of ingestion and sexual activity, it parades the active participation of the body in its material context. From this perspective, the satirical narrative reduces everything that might be heroic and noble to a common level of physical experience.

Epic or tragic *decorum* ritualizes (when it does not suppress) the process of ingestion and sexual activity; as elevated forms, epic and tragedy deign to touch the common physical facts only in connection with suffering and death. Comedy too, even though it concerns itself with bodily needs, accepts these only in order to reconcile them with social forms. I mean that what triumphs in comedy is not the individual appetite but the needs of the community. While codified literary genres like epic and tragedy aim to transcend the wretched limitations of human nature, and while comedy stages these only to bring them back within socially accepted conventions, Petronian satire revels in the physical phenomena condemned by the lofty professions of nobility of characters like Quartilla, the matron of Ephesus, Oenothea, or even Encolpius. This is how the seriousness of high aspirations, once demystified, will dissolve into the laughter that unites opposites and makes the high and the low both phases of a single, complex, process.

This leveling of mind and body redeems the material aspect of life and brings it back from the exile to which the high literary genres had relegated it. Epic and tragedy had tried to contain the energies of life by imposing upon them a rhetoric of form and content, indifferent to the great weight of reality that could not be included in their code. This was also the tendency of the romantic novel which recycled the idealizing demands of these genres. So Petronius' method of operation is to invent a mythomaniac narrator who believes that the conventions of high literary genres are broad enough to contain and interpret all reality. But under the pressure of events, the protagonist's interpretative system, based on the literary rhetoric of epic and tragedy, or great oratory, is revealed as inadequate, as any partial scheme of interpretation of the world must be. Encolpius naively constructs reality to match his desires, but unknown to him the hidden author is transforming him into a catalyst for satire—a catalyst, in fact, in the technical sense, since Encolpius performs the function of breaking open and dissolving the system of codified literary genres, with their claims of comprehensiveness in representing the world and the complexity of life.

Every literary genre implies a way of interpreting the world by imprinting a discursive form upon it. Thus the parodic mixture of genres undermines these very discursive forms, their cultural horizons, their religious and philosophical ideologies, their limited perspectives. What Petronian parody attacks is not the great texts of epic, tragedy and forensic oratory, but rather the cultural authoritarianism that straitjackets reality by imposing upon it the schematic systems of the high literary models. In Petronius' narrative two different cultural paradigms, the orthodox and the alternative, collide and clash: his satire is his way of narrating this collision.

When Petronius satirizes in the *Cena* the uneducated taste-lessness of the newly rich, he is recording the emergence of new social elements and new wealth, but at the same time he is an-nouncing a process of cultural disintegration. We have on the one hand the low forms: mime, the Milesian tale and Menip-pean satire; on the other the lofty genres: epic and tragedy, ora-tory and the philosophical dialogue, even the less elevated con-ventions of the idealizing romantic novel. To juxtapose these incongruous opposites is to override the scholastic hierarchy of literary genres and subvert the traditional precedence of the high over the low. Yet note that a subversion of social hierar-chies moves *pari passu* with this subversion of the hierarchy of literary genres. It is not that Petronius wants to replace the high with the low, the non-material with the material, the incorpo-real with the corporeal, to produce in carnival fashion a "World Turned Upside Down"; rather, he wants to blur the hierarchic divisions themselves and to reduce high and low to the same material level. Nature must again take its place alongside cul-ture, and with equal rights.

Cultural orthodoxy eliminates every possible point of contact between the high and low genres by instituting a firm hierarchy that bars communication; the multiplication of discursive forms activated by Petronius produces instead a continual and disori-enting dialogism between the literary genres. The same new Petronian discourse presents itself on equal terms as one of the many discourses about reality which express limited (and self-interested) perspectives on the world. No longer can any dis-course keep its authority.

The sheer ineptitude of Petronius' protagonist ensures that his scholastic enthusiasms will prove to be inadequate cultural models when put to the test of reality; they are stable and dom-inant, but also incomplete, languages. The real problem of the *Satyricon* (which also raises the problem of realism in the narrative) is that the parody does not work through a direct attack upon the great models of the sublime; instead it is regularly generated by exposing the incongruity of the fantasies that guide the protagonist on his path through the world. These are nothing but melodramatic fancies, literary and declamatory poses which crumble under the parodic pressure of anticlimax that assails Encolpius the scholastic. What begins with the *pathos* and *hypsos* of illusory interpretative schemes falls into the *bathos* of a mediocre reality.

But, as we have often noted, the protagonist is also the narrator, so that the problem of parody becomes the problem of "first person narrative." The "I" in the *Satyricon* is not the author but an unreliable narrator, and the hidden author takes advantage of this ambiguity to create a many-sided discourse, a discourse into which are woven many other discourses. The fact that Encolpius is an unworthy interpreter of the sublime which weighs upon him is enough to show that the great idealized literary forms are incapable of interpreting a changing world. The relativization of truth, and of the sublime forms of literary discourse, is created in the *Satyricon* out of a new polyvalence of languages. These were once considered to be fixed and monovalent (hierarchized, in fact), but now they are paratactically juxtaposed (without a hierarchy). We have seen that in the *Satyricon,* because there is no direct authorial utterance, language suffers an effect of refraction in the distorting perspective of the narrative "I." This is the source of the dominant constitutive ambiguity of the *Satyricon*.

Petronius' challenge to authority can thus parody not only the reigning taste for the literary sublime, pretentious and artificial as it is, but also that moralistic literature which sets itself up as reformative, and which in some respects might seem the natural ally of Petronius' skeptical smile. In fact, the author of the *Satyricon* knows how to guy the moralistic poses of satire itself and the risky normative implications which the genre carries. Already the second book of Horace's *Satires* had stripped the authority from the satiric mask: Ofellus, Damasippus, Catius, Davus, were *doctores inepti,* unworthy spokesmen of the moral message which they claimed to interpret.[11] The *Satyricon* (and this is the difference in its new realism) gives full weight to this contradiction, and turns it into narrative: in a paradoxical maneuver, the satiric mask is worn by unreliable characters who have no hesitation in behaving like censors although they have no right to do so.[12]

Thus Agamemnon, the professor of rhetoric, can inveigh in a moralistic tirade against parasites (characters from theatrical farce, *ficti adulatores* [3.3]) who are always looking for rich men to provide a dinner. He finds an excuse to launch an improvisation in the style of Lucilius (*schedium Lucilianae humilitatis:* the theme itself is a satirical topos) in which he claims to explain the rules which must be obeyed by anyone with literary ambitions. Such a man must not be servile, and above all he must avoid pursuing free dinners from powerful men: *nec curet alto regiam trucem vultu / cliensque cenas impotentium captet*

11. See W. S. Anderson, "The Roman Socrates: Horace and his Satires," now included in W. S. Anderson, *Essays on Roman Satire* (Princeton, 1982), 41–49 (previously in J. P. Sullivan, ed., *Critical Essays on Roman Literature: Satire* [London, 1963], 29–37); N. Rudd, *The Satires of Horace* (Cambridge, 1966), 195–201; see also (from a different perspective) M. Labate, "La Satira di Orazio: Morfologia di un genere irrequieto," introducing *Orazio: Satire* (Milan, 1981), 25–33.

12. Good observations in Beck, "The *Satyricon*: Satire, Narrator and Antecedents," even if his critical perspective differs from mine in important aspects (cf. chapter 1, n. 28). There is already an intuition of this kind in F. F. Abbott, "The Origin of the Realistic Romance among the Romans," *CP* 6 (1911) 257–70, esp. 259–60. One might say that the *Satyricon,* in its own highly individual manner, shows a characteristic of the literary system of the early empire in which "satiric (or, more generally, moralistic) voices" were in fact very numerous and multiplied conspicuously. Satire and moralism were much practiced. The sublime and "enthusiastic" satire of Juvenal will be an unexpected reply to this situation, an attempt to renew the genre.

(5, vv. 4–5). And yet shortly afterwards Agamemnon will be among the most enthusiastic guests at Trimalchio's banquet. In fact, as Encolpius notes ironically during dinner, Agamemnon knows perfectly well how to earn the next invitation (52.7: *Agamemnon qui sciebat quibus meritis revocaretur ad cenam*).[13] The moralistic claims of the *scholasticus* turn out to be nothing but satiric conventions;[14] the character who appropriates them is quite unworthy of the task he has undertaken. Satiric discourse against flattery is reduced (in the parodic intentions of the *Satyricon*) to the same level of adulatory discourse that it seems to attack. Even satire, once diverted from its true nature, itself becomes (like other literary genres) a rhetoric composed of empty words. Alimentary needs easily get the better of false attitudes borrowed from moral greatness.

If Agamemnon shows himself indifferent to the contradictions that arise between his speech and actions, and, as a practicing immoralist, does not hesitate to put on the costume of the satiric moralist, he is certainly not the only one of Petronius' characters to behave with such absurd inconsistency. In this same episode of the *Cena* the most extraordinary character of them all, Trimalchio, both displays unbridled gastronomic luxury and pronounces a poetic tirade against the luxuries of the table and other forms of debauchery (55.5). (According to him, this is supposed to be a quotation from Publilius Syrus, but it is probably a virtuoso imitation of the great mime-writer's style.)[15] This is a real *locus de divitiis,* just like the passage which opens the *Bellum Civile* (119, vv. 1–60). The theme is

13. Agamemnon's flagrant self-contradiction did not escape Walsh, 85 n. 3.

14. See above, chapter 1, n. 2. On Agamemnon see also G. Kennedy, "Encolpius and Agamemnon in Petronius," *AJP* 99 (1978) 171–78.

15. The restoration *Publilium,* due to Bücheler (*Publium* codd.), heals the text. Naturally it is very unlikely that this is a true citation from the works of Publilius Syrus: see, more recently, H. Petersmann, "Petrons 'Satyrica,'" in

also one of the most common in satiric poetry, so conventional
that Trimalchio cannot resist appropriating it, indifferent to the
fact that these verses sound like a violent indictment of himself.[16] The rich ignoramus has even bought himself the right to
improvise like a satiric censor. Not only the guest Agamemnon
but also the host endures the author's ironic attack. Both, while
the triumph of food is celebrated, or is supposed to be celebrated, exploit literature to discredit with the power of words
the opposing power of food. So the two authors evoked by
Agamemnon and Trimalchio (Lucilius and Publilius, both crucial figures in the moralizing tradition) become mere empty
names, made inert by the author's strategy.

We know that the *Cena* is in many respects designed as an inversion of Plato's *Symposium*;[17] there are numerous pointers,
even if—in my view—it is not helpful to see the Petronian text
as a faithful and continuous rewriting of the Platonic model. Instead, I believe that the model (and this is the general pattern in
the *Satyricon*) shows through like a barely perceptible tracing:
at some points the pattern becomes more explicit, but then the
two texts diverge to leave room for the autonomy of the new
text. In the high tradition of sympotic literature food was left
offstage, as if censored. The symposium began just when the

J. Adamietz, ed., *Die römische Satire* (Darmstadt, 1986), 409–10; and N. W.
Slater, *Reading Petronius* (Baltimore and London, 1990), 185–86.

16. Trimalchio's inconsistency is noticed by G. N. Sandy, "Publilius Syrus
and *Satyricon* 55.5–6," *RhM* 119 (1976) 286–87, but in fact it had not
escaped E. Hauler, "Die in Ciceros Galliana erwähnten convivia poetarum
ac philosophorum und ihr Verfasser," *WSt* 27 (1905) 95–105, esp. 103 n. 3,
or F. Giancotti, *Mimo e gnome. Studio su Decimo Laberio e Publilio Siro*
(Messina and Firenze, 1967), 244.

17. Cf. A. Cameron, "Petronius and Plato," *CQ* 19 (1969) 367–70;
F. Dupont, *Le plaisir et la loi: Du Banquet de Platon au Satyricon* (Paris,
1977), esp. the third chapter, 61–89 (there are also various useful observations in the second part of the book, chapters 4 and 5); some interesting details in F. Bessone, "Discorsi dei liberti e parodia del 'Simposio' platonico nella 'Cena Trimalchionis,'" *MD* 30 (1993) 63–86 (with extensive
bibliography).

banquet ended: speech triumphed over food.[18] Here the exact opposite happens.

However, the great Platonic text that had represented the triumph of philosophical speech and the new Petronian text which represents the triumph of food *do* intersect. The intersection becomes obvious when Habinnas' entry (chapter 65) repeats in many details the entrance of Alcibiades. But Habinnas is the anti-model of Alcibiades. Alcibiades intervened to recharge the dialogue, to enliven and lift the running themes of the conversation; the only ingredient of Habinnas' speech is food, and he offers a review of all he has just eaten at a previous feast. He talks about pork and bear-meat, about sausages and black puddings, honey cakes, chickpeas and lupin beans, cheese and chicken livers, eggs and turnips.[19] It is not just ingestion that dominates Habinnas' speech. He is no less preoccupied with the end of the digestive process, and he reassures his friends that he has eaten whole meal bread as a precaution. This is the triumph of the physical. In a sense, Habinnas' report duplicates—as a miniature narration—the whole narrative of the *Cena*, since it sets out in condensed form the whole gastronomic array with which Trimalchio assails his guests.

If food celebrates itself throughout the *Cena* and reigns unchallenged by making itself the material of spectacle and speech, only money competes with it for pride of place in this representation of the world. The exuberance of Trimalchio's wealth assails the guests with the flash of gold and silver; many of the diners possess (or once possessed) dazzling inheritances. When the conversation is not concerned with meals past and

18. See M. Jeanneret, *Les Mets et les Mots* (Paris, 1987), 146–51.

19. Cf. Dupont, 77–79, but her attempts, here and elsewhere, to find in the contrast between the two texts a basis for a sociological interpretation (from the freedom of speech of the *polis* to the denial of speech in Roman society) seem misplaced. This process of reduction of "convivial discourse" was already set in motion, of course, by the Nasidienus Satire (2.8) of Horace.

present, it slips easily into the theme of money. The identity of these characters—the horizon that defines their existence—can be expressed only in terms of food and money:[20] these are the parameters that determine the value of men. In such a value system food and wealth stand in a relation of equivalence to each other.

Trimalchio's feast becomes an exhaustive mapping of the world:[21] "the loaded table" represents the geography of the various scattered estates which the Master possesses and which supply him with one food or another. Every place can be marked by a dish, and conversely every dish is the mark of a place: geography has become gastronomy. Even the heavens, the stars and planets, are marked out in a gastronomic code; the zodiac (35.2–5) becomes a "concordance" between foods and constellations: for the twins there are two testicles and two kidneys, for the lion an African fig, and so on.[22] If Aratus and Hipparchus had described the heavens with words and numbers, Trimalchio now redescribes them with food; now even the celestial spheres talk the language of the kitchen, and the *scholastici* are forced to applaud (40.1).

Even Trimalchio's time is articulated by gastronomic rhythms. On arrival, the guests are welcomed by a board on which the Master's engagements are recorded: "on the 30 and

20. Cf. 38.15: *solebat sic cenare quomodo rex* (cf. also, conversely, 44.2–3) or 77.6: *credite mihi: assem habeas, assem valeas: habes, habeberis.*

21. Refined gastronomy was expected to exploit the delicacies of all the known world. But in literature this practice was a favorite target of the moral and satiric tradition: cf. E. Courtney, *A Commentary on the Satires of Juvenal*, on *Sat.* 4.142; for a full discussion see S. Citroni Marchetti, *Plinio il Vecchio e la tradizione del moralismo romano* (Pisa, 1991), esp. 209–13; C. Edwards, *The Politics of Immorality in Ancient Rome* (Cambridge, 1993), 186–87; E. Gowers, *The Loaded Table* (Oxford, 1993), 9–20, 194, 207–208.

22. See M. Grondona, *La religione e la superstizione nella Cena Trimalchionis*, Collection Latomus 171 (Brussels, 1980), 17–25; see also J. G. V. M. de Vreese, *Petron 39 und die Astrologie* (Amsterdam, 1927).

31 December Gaius is dining out" (30.3). Only the ingestion of food can serve as an appropriate frame of reference for the Master. Days ahead will be marked by Trimalchio with what he will eat, days past with what he has already eaten. Thus in 76.11 he mentions an astrologer so smart that he seemed even to understand Trimalchio's intestines: "He almost told me what I had eaten the day before." Here is a life completely subordinated to the needs of the body, a life in which food becomes a Protagorean "measure of all things."

The inventive grandiosity that marks Trimalchio's dinner lies precisely in the extraordinary power of food, which finally reigns supreme. This is not just because the Master is solely, or even principally, interested in imposing food on his guests as a display of his own wealth or his own gastronomic art; the reason is rather that the material nature of food is the only form which gives expression to the intellectual and cultural ambitions of Trimalchio himself. The *Cena* presents a paradox. In the intentions of the *scholastici,* it is just a chance to exploit their prestige in order to satisfy their alimentary needs. For their host, it is a special opportunity to show off the witty and amazing discoveries of his own talent. Indeed for Trimalchio—as for a tyrannical stage director—what matters is to put on a show for a public that is finally worthy of him. Instead of finding satisfaction in abundant and delicious food, the *scholastici* find themselves taking part in a symposium with intellectual ambitions. The distaste for food which rises progressively in Encolpius and in the narrative itself[23] is the distaste felt by someone who has not been able to dominate the mechanism which controls the dinner; I mean that his distaste is *simply a*

---

23. Cf. 65.1: *hanc humanitatem insecutae sunt matteae quarum etiam recordatio me . . . offendit;* 69.7: *et haec quidem tolerabilia erant si non ferculum longe monstrosius effecisset ut vel fame perire mallemus;* 72.5: *ego enim si videro balneum, statim expirabo.*

by-product of the intellectual pretensions of a host who does not know how to talk except through the medium of food.[24] Even here the hidden author and the complicit reader retain their ironic distance from the narrator and protagonist and amuse themselves over his misfortunes.

There is surely a significant intertextual link between Trimalchio and his satiric predecessors Granius and Nasidienus (and indeed other possible representatives of the anti-symposiastic Menippean tradition),[25] but if Trimalchio is more vulgar than they are, this is precisely why he also succeeds in becoming the real victor of the *Cena*. Horace's Nasidienus (*Sat.* 2.8) is also a rich boor who wants to make a fine impression on a group of intellectuals: to honor Maecenas he has invited three men of let-

24. The food served to those at table, even more than an exhibition of *lautitiae*, is for Trimalchio the medium of intellectual communication. It is enough to consider the dishes which are gastronomically most demanding, those which by their sheer accumulation will drive Encolpius and his companions to disgust. The enormous wild boar which is served to the guests in chapters 40–41 is for Trimalchio mainly a *pretext* to surprise his guests with a hunting scene in the dining room and to amuse them with a witty riddle (the *Aper pilleatus*) and a pun (*etiam videte quam porcus ille silvaticus lotam comederit glandem*). It is just the same with the (perhaps even bigger) sow, presented in 47.8–11 and dressed in chapter 49: this serves above all to amaze the guests with the incredible speed of its cooking, but it also aids the ingenious little scene between the cook Daedalus and Trimalchio, which first confuses the guests and then astounds them with the discovery that the innards have already been turned into sausages. Finally, if Trimalchio does not offer thrushes as *matteae*, but rather one hen each and "hooded" eggs (65.1–2), this is not so much to wallow in vulgar abundance as to make possible the next of the endless jokes: he had worked out that the eggs could be wittily described as "boneless chicken" and was supplying a convivial context to support his invention (cf. the neat exegesis of L. Friedländer, *Petronii Cena Trimalchionis, mit deutschen Uebersetzung und erklaerenden Anmerkungen* [Leipzig, 1906², repr. Amsterdam, 1960]. *ad loc.*). Here too the guests' disgust is the price they must pay for the "intellectual" ambitions of Trimalchio.

25. See Collignon, 254–56; J. Révay, "Horaz und Petron," *CP* 17 (1922) 202–12; L. R. Shero, "The Cena in Roman Satire," *CP* 18 (1923) 134–39; Sullivan, 82, 92, 126ff.; Walsh, 39; more recently, see M. Coccia, "Cena di Nasidieno e cena di Trimalchione," in R. Uglione, ed., *Atti del convegno nazionale di studi su Orazio* (Torino, 1993), 131–48 (with further bibliography).

ters, Viscus, Fundanius and Varius. But in Horace the dinner
and its host are a mixture of luxurious prodigality and unwitting stinginess, of pedantic ostentation and ridiculous naivety,
and the intellectuals never lose their position of acknowledged
prestige. They will abandon the dinner, but only to leave Nasidienus in discomfort, thus condemning his banquet to failure.
During the dinner they laugh more or less openly and make fun
of the ridiculous host's pretentious inventions: at 63 Varius
stifles his laughter behind a napkin, and as he listens to the
tale told by Fundanius (a comic poet!) Horace too laughs to
think of the guffaws his friends must have enjoyed (79–80).
Every guffaw is the reaffirmation of the amused superiority with
which the group of intellectuals observes the failures of poor
Nasidienus.

Trimalchio is not Nasidienus, if only because Encolpius and
his companions are not comparable to Maecenas' set. The
scholastici of the *Satyricon* deceived themselves in thinking they
could make fun of the hosts and his companions: they went to
dinner confident of their assumed superiority (10.6: *tamquam
scholastici ad cenam promisimus*). But this illusion does not last
long. Only at the beginning do they manage to act like people
enjoying the tidbits while laughing at their curious host (32.1:
*in his eramus lautitiis, cum ipse Trimalchio ad symphoniam al-
latus est positusque inter cervicalia munitissima expressit im-
prudentibus risum*). There will be another chance for them to
laugh at Trimalchio's extravagant and vulgar preoccupations in
47.7–8, where only the afterknowledge of the narrating "I"
marks the illusion of a participant who did not realize that
the pleasures of the banquet were really meant to turn into an
exhausting ordeal. But we shall soon see that they are really
powerless victims of the aggression which the world of the
freedmen commits against them.

Scholastic instruction cannot guarantee them the slightest

protection. Confronted with lavish supplies of food and money, they remain confused. One of the freedmen, the rag picker Echion, shows that he is not at all intimidated by their *litterae,* and he exploits their embarrassment. He does not hesitate to accuse Agamemnon of *fatuitas* (46.1): schoolmen can easily lose their senses living among books, recitations and declamations. But then Echion allows himself a more generous attitude towards the scholastic skills of the rhetor Agamemnon: even his own little son loves to study, and as a father he is happy, since a little education is handy if it can bring the kind of wealth it brought the lawyer Phileros, once a poor porter and now a respected citizen. Money is what really matters. The crudity of the ignorant parvenu puts a cash value on the skills of the *scholastici* and simply reduces them to his own materialist code.[26]

Even when Ascyltus thinks he can show his superiority by laughing openly at his fellow guests with their trivial amusements, the freedman's violent reaction easily deals with him, and with Giton, too, who was unable to control a second reaction of contempt (57–58). Only the intervention of Trimalchio restores calm; like an Olympian father of the gods he controls the situation and calms tempers. He has the last word: he is impressed by the example of eloquence Hermeros has presented (a freedman more eloquent than a *scholasticus!*)—a vulgar kind of *eloquentia,* compounded of insults and aggression, but still carrying the day. How could such eloquence not triumph in the *Cena,* when it opposes the despised values of education with the

26. Rich men do not even know what a poor man is: Trimalchio, to be witty, pretends to be astounded when Agamemnon tells him he declaimed a controversia entitled, "a poor man and a rich man were enemies." *Quid est pauper?*—Trimalchio interrupts arrogantly (48.5), exploiting the ambiguity of his question: apparently he is following the real procedure of rhetoric by defining (*horismos*) the terms of debate, but he is pretending that, like his rich friends, he cannot even form an idea of what a person could be without money.

arrogant value system of food and money which are the dominant parameters of social evaluation?[27]

At this point Trimalchio can resume the theatrical program and bring on the *Homeristae,* a little culture to show off. Satisfied, he can even make a display of his mythological education (59.3–4): Diomedes and Ganymede were two brothers (the rhyme makes them kin), their sister was Helen, and she was carried off by Agamemnon—here is a fine beginning for the Trojan war! Hadn't he declared much earlier, "even at dinner one should show a little expertise in literature" (*oportet etiam inter cenandum philologiam nosse* [39.4])? His knowledge of literature, however monstrously absurd, is enough to make him feel at ease among the *scholastici,* so much so, in fact, that they are discomfited. In their confusion they fall silent.[28]

Caught in the dense net of money and food which Trimalchio and his cronies throw around them, the *scholastici* seem at first embarrassed, then downright terrified; the tyranny[29] of the host keeps them passive. The intellectuals of the Horatian satire knew how to punish Nasidienus by abandoning the banquet without touching his food; to flee was a gesture of contempt which gave definitive form to their superiority. In contrast, Encolpius and his companions are driven to take flight, or rather they try more than once to flee, only succeeding at the

27. *Satyr.* 58.7–14: *non didici geometrias, critica et alogas naenias . . . iam scies patrem tuum mercedes perdidisse quamvis et rhetoricam scis . . . Eamus in forum et pecunias mutuemur: iam scies hoc ferrum fidem habere . . . Ego, quod me sic vides, propter artificium meum diis gratias ago.* The only one of the freedmen who seems to fear the culture of the *scholastici* is Niceros (61.2): in every battle there is a coward!

28. It seems appropriate that the *scholastici* in the *Cena* are apparently born under an evil star. Trimalchio had already warned them of this in his astrology: *caput praeterea durum, frontem expudoratum, cornum acutum. Plurimi hoc signo scholastici nascuntur et arietilli* (39.5).

29. Cf. 41.9: *nos libertatem sine tyranno nacti.*

end in emerging from the labyrinth where they feel ensnared.[30] Their inferiority is obvious from the beginning. They entered Trimalchio's house with the disdainful condescension of *scholastici,* but found themselves constantly forced to endure the inventiveness of Trimalchio and his fellow freedmen without ever being able to impose upon them the cultural superiority which they claimed to enjoy. Compared with the intellectuals of the *Cena Nasidieni,* their position is the complete reverse.

I am claiming that Encolpius and his companions would dearly like to repeat the behavior of their Horatian predecessors.[31] But Horatian satire also showed how an intellectual, Fundanius, could report with lordly indifference the failures of a clumsy host. Victim of his own mythomania, Encolpius, for whom Horatian satire must have belonged to the Parnassus of great literature studied at school, now aims to put on the role of Fundanius, the narrating voice of Nasidienus' dinner party. Horace's famous satire tempts him, as epic, tragedy, and great oratory tempt him elsewhere. This explains the snobbishly critical attitude that Encolpius maintains in his report, which is not without irony and sarcastic (we might say satiric) detail.[32] In

30. Cf. 73.1: *quid faciamus homines miserrimi et novi generis labyrintho inclusi?*

31. A long literary tradition (Menippean and satiric) found fun in mocking unrefined and pretentious hosts: cf. J. Martin, *Symposion. Geschichte einer literarischen Form* (Paderborn, 1931), 36–51; this must have been the case with the Lucilian Cena of Granius also. Once given the chance, as he is after being abandoned by Giton (80.9), Encolpius shows himself well able to put on the diatribic pose of the cynic philosopher: see the discussion in chapter 3, p. 82.

32. A complete list would be too long: enough to mention the most representative cases, *pantomimi chorum, non patris familiae triclinium crederes* (31.7); *ipse etiam taeterrima voce de Laserpiciario mimo canticum extorsit* (35.6); *ego, crudelissimae severitatis, non potui me tenere,* etc. (49.7); *expectabam, ut pro reliqua insolentia diceret sibi vasa Corintho afferri* (50.3); (referring to Trimalchio) *nihil autem tam inaequale erat* (52.11); also 54.1, 68.5, 69.6, 69.7, 70.8, 70.12–13, 73.2–3, 78.5. Some critics have thought they could interpret these ironic comments which (implicitly or explicitly) reject the vulgarity of Trimalchio and his world as comments that the author

short, as men of letters the *scholastici* would like to occupy a superior position, but time after time their pretensions are contradicted by the humiliating passivity to which they are gradually condemned during the dinner. Encolpius himself, while telling the tale, is forced to bear witness to his own lack of impact as *scholasticus* and to the triumph of the freedmen. To be sure, his sarcastic comments are satiric ploys that polemically attack the vulgar pettiness of his fellow guests, but above all they indicate the failure of anyone who, like himself, thought he could easily impose on Trimalchio and his company. The author has provided his narrator and protagonist with material worthy of satire, but he has also ironically ensured that the narrator himself collapses when confronted with the world around him.[33]

This is the real theme of Petronian representation: to show how fallible is the culture of the *scholastici* when they claim to know how to deal with the real world on the strength of their education.[34] Schooling, if it pretends to reduce the complexity

---

lends to the narrator; cf. P. Veyne, "Le 'je' dans le *Satyricon,*" *REL* 42 (1964) 303–309: the narrator Encolpius would be the author's spokesman during the *Cena*. R. Beck, "Encolpius at the *Cena,*" *Phoenix* 29 (1975) 271–83, esp. 280–83, is right to reject Veyne's position, but we cannot deny the snobbishness (however wishful) and "satiric" aspirations of Encolpius' comments.

33. Some have even thought that the ironic comments are to be attributed to the thought of the author even if they are mediated by the voice of a discredited character like Encolpius. They would see these comments as marking Petronius' limitations as a realistic novelist, inasmuch as they are the residue of a moralistic or satirical inheritance which ultimately undermines the autonomous narrative representation of events and persons. This is the position of J. P. Sullivan, first advanced in "Satire and Realism in Petronius," in J. P. Sullivan, ed., *Critical Essays on Roman Literature,* 88–90, then argued more fully in the monograph, *The Satyricon of Petronius,* 125–57. One can argue against Sullivan that however well defined the limits of Petronius' narrative realism, they are not simply content with the satiric inheritance. The complex strategy of the narrative can reabsorb and revitalize the whole satiric model.

34. Thus culture is felt as a tool of practical utility. At bottom, this idea is common to all the characters of the *Satyricon,* if even the ragpicker Echion, one of Trimalchio's guests, can declare with solemn banality, "Education is a treasure and a profession lasts forever" (*Litterae thesaurum est, et artificium numquam moritur* [46.8]). This is the smug conclusion of the speech ad-

of the world to its own parameters, can only offer illusions which are doomed to frustration as soon as they are confronted with facts. Encolpius, the narrator and protagonist of the *Cena*, knows (for Horace the satirist guarantees it) that intellectuals can attend a banquet of uneducated parvenus while maintaining their own smile of effortless superiority. But unfortunately for them, Petronius has not allowed Encolpius and his companions to be like Fundanius, Varius and Viscus. He has made them feeble, enclosed in their pretentious but ineffectual scholasticism; he has made them victims of the overwhelming vulgarity of Trimalchio's world. Their final flight will be precisely an admission of defeat, not a gesture of contempt or affirmation of superiority.

So, when Petronius' *scholastici* run defeated from the inferno of Trimalchio's house, the text of the *Satyricon* forces them to copy (but with opposite results) the example of Horace's intellectuals, who had left Nasidienus' house as victors. Petronius had already marked the intellectual links of Trimalchio's *cena* with Horace *Satires* 2.8 when the accident which brought the young acrobat down on Trimalchio's head (54.1) more or less repeated the collapse of the canopy covering Nasidienus' table (54–85). What matters here is to notice the real difference between Trimalchio's reaction and that of Nasidienus. Nasidienus is desperate (one of his friends bursts into tears as if he had lost a son), but someone intervenes with a speech about Fortune which mocks human enterprises and the poor host feels consoled by such sympathy. Yet the laughter of the intellectuals confirms that he is the victim not only of fortune but also of the most merciless sarcasm.

---

dressed by Echion to Agamemnon; as a professor of rhetoric, he can understand the importance of education, even if it seems—and this is the reproach he makes against Agamemnon—that culture has gone to his professor's head: perhaps out of arrogance Agamemnon is making fun of the humble sayings of Trimalchio's ignorant guests. Cf. also Trimalchio's remark at 56.1: *quod autem, inquit, putamus, secundum litteras difficillimum esse artificium?*

Trimalchio, on the other hand, once he has recovered, resumes full control of the situation—Encolpius even begins to suspect that the whole episode was orchestrated as a spectacle by the host—and he decrees that the boy must be immediately freed "so that no one can say such a great gentleman was struck by a slave" (54.5). As if that were not enough, he ventures to improvise a limping epigram—again on the subject of Fortune. The accident gives him a chance to show wit and even to exercise (why shouldn't he?) his skills as a poet. His arrogant confidence, which keeps the *scholastici* at bay, never lags: he controls not only everything he has programmed but even the unforeseen. Indeed, his superstition contributes to the spectacular success of the dinner: in the night a cock suddenly crows, thus disturbing Trimalchio by its ill omen (a fire in the neighborhood? a neighbor dying?); he immediately orders the poor bird to be caught and put in the pot (*in caccabum est coniectus* [74.5]). It too undergoes the *ius cenae* proclaimed by Trimalchio (35.7):[35] it is turned into food.

Of course, our point of departure is the holiest of scholastic texts, Homer. The epic-heroic scenario entrusted to the *Homeristae* is interrupted first by Trimalchio's implausible display of learning, as he invents mythological stories and kinships and then transposes them directly into gastronomic terms. As soon as Ajax is named, a new *Aias mainomenos* comes forward into the dining room *stricto gladio*. But the figure who bursts in is really a clever carver in costume, who pretends to be mad (*tamquam insaniret*) and lunges at a stewed calf with his sword, slicing it up and distributing the slices to the guests (59.6–7).[36] Trimalchio prepares his guests for the sublime exaltations of heroic delirium, but degrades them to mere food.

35. The reading has been convincingly defended by W. T. Avery, "*Cena Trimalchionis* 35.7: *hoc est ius cenae*," *CP* 55 (1960) 115–18.

36. This would seem to be the parodic reworking of a tragic scene—more precisely, a scene of pantomime. Ajax's madness must have been a favorite

Trimalchio's tyrannical gastronomic code can tackle and appropriate the entire world of classical *paideia*. He even has a minister to assist him in the operation: Daedalus the cook, an artist worthy of his mythical name, skillful disguiser of reality, embodiment of the mimetic power of sophisticated gastronomy, who with his culinary skills can transform a pig into a goose (70.12: *qui de porco anserem fecerat*).[37] Towards the end of the *Cena,* Daedalus makes his entrance, sits down beside Encolpius, and starts to imitate the tragic actor Ephesus (70.13). He is an important figure, at least as important as a professor of rhetoric, if we can rely on Trimalchio, who proclaimed in his cosmology that *rhetores* and *obsonatores* (cooks or their assistants who did the shopping) are born under the same star (39.13): this common origin binds together their arts and their destinies.

But the bond, even the analogy, between rhetoric and cookery goes far beyond Trimalchio's fantasies. The rhetoric that has taken over literature and oratory begins to seem like a kind of cookery that treats its products like *Delikatessen* for gourmets. At the beginning of our excerpts, in their initial encounter immediately outside the school, Encolpius and Agamemnon agree on a gastronomic interpretation of the studies that are now in fashion among *scholastici.* The narrator and protagonist gives vent to a lofty-sounding tirade lamenting the lost values of the great sublime literature (Sophocles, Euripides, Pindar) and

---

theme of pantomime performance, just because the mimesis of madness allowed the actor to obtain remarkable effects of pathos. Lucian (*De saltat.*: 82–84) recalls a pantomime who, while dancing the role of Ajax, over-identified and went beyond the limits of feigned madness and began striking the other actors violently: "as in rhetorical speeches, so even in pantomime there is the so-called affectation of those who overdo imitation and become more exalted than they should [. . .]. Some were amazed at this event, others laughed, others thought the excess of imitation had really driven the actor mad."

37. Trimalchio composes the elogium of his great illusionist in these terms: *volueris, de vulva faciet piscem, de lardo palumbum, de perna turturem, de colaepio gallinam* (70.2).

the great oratory (Plato, Demosthenes, Thucydides, Hyperides [2.3–8]) of the past. Today—so the accusation goes—young men are nurtured with the bombast of absurd themes and empty phrases (1.2: *nunc et rerum tumore et sententiarum vanissimo strepitu hoc tantum proficiunt ut, cum in forum venerint, putent se in alium orbem terrarum delatos*), while they exercise their eloquence against unlikely pirates and tyrants, waxing emotional over oracles that order the sacrifice of innocent virgins. They confect sentences as honeyed as if they were sweetmeats or candies (1.3: *mellitos verborum globulos et omnia dicta factaque quasi papavere et sesamo sparsa*). And the result? They stink of the kitchen like scullions: *non magis sapere possunt quam bene olere qui in culina habitant* (2.1).

The term *culina*, kitchen,[38] is a powerful and undignified intrusion into Encolpius' lofty context, a kind of involuntary lapse in a speech with great critical aspirations.[39] The incompetent preacher launches into a theme worthy of a voice far superior to his own; in fact, he puts on the noble and impassioned pose assumed by Pseudo-Longinus, and later Tacitus, precisely

---

38. In defense of *culina* against the conjecture *coriaria* of Van Thiel, see my "Petr. *Satyr.* 141," 311–12, n. 1. Stylistically the word is of conspicuously low status (cf. also N. C. Conomis, "Graeco-Latina in Charisius," *Glotta* 46 [1968] 178); it is absent from the entire corpus of Cicero's works, except in his letters where it has humorous intent: cf. *Fam.* 15.18.1 with the commentary of D. R. Shackleton Bailey, ed., *Cicero Epistulae ad familiares* (Cambridge, 1977). Even Pliny the Elder shows some embarrassment in using it: *et alia genera similiter, ne culinarum censura peragatur* (*Nat.* 9.169). Culinary terminology was carefully avoided in literature with lofty pretensions: cf. Gowers, esp. 22–23. This purist principle must have been very banal if even Eumolpus, in his poetic manifesto (on which see chapter 2, pp. 68–72) says, *refugiendum est ab omni verborum, ut ita dicam, vilitate et sumendae voces a plebe summotae* (118.4).

39. Thus an ironic gap is opened up comparable to the case we examined in chapter 1 (p. 10), *et ne infirmitas militiam perderet largioribus cibis excito vires* (82.1). The persistent use of culinary metaphors, and especially of *culina*, is incidentally a good indicator of the correct interpetation of Encolpius' impassioned speech on the causes of *corrupta eloquentia*, a speech dictated by the hidden author with parodic intention. The ideas expounded by the pro-

when they confront the theme *de causis corruptae eloquentiae.*[40] Admittedly, serious literary criticism also made use of gastronomic images and metaphors (for example, *oratio condita,* or *salsa* or *ieiuna,* and even, with a double meaning, *sapor/sapio,* just as in Greek a whole series of epithets refer to the "taste" of literary style: δριμύς, πικρός, γλυκύς);[41] but here Encolpius goes too far, and seems inadvertently to exemplify these same vices of the new art of rhetoric. This was an art which, in its degraded forms, was in many ways comparable to cookery.[42]

Plato, the first enemy of *corrupta eloquentia,* had in the *Gorgias* developed the theme that rhetoric, in particular the sophistic practiced by Gorgias' pupils, was an analog of the culinary

---

tagonist are contradicted by the language in which they are couched, and there is no way that chapters 1–5 of the *Satyricon* can be transformed into a manifesto of Petronian poetics. On this consult P. A. George, "Style and Character in the *Satyricon,*" *Arion* 5 (1966) 336–58; E. Cizek, "À propos des premiers chapitres du *Satyricon,*" *Latomus* 34 (1975) 197–202; and best of all G. Kennedy, "Encolpius and Agamemnon"; some good material in W. Kissel, "Petrons Critik der Rhetorik (*Sat.* 1–5)," *RhM* 121 (1978) 311–28, though I do not understand how he can persist in seeing behind these words of Encolpius the more or less direct intentions of the author. There is a full synthesis in Soverini, 1706–79, esp. 1706–38. See also the discussion in chapter 2, pp. 44–45, 50–52, 59–64.

40. The congruences and analogies are particularly strong with *On the Sublime;* cf. L. Alfonsi, "Petronio e i Teodorei," *RFIC* 76 (1948) 46–53, and Cosci, 201–207.

41. On the use of culinary images in literary criticism see the classic pages of J. C. Bramble, *Persius and the Programatic Satire: A Study in Form and Imagery* (Cambridge, 1974), 45–59; add now Gowers, 41, 182ff. (indeed this whole book should be read on this issue, though with some caution).

42. In a sense we can say that Encolpius gets his just deserts (not desserts!) in the *Cena:* the spectacular gastronomy of Trimalchio is a revenge upon someone who is inclined to the degraded (gastronomic) rhetoric of his time. For a *scholasticus* it would have been more honorable to glut himself with talk instead of food, as happened to the *scholastici* in one of Varro's *Menippeae,* the *Eumenides*—note that they too were clearly the object of humor, though of less cruelty: *et ceteri scholastici saturis auribus scolica dape atque ebriis sophistice aperantologia consurgimus ieiunis oculis* (fr. 144 Büch.).

art; it too was an illusionist art, able to disguise reality with every kind of artifice. Both arts adulterated (or "sophisticated") things by means of flattery of the senses and the spirit.[43] In the finale of the *Satyricon,* an obscure figure will appear who tries to convince the *captatores* of Croton to implement the monstrous clause in Eumolpus' will, namely to eat the flesh of his corpse.[44] This figure has the "speaking name" of Gorgias, and he shows himself to be an impartial patron of the two arts of rhetoric and cookery. His entire *inventio* seeks out new ways of beguiling and distracting the palate, not to mention the mind, of men: *inveniemus blandimenta quibus saporem mutemus* (141.8), a unique utterance which combines all the elements of ambiguity carried, from Plato onwards, by the figure

43. Platonic doctrine was fully received by Latin culture at various levels, and it inevitably exercized a negative influence on the image of the historic Gorgias: see Conte, "Petr. *Satyr.* 141," 306–309; and as an attempted reaction Cic. *De Orat.* 3.129, Quint. *Inst* 2.15.24–25. But on the ambiguity of the figure of Gorgias caught between historical reality and antisophistic polemic see L. Bianchi, "A proposito del giudizio di Platone su Gorgia," *Maia* 6 (1953) 271–82; E. L. Harrison, "Was Gorgias a Sophist?" *Phoenix* 18 (1964) 183–92; P. A. Bernardini and A. Veneri, "Il Gorgia di Platone nel giudizio di Gorgia e l''aureo' Gorgia nel giudizio di Platone (*Athen.* 11, 505d-e)," *QUCC* 7 (1981) 149–60.

44. It seems obvious that the speech which ends the surviving part of the novel must belong not to Eumolpus as is often thought, but to the character Gorgias: cf. Conte, "Petr. *Satyr.* 141," 307–308. There is simple guesswork about the relationship between the historic Gorgias, object of Plato's polemic, and the Gorgias of the *Satyricon* in H. J. Shey, "Petronius and Plato's Gorgias," *CB* 47 (1971) 81–84, esp. 84. But discussion has recognized the "sophistic" resonances of the character Gorgias and his speech: cf. Ciaffi, 125; Walsh, 108–109. On the final scene and the cultural context in which it is inserted, cf. H. Rankin, "'Eating People is Right': Petronius 141 and a TOPOS," *Hermes* 97 (1969) 381–84, reprinted in H. Rankin, *Petronius, the Artist: Essays on the Satyricon and its Author* (The Hague, 1971), 100–101. What the Petronian Gorgias recommends to his audience is that they overcome their natural abomination of anthropophagy: they should "correct" the usual disgusting taste of human flesh. Isn't this precisely the cook's professional skill, as well as being the art of the rhetor? Hence the need to read *corrigitur,* proposed perhaps by the younger Junius, reported in Bücheler's apparatus, but subsequently lost in successive editions: cf. Conte, "Petr. *Satyr.* 141," 304 n. 1.

of the rhetorician-cook.[45] The new Gorgias is the direct heir of the homonymous proto-sophist, whom even Aristophanes teased as founder of a sect of ἐγγλωττογάστορες, "men who use the tongue to fill the belly" (*Av.* 1695f., 1702f.).

The kinship between the art of language and the art of cookery has its own story in the *Satyricon*. We have seen that in the first chapters the two arts were juxtaposed and contrasted. Later, in the *Cena Trimalchionis,* the art of cooking assimilates literary rhetoric to itself, and seems to be gaining the upper hand. At the end, in the last scene of the novel, the two arts converge and coincide. This is the scene which sees Gorgias among the *heredipetae* who are gathered for the reading of Eumolpus' will. Now it is obvious that Roman society was not composed merely of *captati* and *captatores,* as some exaggerated and bitter passages of Horace, Seneca and Juvenal might suggest.[46] But literature, beguiled by the power of the image, had eagerly welcomed the model developed by the moralistic tradition.

If we assume the equation of food and money, and of money

45. *Inventio* was an important part of both rhetoric and cookery: cf. Gowers, 80–83. Pliny the Elder also lays much (polemical) stress on the *inventa* produced by the unwearying fantasy of gastronomes: cf. Citroni Marchetti, esp. 200–229 (for other forms of *luxuria* also); *ingeniosa gula est*—as the epic poet Eumolpus would say (*Satyr.* 119, v. 33). And what Gorgias is intent on "inventing" are *blandimenta* for the mind as well as for the palate of the *captatores.* *Blandimentum* in the sense of "condiment" is relatively rare, and the semantics of *blandior* stay active in the word. In Petronius' case, the concept of κολακεία elaborated by Plato in the *Gorgias* and elsewhere is important. There is here the same language which Apuleius (?) *De Platone et eius dogmate,* 2.8.231–33, uses to translate into Latin the Platonic concept, *captatrix, blanda,* etc. The gesture of the rhetor Gorgias, who calls condiments *blandimenta,* is comparable in reverse to that of Gellius who, perhaps on the model of Lucilius, calls the artifices of ornate speech, such as assonance, rhyme and alliteration, *scitamenta,* "tidbits," "gourmandises" (Gell. 18.8.1). It is well known that the cook, especially in comedy, is an ambiguous figure, often the producer of parody, even, or especially, in relation to literature: cf. H. Dohm, *Mageiros. Die Rolle des Kochs in der griechisch-römischen Komödie* (München, 1964).

46. Cf. E. J. Champlin, *Final Judgment: Duty and Emotion in Roman Wills 200 B.C.–A.D 250* (Berkeley, 1991), esp. 86–102.

and man, cannibalism becomes, through a transitive association, the extreme pathological case of covetousness.[47] To say *captator* and *captatus* is like saying hunter and hunted, breeder and fattened livestock. The *captator* of Roman satire (under the influence of diatribe and moralistic literature in general) is a clever character who puts the old men whose inheritance he desires into large nurseries (cf. Horace, *Ep.* 1.1.79: *in vivaria mittunt*) and, when the will of the old *captatus* is opened, waits like a carrion crow with his mouth gaping to get his share of the prey (*plerumque recoctus / scriba ex quinqueviro corvum deludet hiantem / captatorque dabit risus Nasica Corano*, Hor. *Sat.* 2.5.55–57; but one should also read the vignette in Lucian *Timon* 21–23).[48]

The episode of the *heredipetae* is constructed from language already given a metaphorical charge by satire, but it seeks out the path of paradox; it becomes satire raised to the nth degree. "To devour a person" changes from being a harsh metaphor of the moralistic imagination into a real physical act: the language is reified. Gorgias too ends up caught in this linguistic mechanism. His efforts at rhetorical persuasion consist in restoring the signifiers to their original metaphorical level. "Imagine," he says, "that you are eating ten millions sesterces" (*finge . . . centies sestertium comesse*). The reduction of the spiritual to the material ends up corresponding to the reduction of the meta-

47. The misers described by Horace sleep on their sacks of money with open mouths, as if yearning to consume it even while asleep, or else they melt costly pearls in vinegar in order to swallow them. Pliny the Elder too will recall rich bon vivants who chew cups of inestimable value; in the pathology of greed, money becomes an object of physical hunger. Even cannibal urges belong of course to the pathology of greed, as one of its final stages; this depends upon the equation between man and money, another favorite claim of moralistic polemic. This sequence is admirably reconstructed by Citroni Marchetti, esp. 90–173, 235–78, which should be consulted for testimonia and bibliography.

48. For a useful synthesis of materials cf. V. A. Tracy, "*Aut captantur aut captant,*" *Latomus* 39 (1980) 399–402. Tracy's article illustrates how often *captatores* are foiled: Eumolpus would fit into a long tradition of tricksters.

phorical to the literal. Satiric language works in idioms and clichés, *idées reçues* of the satiric moralistic tradition, so as to restore figurative pretensions back to their common denominator of the body.[49] *Devorare patrimonium, comesse pecuniam* were traditional idioms of comic speech and satiric invective.[50] Petronian invention follows the tracks of the tradition, but transforms the phraseology of the common imagination into narrative. With his gift for fantastic fiction Petronius redeems the banality of the image by discarding its original moral harshness; from that point he has complete freedom to construct a new romantic adventure, and one with a smile on its face.

Gorgias, the new impromptu rhetor, is in complete agreement with the Eumolpus of chapter 140 (if it is he who is talking) and with the rhetor Agamemnon of the opening chapters of the *Satyricon:* men are caught only when there is good bait.[51] Eumolpus and Agamemnon share the ability to parade respectable moral banalities which they will be expert at not practicing.[52] The hidden author smiles at them both.

49. I tried to show in "Petronius, *Sat.* 141.4," *CQ* 37 (1987) 532 how the text of 141.4 should be corrected to *quibus animis devorarint spiritum meum, eisdem etiam corpus consumant:* to feed on the truth of a wise man becomes, in the satiric reduction of the metaphorical to the literal, to feed on the body itself.

50. Countless examples can be found in *TLL* s.v. *comedo*, 3.1767, and s.v. *devoro*, 5.1.876.

51. *Satyr.* 140.15: *sicut animalia cibo inescantur, sic homines non caperentur nisi spe aliquid morderent;* cf. 3.4: *sic eloquentiae magister, nisi tamquam piscator eam imposuerit hamis escam, quam scierit appetituros esse pisciculos, sine spe praedae morabitur in scopulo.* Plato too, with polemic intent, had compared sophistic rhetoric, as a technique of flattery for profit, with the art of the fisherman with rod and line: cf. *Soph.* 221d-223a. The motif is inherited by [Xenophon], *De venatione* 13, and Philostratus, *Vit. Soph.* 1.12.

52. The craving for inheritances is one of the contemporary vices that Eumolpus, in his speech of introduction to Encolpius, particularly criticizes: *ac ne bonam quidem mentem aut valetudinem petunt, sed statim antequam limen [Capitolii] tangant, alius donum promittit, si propinquum divitem extulerit, alius, si thesaurum effoderit, alius si ad trecenties sestertium salvus pervenerit* (88.8).

The materialistic power of food and money dominates the Petronian vision to a point where they even found a city. In the antimythical perspective of the *Satyricon*, Croton, once adoptive home of Pythagoras the wise vegetarian,[53] and symbol of a community founded on the principles of healthy diet, has, through a process of parodic reversal, become a new world in which there are only *cadavera quae lacerantur aut corvi qui lacerant* (116.9). Here, as elsewhere in the *Satyricon*, nothing is left of the myths except bare names, the last residues of a paradoxical transformation: Polyaenus, Circe, Proselenus, Philomela, and now, lastly, Gorgias.

53. The discipline of vegetarianism had found famous adherents in the school of the Sextii (Seneca too followed them in his youth) in the first century A.D. The ideas of Pythagoras, albeit in new and more popular forms, must have circulated widely: cf. L. Ferrero, *Storia del Pitagorismo nel mondo romano (dalle origini alle fine della Repubblica)* (Torino, 1955), 374–75. The paradoxical and parodic inversion of Pythagorean Croton (on which see Conte, "Petr. *Satyr.* 141," 309 n. 1) could hardly have escaped the notice of the Roman reader.

CHAPTER FIVE

The Quest for a Genre
(or Chasing Will o' the Wisps?)

*Some Skeptical Thoughts
on Menippean Satire*

If we consider the *Satyricon* in purely formal terms, its most obvious characteristic is surely the alternation of passages in prose and in verse. The versified sections provide a constant counterpoint to the prose narrative and seem completely integrated in the discourse: sometimes they continue it, sometimes they comment upon it, and very often they add elements which make explicit or complete the action.[1] This alternation of prose and verse becomes the marked aspect of a dual narrative structure; in this way the real narrative (in prose) can be enriched with secondary connotations (expressed in verse). Thus the narration emerges as a composite of both "events" and

---

1. A special case is that of the long metrical passages (*Troiae Halosis* and *Bellum Civile*), or excerpts like the *Elegidarion* (109.9), or else the *schedium* (5), which the characters themselves present as recitations: cf. below, p. 154 n. 15. In 133.2 Bücheler accepts the traditional reading, *deprecatus sum numina versu:* with these words Encolpius would begin his prayer to the god Priapus by proclaiming *explicitly* that he will express himself in hexameter verse. But probably (as Müller has in his text) we should accept the emendation *numen aversum* as recorded in Burman[2] (the Anonymus who put forward this emendation should be identified with Janus Mellerus Palmerius, as proposed by my learned friend Ernesto Stagni). *numen aversum* offers an excellent cretic-trochaic clausula instead of the improper heroic rhythm. Thus the transition from prose to verse is not signalled by any metalinguistic comment.

"representations." It allows us to perceive, more directly and openly than can occur in the prose sections, the systems by which the events are construed by the participating characters—and these are mostly stereotypical categories and scholastic codes. In this way too, in a sense, the metrical insets function as a signal for the reader: they are frequent where they reveal the characters' tendency to "live" the various narrative situations according to conventional models, whereas they are almost completely absent from the realistic account of the *Cena*.[2]

It is understandable that such a remarkable peculiarity should become a fundamental problem for any critic who seeks to situate Petronius' work in a literary genre and thus reconstruct the nature of the original project. Indeed, it is intuitively obvious that the work's prosimetric form is one of the author's programmatic choices. It reflects the double nature of a text which communicates through the ambiguous language of parody. But every attempt to confine Petronius' indefatigable creativity within a generic category—even a mixed genre like Menippean satire—must ultimately be unsatisfactory, since the chief purpose of this text is precisely the accumulation of languages, the grafting of one genre upon another, the inexhaustible contamination of different literary forms. The presence of literature in the *Satyricon* is vital, incessant, almost obsessive. In the *Satyricon,* the Greek romance of love and adventure, the heroic epic, grand oratory and declamation, and tragic pantomime are not only used as means of expression, they are also crucial features of the discourse. What I mean is that Petronius' work does not aim to speak *through* these genres but, rather, to speak *about* them. They are, in fact, themes in

2. Verses occur more often in the sections based on assumed roles, more infrequently in the *Cena:* cf. A. M. Cameron, "Myth and Meaning in Petronius: Some Modern Comparisons," *Latomus* 29 (1970) 397–425, esp. 418; F. Jones, "The Narrator and Narrative of the *Satyrica*," *Latomus* 46 (1987) 810–19, esp. 816–17.

themselves besides being vehicles of parody. To recognize the models underlying a text of this kind means dissecting this extraordinary literary product to discover its dominant traits, to determine the directions in which Petronius has oriented the elements of his culture and writing. So this is a quest for meanings, if it is true that the meaning of a text arises from the central intention that subordinates the constitutive elements of the discourse. The genre, or, rather, genres, which work together in different ways to form the *Satyricon* serve the author as ideal landmarks, and in addition guide the reader as strategies of composition which have become part of the text's form. An undertaking like this does not necessarily have to be mere source-hunting; even in recent times, there has been no lack of *Quellenforschung* on the question of prosimetrum and its origins.[3]

3. On the classification of the *Satyricon* I limit myself to the report, "The Romance of the Novel," by E. L. Bowie and S. J. Harrison, in *JRS* 83 (1993) 159–78 (esp. 166–69); but for critical balance we should cite Horsfall, "'Generic Composition,'" 130–38, which also provides useful access to previous bibliography. Most recently G. Schmeling, *"Quid attinet veritatem per interpretem quarere? Interpretes* and the *Satyricon,"* *Ramus* 23 (1994) 144–68, presents a critical history of interpretations of the *Satyricon* from antiquity to present times (144–51) and rightly distinguishes (152) "three special and intertwined problem areas . . . (1) the unreliable narrator, (2) the thick literary texture and (3) genre." One particularly attractive idea (160–61) is that in the narratives of antiquity, especially the *Satyricon,* a technique that produces "generic confusion" can be assimilated to the trope of syllepsis. Otherwise, I would prefer to concentrate my attention on a few works, particularly those more recent and representative. One of the most recent treatments of the relationship between the *Satyricon* and *Satura Menippea,* besides Relihan's study (for which see n. 5), will be found in K. Korus, "Wokoł Teorii Satyry Menippejskiej," *Eos* 78 (1990) 119–31. According to the German synopsis, the author (who rightly criticizes the tendency to see in Menippean satire an absolute freedom from convention) stresses the inclusion of the *Satyricon* in the genre. In his view Petronius' work shares all its basic features: besides prosimetrum, it has the comic aspect, the aggressive character of satiric invective, and a moralistic vein. But I believe that to give an adequate definition of Menippean satire, it is best to rely on the individuation of precise formal features which can function as real conventions. Thus, among the conspicuously Roman, we might say "Varronian," characteristics (cf. below, note 5), there is

We must assume, I believe, that even for the first readers of Petronius the prosimetric form was a crucial, perhaps even decisive, element which directed their expectations and set the work in a generic frame. So how does it appear to a modern critic? What is likely to be his first reaction when faced by the prosimetric form of the *Satyricon*? It seems natural, even inevitable, for the *Satyricon* to be assessed against the model of the Menippean tradition. It is true that some critics have shown caution and have made the Menippean genre only one ingredient of the Petronian text, albeit an essential one within the highly original mélange of various competing literary forms; besides Menippean satire, indeed even ahead of it, one must bear in mind the *Triviallitteratur* represented by the Greek novel of love and adventure, but also by the *Fabula Milesia* and the mime. To declare my own position at the outset, I simply do not believe one can turn Menippean satire into *the* structural model of the *Satyricon*. Nor do I think the current identification of prosimetrum and Menippean is valid, either absolutely or in this specific instance.

Some more recent discussions of Menippean satire, whether written or inspired by M. Bakhtin,[4] have considerably ex-

---

an appetite for contrast, an almost anarchic mixture, the constant use of Greek words and quotations, which are noticeably absent in Petronius. Nor does it seem to me useful to stress the aggressive character of supposed Petronian satire, or to give too much weight to bouts of "moralization," since in fact these are dominated and reorientated by the narrative structure and the characterization of the agents, as I have tried to show in the preceding chapters. We do not find in Petronius one fundamental constitutive feature of satire, namely the satiric *persona*. Nor can we apply to Petronius the canons of *spoudogeloion*. Under the guise of comic aggression, the objects of discussion in Menippean satire were undoubtedly serious, if only with a view to demolishing current opinion.

4. Cf. esp. M. Bakhtin, *Rabelais and his World*, trans. H. Iswolsky (Bloomington, Indiana, 1984); *Esthétique et Théorie du Roman*, trans. D. Olivier (Paris, 1987). On the application of Bakhtin's theories to classical texts see H. K. Riikonen, *Menippean Satire as a Literary Genre, with special reference to Seneca's Apocolocyntosis, Commentationes Humanarum Litterarum* 83, Helsinki, 1987, esp. 17–31.

panded, or perhaps distorted, the idea of this genre as it was once formulated (often in half-conscious terms) by classicists. Bakhtin's immense authority has had the result that Menippean satire has become a sort of protean super-genre, able to absorb into itself, through parody, the characteristics of a multitude of genres. In recent times the temptation has developed to explain Petronius' problematic choice by transforming questions into answers. Surely the *Satyricon* cannot be reduced to a single genre? Surely different individual genres can be distinguished in the text (juxtaposed without mediation or hierarchization), in the form of passages each serially classifiable and often exposed to the filter of parody? Then, following this line of reasoning, the very irreducibility of the work, not to mention the mélange of tidbits of variable literary quality (*ekphraseis,* epic poems, novelistic reversals, declamations, epigrams, excerpts of historiographical or juridical language), become in the end the *sure mark* of a deeply and authentically Menippean inspiration. Such an explanation is only superficially satisfying; we are in danger of attributing a distinct identity to a creature whose generic characteristics are so indefinite as to be unrecognizable by any reader.

I do not intend to review systematically modern criticism of Menippean satire.[5] I would rather start from the view of Quin-

5. This has been done most recently by J. C. Relihan, *Ancient Menippean Satire* (Baltimore and London, 1993), one of the most useful studies on this issue. Relihan is rightly concerned to establish a more restrictive definition of Menippean satire that would stay closer to ancient literary theory and practice. Even when I do not refer to it explicitly, and although there are many points on which I differ, including some found in the chapter on Petronius (91–99), this book is important to the present discussion because of its review of Menippean satire as a genre, and its attempt to find its basic principles as well as tracing its historical development in the classical literatures. The definition put forward in Relihan's first chapter attempts to identify the distinctive, recurrent features of Menippean satire so as to include both Greek and Latin authors, even those coming late in Latin literature (Martianus Capella, Fulgentius, Ennodius and Boethius). In reality, however, he cannot formulate definite formal constants beyond the mere prosimetric structure.

tilian that the Menippean was simply one particular form of satire.[6] Nor do I intend to discuss the relationship which scholars have until recently thought they could establish between Menippean satire and our *Satyricon* (including the title).[7] I would simply like to set limits to what I believe should remain problematic, but at the same time make problematic what has too hastily been taken for granted.

Perhaps it will be more convenient, and certainly more straightforward, to adopt a process of *negative* definition. To exclude the presence of features that are genuinely Menippean seems to me a more productive approach than to define *positively* the specific literary components that can be recognized in the *Satyricon*—beginning with realism of representation, which deserves separate discussion (see chapter 6). Here I can only say that the realism of the *Satyricon* cannot be explained by means

---

Throughout this chapter I have therefore preferred to adopt an image of Menippean satire which I would call "Varronian" and "Latin" (Relihan is himself well aware of Varro's role as innovator but also as influential and authoritative model). This induces me to base my comparisons mainly on Varro and Seneca, and only cautiously on Lucian, and to disregard the literature of Late Antiquity; nor do I claim to reconstruct an "archetype." It is not my task to understand whether, or to what extent, later authors have respected, recast or violated the original modes of the founder Menippus (who is named in the title of Varro's own work).

6. Quint. *Inst.* 10.1.95: *alterum illud etiam prius saturae genus, sed non sola carminum varietate mixtum, condidit Terentius Varro, vir Romanorum eruditissimus. Plurimos libros et doctissimos composuit, peritissimus linguae Latinae et omnis antiquitatis et rerum Graecarum nostrarumque, plus tamen scientiae collaturus quam eloquentiae.* (See J. C. Relihan, *A History of Menippean Satire to A.D. 524* [Diss. Univ. of Wisconsin, Madison, 1985, Ann Arbor, 1989], 9–11 and notes, pp. 53–54, on the controversial interpretation of this passage.) For the relationship between Petronius and Roman satire, especially but not only Menippean, see H. Petersmann, "Petrons *Satyrica*," 395–400 (with essential bibliography). Among the most balanced assessments I would mention that of Walsh, 21–24, who succeeds in identifying the authentically satiric motifs and placing them in their proper role within the general structure of the *Satyricon*.

7. The problem has been aggravated by the fact that *Saturae* was the title recognized by the most authoritative edition until thirty-five years ago. See below, n. 23.

of the quite idiosyncratic realism of the Menippean (as the theories of Bakhtin might invite us to do). As I implied, and as I will repeat somewhat tediously, no one can define precisely the limits and achievements of the *Satyricon*'s originality, not only in literal positivistic terms, but simply because of the disappearance beyond recall of so much ancient popular (and low-level) book production, which would have been a control of primary importance for understanding the literary operation undertaken by Petronius.

But once Petronius is granted autonomy and innovative ability, we should probably be content with the affirmation that the *Satyricon* cannot be reduced to too rigid a scheme. An author such as we have studied in the preceding chapters appears ambiguous, multiform, elusive, certainly not to be reduced to a single discursive purpose. This conclusion seems in harmony with the extraordinary awareness shown, for example, in the functional exploitation of the narrating "I." To pick on this (real or theoretical) irreducibility, which is a characteristic of the entire Menippean genre, seems to me a careless shortcut. What is really fruitful is to get down to details, to analyze concretely the manner and above all the limits in which Menippean license expressed itself. The arguments we have to resist, as I said, are those which go more or less like this: "Petronius chose the Menippean because it allowed him to do anything and everything." Worse still would be to argue by inverting the terms of the question: "since Petronius does anything and everything, he must be putting himself in the Menippean tradition." The absence of limits cannot in itself be a distinguishing criterion.

In any case, we might reach a worthwhile result by acknowledging that the Menippean has often been considered an essential component of the *Satyricon* precisely because it is a literary construct characterized by prosimetrum and parody. In fact, these features are not confined to the Menippean, since they are perfectly possible in other literary forms. We can grant that Petronius derived from Menippean satire some important structural features; at any rate, he will have been able to exploit it (on the same basis as satire in general) as one literary genre among many, most of all as a rich treasure trove of motifs, situations, profitable conventions—and here I would include even a certain use of prosimetrum. What I must underline is simply that it would be hasty to see in the Menippean the obligatory vehicle or medium of every parody, as of all prosimetrum.[8]

Other arguments also prevent us from including Petronius within the Menippean category on the grounds that it is a genre able to absorb and exhaust all the functions of his discourse. Even Menippean satire must have institutional limits and conventions. It may well absorb everything in its parodic function, but not without discrimination. It transforms the elements derived from outside, but it does not deprive them of an identity that can be recognized and isolated (even though modified, distorted and inverted). Indeed it exalts their identity. It does not limit itself to a chaotic mingling or juxtaposing as Petronius seems to do, and above all (unlike Petronius), it does not renounce all expression of its own chosen stance. Let us consider the cynical aggression of Menippus as it emerges from the ancient testimonia or the literary images provided by Lucian's character, or suppose we consider the pamphletistic attack of the *Apocolocyntosis,* or the moralizing and authentically satiric aggression which can be gathered from the surviving fragments

---

8. In any case the Menippean elements cannot have the same function in the *Satyricon* as the epic, tragic or elegiac elements that Petronius imitates, dismantles and reassembles. These last—elements of the literary sublime—are noble frameworks projected by the romantic imagination of the characters, who thus expose themselves to parody. The other elements, those of Menippean type, behave differently: they are the instruments of the game set in motion by the ironic author against the projections of his characters.

of Varro. In every one of these cases, the celebrated Menippean polyphony, even while displaying a plurality of points of view, always chooses one precise position and never hides the direction of its aggression; indeed, in the end, there emerges the univocal message of the author whose presence the work advertises. Menippean satire does not confuse the reader by unfolding before him a more complex image of the world; rather, it is more like a bow shooting arrows, and arrows with a definite trajectory that can be reconstructed. Its primary intent is to make some precise issue the subject of debate, something that has been too drastically fixed or too uncritically accepted. In it the facetious and the serious coexist, in line with the moral tradition of the *spoudogeloion*.

In a quite different way, as I said, the *Satyricon* seems to prefer juxtaposition—an ambiguity of language which leaves confrontations unresolved, which refuses univocality of meaning and keeps the author concealed. This is why its parody, at least in some manifestations, seems so elusive. It is almost unnecessary to recall the disputes on the meaning of the *Troiae Halosis* and above all of the *Bellum Civile*. Are these really parodies? What would their object be? In what way would the parodic joke be conveyed? Certainly there are features that bring the *Satyricon* and Menippean satire together, but we should not overlook the fact that the intent of the Menippean is not that of gratuitously juxtaposing parodies of different discourses in order to offer a kind of parade of different worlds. What it seeks to do is to degrade the "elevated." In Menippean satire, cynic ideology works to redefine the scale of values and to legitimize everything that common ideology has censured as vile and ignoble, by restoring it to the same level as the constitutionally "elevated."

We must be careful not to attribute to the ancient Menippean the intention of producing a blurred amalgam. In contrast with the travesty of Petronius' petty characters who aim to rise to a more elevated level, Menippean discourse aims to debase the models on which it operates in a precise and direct manner: it assaults them and tries to drag them down. It is no accident that the comic effect most often exploited by Lucian and Seneca, and probably also by Varro before them, consists of making gods speak like men, attributing to them the most earthy of preoccupations. The scene may be set on the summit of Olympus or in Hades or on the Moon: in each case we have to face the ultimate questions of eschatology and try to resolve serious moral problems. This is what gives the leap from the great to the small its effect. In short, what is characteristic here is the choice of eccentric perspectives, of other places from which to criticize the world, of Utopian abodes that create contrast and alienation.[9] What we don't find in the Menippean is a concern for verisimilitude and credibility of situation. Crucially, what we *do* find instead is a lively taste for the paradoxical, an exaggerated indulgence of fantastic and bizarre invention, as in the best Attic old comedy.[10] It is difficult to imagine a more radical form of debasement. Homeric gods, mythical figures, fantastic personifications—all suffer an uncomfortable leveling down to an everyday world unenclined to spare them.

Matters are quite different in Petronius. Neither deities nor heroic figures are degraded. Nor is there any debasing of the great models of sublime literature. Instead there is *parody of the debasement* which they have already endured. What is represented and parodied is anyone whose way of life debases these

9. See W. von Koppenfels, "*Mundus alter et idem*. Utopiefiktion und menippeische Satire," *Poetica* 13 (1981) 16–66, esp. 26–28, where the consciously ironic presentation of fiction and eccentric spatiality are judged to be constitutive factors of Menippean satire. It is just this eccentric perspective which has allowed us to recognize in the fifth satire of Horace's second book an experiment close to the Menippean genre: Tiresias and Ulysses, in a new version of the *Nekyia*, are made to occupy themselves with a squalid practice of earthlings, the hunt for inheritances.

10. The examples are infinite and I would abuse the patience of my readers if I cited even one.

great models by reducing them to his own trivial pettiness. In short, the attack is not against the grand forms of epic and tragedy or high forensic oratory, but against their degraded forms, that is, romanticizing novels and *Trivialliteratur,* the melodrama of pantomime, the excesses of scholastic declamation. The general atmosphere, the use of the mythomaniac narrator's persona, and the realism or lifelike color of the action all combine so that when the noble models try to break out and reclaim their original form, reality itself catches them out. While the *scholastici* deceive themselves in aspiring to the sublime, the author dismisses them as follows: "All of you, Encolpius, Ascyltus, Giton and your crew can at best be the characters of a novel, a mime, a Milesian tale, a stage melodrama, but if you realized it yourselves, you would fall apart immediately. The sublime is far beyond you. A phrase, a gesture, a flourish is not enough to turn you into an Achilles, an Aeneas, a Lucretia, a Cicero."

Petronius' strategy is very different from that of the Menippean, virtually its opposite in fact. It is not a matter of reaching for the heights of divinity in order to debase them with the corrosive power of paradox; Petronius does not degrade the sublime texts that are cited or parodied from time to time, and above all he does not directly debase divine, mythological or heroic roles. Rather, he brings down to earth an ordinary humanity which had sought to scale heights to which it had no right. Moreover, unlike Menippean satire, Petronius has absolutely no intention of providing representations of universal or symbolic value. So the entire narrative is depressed to this "low" level, despite the struggles of its characters to disengage themselves. There are no gods, as in Menippean satire, who discuss terrestrial problems; there are no divine councils,[11] no

11. This is a theme which, with due adaptations and variations, must have been particularly popular in Menippean satire (as in other genres). After

meetings with great men in the Underworld, nor are the extreme questions of the human condition raised for discussion. Instead, there is a primary narrativity based on real events and centered on characters playing out their daily lives in their most sordid and thus, in a sense, most authentic aspects. Nor is there any collapse: the level of action is low from the start. The ambitious acrobatics of the characters are not enough to raise them off the ground.

We would never catch Petronius constructing situations and reversals by neglecting the verisimilitude of his narrative or the internal consistency of his narrator. Menippean satire, on the other hand, shows the greatest indifference to all that—indeed, such indifference is the real distinguishing feature of the genre. Verisimilitude is so far from the fantastic drive of Menippean satire that a narrator can compose a prologue like that of the *Apocolocyntosis,* based on a mocking indifference to the truth, as if to say, "I am going to tell you a true story: if it turns out not to be true, listen just the same." Here the Menippean Seneca gives the canonical assurances of impartiality and truthfulness, but only to repeat sarcastically the conventional framework of serious historiography—and he does it at the very moment when he is boldly swaggering into the realm of the miraculous and the incredible.

In the *Satyricon* there is nothing like these metaliterary jokes; rather we have the direct narrative of stories that could happen in this world, on any day, however hackneyed or extravagant

---

Menippus one should remember, amongst others, the two chronological extremes of the satirist Lucilius and the late Menippean Julian, author of the *Caesares;* along with them, Lucian, Varro with his *Pseudulus Apollo,* περὶ θεῶν διαγνώσεως, and naturally Seneca, all seem to presuppose the problem of "false gods." But it should be noted that the theme of the "Council of the Gods" has received a disproportionate emphasis in the reconstructions of Menippean satire made by modern critics: it is the accident of survival that has left us the *Apocolocyntosis* as the most complete instance of the genre, and we should not generalize too much on that basis.

they may be. In Petronius, there are no paradoxical elements or pure fantasies, no brilliant inventions such as the titles of certain Varronian satires seem to imply (*Endymiones, sexagesis, Bimarcus* and others); in Petronius there are no men who wake up after years of sleep, no personalities split into two parts which converse with each other, no fantastic situations of this kind.

But there is something else. As has often been noted, textual citations, or even simple parodies which play on the parodied texts by near-quotation of the models, are absent from Petronius. Just this kind of "parasitic parody" is widespread in Seneca, although he is not without his own poetic inventions (and *pastiches,* of a kind which probably also occurred in the original Menippean satire, not to mention Varro).[12] But what matters is that in true Menippean satire, quotations (like the less pretentious proverbs) are very common, almost constantly inserted in the body of its prose; and this is true both for the language of the narrator and for that of the characters. In short, in contrast with Petronius, the poetic insets into Menippean lay violent hands upon the illustrious model, which at the very moment of citation is either overthrown and humbled or manipulated and distorted. The Menippean cites poetry only to infect it, to desacralize it, only to indicate how absurd it is to speak in poetry: it is fully aware that the fact of speaking in poetry already signifies something in itself.

Indeed this is the condition for a common type of metaliter-

12. Lucian too quotes Homeric verses, sometimes only slightly modified or modified just enough to adjust them to the context. Indeed in his Menippean works original verses are not to be found. On the prosimetry and quotations in Varro, cf. E. Woytek, "Varro," in J. Adamietz, ed., *Die römische Satire* (Darmstadt, 1986), 311–55, esp. 348–49. See also the excellent paper of M. Fusillo, "La citazione menippea (sondaggi su Luciano)," in A. de Vivo and L. Spina, edd., *"Come dice il poeta." Percorsi greci e latini di parole poetiche* (Napoli, 1992), 21–42; see also D. Bartoňková, *"Prosimetrum:* The Mixed Style in Ancient Literature," *Eirene* 14 (1976) 65–92.

ary joke that thematizes the double nature of prosimetric composition: it makes it conspicuous that there is poetry in the
prose and marks *explicitly* when the person writing or talking
abandons prose to set himself up as a poet (here it is enough for
me to mention the prologue of the *Apocolocyntosis* yet again).
The change of medium, from prose to verse, becomes a problematic feature to be discussed, of which the narrator shows
complete awareness. A good example is in the *Apocolocyntosis,*
before the paratragic senarii pronounced by Hercules (7.1),
when Seneca says, *et quo terribilior esset, tragicus fit et ait.* This
kind of *metalinguistic* reflexivity seems a fundamental feature of
Menippean satire.[13] Lucian highlights this when the personification of the Menippean Dialogue, a monstrous hybrid constructed to subvert the hierarchy of literary discourse, openly
accuses its author: "but the most absurd thing is that I
have been transformed into a paradoxical blend (κρᾶσίν τινα
παράδοξον) and I am neither infantry nor cavalry, marching
neither in prose nor verse (οὔτε πεζός εἰμι οὔτε ἐπὶ τῶν μέτρων
βέβηκα) but, like a centaur, I appear before my public as a
bizarre composite creature."[14] The Menippean is an eccentric
form, and the metaphor that expresses it has to be a fantastic
monster like the centaur.

There is nothing like this in Petronius. We will see below how
he prefers to the "poetics of contrast," which seems to be typical of the Menippean, a "poetics of *continuity,*" that is, a type
of discourse which, while alternating passages in prose with
passages in verse, calmly accepts the double medium and does
not raise difficult questions—with self-reflexive implications—

13. In all probability such metalinguistic reflexivity should be recognized
even in Varro, especially in fragment 57 A from *Bimarcus* (and cf. also fr. 58):
see J.-P. Cèbe, *Varron, Satires Ménippées,* vol. 2 (Rome, 1974), 244.

14. *Bis Accusatus* 33. The metaphor of the centaur recurs in another programmatic work of Lucian (*Prometheus es in verbis,* 5), where however it
refers to the contamination of dialogue and comedy: cf. R. B. Branham, "Introducing a Sophist: Lucian's Prologues," *TAPA* 115 (1985) 237–43.

about its own hybrid nature. As I said, Petronius lacks an explicit metalinguistic organization: the narrative text runs on placidly from prose into poetry, to resume in turn its prosaic flow. No steps or thresholds are marked between the two forms of discourse, except for the cases in which poetic speech is introduced as part of the narrated action, and so is preceded by an explicit introduction of the type, "and then he delivered these verses." (Let us not forget the poets who have roles in the *Satyricon,* especially Eumolpus and his many rivals.)[15] In short, it is as though poetry were simply a continuation of prose by other means.

Petronius does not work like a literary parasite: he seldom recycles pre-existing linguistic material and he usually avoids word-play, of which Menippean satire, on the other hand, is

15. See for example *Satyr.4.5*: *et ipse carmine effingam;* 23.2: *et eiusmodi carmina effudit;* 89: *itaque conabor opus versibus pandere;* 109.8: *coepitque capillorum elegidarion dicere;* 119–24: *tamquam si placet hic impetus.* It is not accidental that the joking or even sarcastic stress on the production of verse in Petronius always finds expression after the event, *a posteriori,* as a reaction to the behavior of the people employed in versifying (I think for instance of felicitous phrases like that uttered by Encolpius against Eumolpus in 90.3: *saepius poetice quam humane locutus es;* cf. also 115.5: *inicio ego phrenetico manum* and *poetam mugientem*). In Seneca, on the other hand, it often happens that the poetic intrusion is marked *beforehand,* or at any rate with a metalinguistic comment that stresses the double option of prosimetric expression. In Petronius the judgments never affect the mixture of the two expressive systems (in prose and in poetry) but only the *poor quality of the poetry,* which is usually foolish and verbose; cf. 6.1: *in hoc dictorum aestu;* 110.1: *plura . . . et ineptiora praeteritis;* 124.2: *ingenti volubilitate verborum;* note too the reaction of the crowd to the *Troiae Halosis* (90.1–6: they throw stones so violently that Eumolpus makes a promise—which he will not keep—not to compose any more verses; cf. 93.3: *saltem nobis parce, qui te numquam lapidavimus*). Here the ridicule falls on the quasi-professional figure of the poetaster always ready to improvise (obviously Eumolpus, but Agamemnon too), a typical figure of Satire from Lucilius to Juvenal, but also a fixture in real life, as reflected in Seneca Rhetor and above all in the letters of Pliny. Such comments on poetic citations or recitations are never directed towards the verse effusions of the narrator, which seem, in this respect also, to have a quite particular status, differentiated from excerpts recited by other characters.

very fond. The Menippean loves to make educated or half-educated allusions, playing on once hallowed or popular phrases; it seeks to produce burlesque effects, quite often brilliant and surprising, comic effects that are often combined with free and easy parodic recycling. Think of how in *Apocolocyntosis* (1.2) the limping Claudius (*nomen omen*) walks *non passibus aequis*: Virgil provides the verse (*Aen.* 2.724, where Iulus follows his father Aeneas "with shorter steps"). Or one notes how another Virgilian verse, referring with humorous epic solemnity to the king (queen) bee (*Georg.* 4.90: *dede neci: melior vacua sine regnet in aula*), is jestingly restored to the *rex* Claudius and the *aula* of imperial power (3.2). This is the mechanism: the quotation of the noble verse is faithful to the letter of the original but inverts its meaning. The *aprosdoketon* is achieved by purely verbal means. At other times it is the technique of *fulmen in clausula* that creates the parodic effect by the substitution of polar or at least contrasting terms. This is the case with the Homeric verses cited by Lucian, which are almost always slightly distorted or adjusted to the syntactical context or situation. This is the case too with the numerous examples in which Seneca adapts references to divinity to his *fatuus* or *moros*.[16]

In the textual form of the *Satyricon* there is a quite different sensibility with respect to verbal humor. What most pleases Menippean satire, playing with verbal clichés, does not interest Petronius. In the same way, he is not interested in playing with proverbs. (The exception of the *Cena*, which crams the freedmen's speech with sayings and ready-made phrases, is enough to confirm this, inasmuch as their use there has a purely mimetic function; it is not a procedure of the narrating voice.)[17] We

16. Cf. *Apocol.* 7.3, 8.3: in both cases μωροῦ is substituted for the expected θεοῦ.

17. See e.g. Petersmann, 401, who points to a correct interpretation of this "linguistic realism" within the general literary frame of the *Satyricon*. Too often criticism stops short of even trying to insert the *Cena* into the reconstruc-

know only too well how much room is taken up by proverbs in Menippean satire, especially the Roman examples. The *Apocolocyntosis* is full of them. Indeed the work begins with the conspicuous quotation of a proverb which becomes as it were the narrative trigger for the entire story: *suum diem obiit ille, qui verum proverbium fecerat, aut regem aut fatuum nasci oportere* (1.1).[18] What is more, in Varro proverbs were so fundamental to the genre that they appeared in the titles of individual satires, whether in Greek or Latin: e.g., Ὄνος λύρας, Γνῶθι σεαυτόν, Δὶς παῖδες οἱ γέροντες, Τὸ ἐπὶ τῇ φακῇ μύρον, Εὗρεν ἡ λοπὰς τὸ πῶμα, *Mutuum muli scabunt, Cras credo, hodie nihil, Idem Atti quod Tetti, Longe fugit qui suos fugit, Nescis quid vesper serus vehat.*

But what seems especially distinctive in the Menippean prosimetrum is its taste for jarring juxtapositions, for the jarring inequality between lofty quotation and the context which contains it. The sheer loftiness of stylistic register marks the distinguished quotation as a foreign body, *immediately* obvious as something incongruous, perhaps even in conflict with the surrounding prose, which is often of a much lower linguistic level.[19] The comedy depends on the language itself, on grand words only appropriate in epic. This is perhaps best seen in an

---

tion of Petronius' program (on which see below, chapter 6). In the *Satyricon* every character speaks according to his need, knowledge and choice, as much in the *Cena* as in the rest of the work.

18. A list of the proverbs in the *Apocolocyntosis* is most easily found in the general index of P. T. Eden's commentary (Cambridge, 1984), 167 s.v. "Proverbs." Cf. also the analytic index of the commentary and edition of C. F. Russo, *L. Annaei Senecae Divi Claudii Apocolocyntosis* (Firenze, 1985⁶), 174 s.v. "proverbi e fraseologia popolare-gnomica-proverbializzante."

19. This seems the place to insist on the low linguistic tone of Menippean prosimetrum. This is a vulgar level which Seneca's narrator (unlike Encolpius) accepts for himself as much as for his characters, even the illustrious ones— even, indeed, the grandest of the gods. In short, from the characters' point of view, Menippean satire assimilates their language into an undifferentiated mixture; all of them, from the narrator up, seem to speak in the same way, even if there may be poetic flights, usually in the form of parody. Another ele-

author like Lucian, who like Petronius prefers a sober prose, rather than in Varro, who often indulges his linguistic fantasy even in non-metrical passages (though, of course, we must make allowance for the criteria of selection by grammarians and the indirect tradition).

In contrast, the metrical passages of the *Satyricon* do not always (indeed not even often) mark an intended contrast. As we have noted, because the versified sections continue in some manner to report the narrated events, they are like *epigrammatic comments* formulated in a language well adapted to the fundamental urbanity of the narration.[20] For the narrative voice of Encolpius, talking in verse does not represent a significant leap from talking in prose: it is just another way of voicing his mythomania, a more conspicuous, freer way of abandoning himself to the illusory fantasies which also dominate his prose. Many of these metrical excerpts form the last and highest stage in the process of "sublimatizing" which is employed by the hidden author in his cruel game:[21] he lets the characters release their ill-timed exaltation in verse before allowing them to fall into the void of disillusionment.

What have I been trying to establish, and what have I actually

---

ment that is immediately jarring, as we said before, is the continual intrusion of Greek, found in Varro as much as in Seneca, but completely alien to Petronius.

20. The *Satyricon* drastically reduces the number of real quotations, even in comparison with the *Apocolocyntosis* (which surely represents the closest Menippean got to Petronius, especially in view of the last metrical insertion of the *Apocolocyntosis*, 15.1, which has a descriptive function in relation to the narrative).

21. It is part of the hidden author's game that one cannot, and perhaps should not, clearly understand whether the occasional verses are to be attributed to Encolpius as narrator or to Encolpius as character (the narrating "I" or the agent "I"). This ambiguity seems to me very important for the construction of the narrating "I": sometimes it fosters identification (of an emotional kind) between Encolpius as narrator and Encolpius as character, but on other occasions the irony after the fact is too open not to accentuate the distance between them.

managed to achieve in this analysis? I hope I have shown that too many essential features of the real Menippean satire just do not appear in the *Satyricon*.[22] Indeed it would seem that Petronius' expressive technique, as well the inspiration and program of his text, are essentially outside the Menippean tradition, if not downright opposed to it. Any attempt to define the literary genre of a work has only a heuristic value. To fix the signifying features of a complex and elusive work like the *Satyricon* is only useful if the attempt at classification—which is a working hypothesis—succeeds in capturing the essential significance of the text, that is, only if it succeeds in making itself an *interpretation*. In any case there is a great risk of arbitrariness. You will understand my difficulty in proposing an alternative hypothesis to that of Menippean satire. No claim has been made that the model of the novel, for all that it may appear more satisfying, can succeed in solving all the problems.

The tendency to oppose as principal constitutive models these two genres—Menippean satire and the novel—lurks in all the vast bibliography. The hypothesis of compromise, which makes the *Satyricon* the product of a mélange of the two differing components, is just as common.[23] Anyone who has exhaus-

22. In recent bibliography one of the most balanced critical discussions seems to me that of Petersmann, 396 (even if he tends to dwell excessively on the satiric intent). This article should also be consulted, especially 396–400, for the discussion of the technique, the function and the typology of the poetic insets in comparison with the practices of the novel. For example, the differences from Chariton are quite clear: verse insets in Chariton are only quotations, and short ones at that. It is still somewhat surprising that Petersmann, while refuting the exclusively Menippean origin of prosimetrum and suggesting the influence of the novel, decides to illustrate the characteristics of the phenomenon in Petronius by contrasting him with Chariton, even if he recognizes these important differences, as we do. He ignores the more convincing parallels that can be traced even in other narrative genres; see below, esp. nn. 28–30. Perhaps Petersmann's rather negative judgment on Astbury's article has led him to underestimate the more solid gains it has made. More persuasive and stimulating views are put forward by Holzberg, 64.

23. It is not unlikely that the title reflects a similar intention on the part of the author himself, but, as it were, one which is more connotative than deno-

tively explored this crude opposition of the two genres, while sustaining the thesis of an essentially Menippean Petronius, has really conducted a kind of mirror operation to my own:[24] such a scholar will have emphasized the lack of certain important elements in the novel and by contrast will have has proposed that certain features commonly believed to belong to the novel can be better understood in the light of other literary traditions, first and foremost the satiric and in particular the Menippean tradition.

Inevitably those who deny the model of the novel strive to devalue the role of the intrigue in the *Satyricon*. In contrast, they

---

tative. The reader, who probably will be surprised to find urbane rather than obscene language, must expect a narrative work (as suggested by the suffix *-i(a)ca*, as in *Milesiaca*, etc.; cf. above, chapter 3, p. 74, n. 1) with an erotic and indeed scurrilous plot (cf. Walsh, 72–73 and Petersmann, 388–90). I admit that with this title Petronius may have intended to direct the readers' expectations towards satire as well, in a more or less broad sense, inasmuch as this signifies wordplay on the etymological value of *satura* and on interpretations of it offered by antiquity. But this is not enough to make us consider the *Satyricon* as a collection of real satires or, even worse, as a single satire of immense proportions (cf. *infra*, n. 26). In general, scholars such as E. Courtney ("Parody and Literary Allusion in Menippean Satire") and Walsh, esp. 17–30 and chapter 4, have argued for a compromise between satire and the novel, or have itemized satiric and in particular Menippean elements in the *Satyricon*. The consequences of the position that demands the identification of prosimetrum with Menippean satire (which seems to me ruled out by new papyrus finds containing narratives in prosimetric form: see below, p. 163ff.) are clear in Sullivan, *The Satyricon*, especially in the chapter, "The Choice of Form." The section, "The Choice of Menippean Satire," esp. p. 90, argues that the preliminary choice of Menippean form, dictated by the type of message and public which Petronius had in mind, would inevitably involve satiric features. But this is aprioristic reasoning, which starts from extratextual elements in order to define the nature of the text; it is clear from 97ff. how prejudicial this kind of presupposition can be.

24. The position is expressed in its fullest form by J. Adamietz, "Zum Literarischen Charakter von Petrons Satyrica," *RhM* 130 (1987) 329–46. See now Adamietz's recent article, "Circe in den Satyrica Petrons und das Wesen dieses Werkes," *Hermes* 123 (1995) 320–34, where he reasserts his theory, especially in his attempt to deny that the Circe episode has a novel-like quality. Conversely, the most recent papers of G. Schmeling insist on the (admittedly problematic) narrative nature of the *Satyricon*: see esp. the discussion in

exalt the function of digressions, the multiplicity of themes treated by the text and the diversity of forms in which it expresses itself (discourses on rhetoric, art and poetry on the one hand and parodistic insertions on the other). This seems to me a quite improper procedure: the intrigue cannot be seen as a more or less accidental framework, imposed from without on a satiric text in order to achieve results different from those intended by the pure satiric tradition. The result of this method of argument is to destroy the effects which the author *does* intend to produce from his narrative through that extraordinarily effective instrument, the personality of the narrating "I."

Despite the damage that *excerptio* has imposed on the tissue of the Petronian narrative, what I defined above as "primary narrativity" seems to me undeniable, and is even the most obvious feature of the *Satyricon*.[25] The objective structure of the work requires it to be conceived as a novel. Even the internal form of the text, programmed in cooperation with a reader ca-

---

"*Quid attinet*" at 151–56. He also discusses the most appropriate classification of Petronius within the category "Continuous Forms: Prose Fiction" established by Northrop Frye (note that Frye includes the Menippean as well in the subgenre "anatomy"): Schmeling privileges the subgenre "confession" (153–56). In this connection see also Schmeling, "Confessor Gloriosus: A Role of Encolpius in the *Satyrica*," *Würzburger Jahrbücher für die altertumswissenschaft*, N.F. 20 (1994/1995) 207–24. This starts from the fundamental work of Beck, "Some Observations on the Narrative Technique of Petronius," *Phoenix* 27 (1973) 42–61, and develops ideas in many ways similar to our own (especially 207–12) concerning the unreliability of the narrator Encolpius, whose imagination, fed entirely on literary models, displays that character trait which I have defined as "mythomania."

25. In this sense I find particularly significant the judgment of Macrobius (a reader who knew the whole *Satyricon* and felt entitled to compare it with that of Apuleius) in *Comm. Somn. Scip.* 1.2.8: *fabulae, quarum nomen indicat falsi professionem, aut tantum conciliandae auribus voluptatis aut adhortationis quoque in bonam frugem gratia repertae sunt. Auditum mulcent, vel comoediae, quales Menander eiusve imitatores agendas dederunt, vel argumenta fictis casibus amatorum referta, quibus vel multum se Arbiter exercuit vel Apuleium nonnumquam lusisse miramur.* According to Macrobius, then, erotic content predominates in the *Satyricon* and the aim of the text is to give pleasure to the reader.

pable of recognizing the recursivity of the narrative and the links between the various episodes, demands that the *Satyricon* be read as the continuous narrative of a tale and not as an elaboration of individual satiric themes; if the latter were the case, the whole tale would disintegrate into anecdotal episodes, vignettes about manners, pretexts for meditation and occasional comic schemes. The substance of Petronius' work is not a discussion on various themes that has been tricked out in a narrative disguise—it cannot be reduced to satiric discursivity or to the dialogue. There is no author who aims, either directly or through the satiric persona, to express himself, his tastes, his opinions, his aversions, in short his own ideological or critical stance.

All the more reason, then, why we cannot turn the *Satyricon* into a collection of satires, a collage of individual satiric pieces, that would treat the most disparate arguments enclosed in narrative framework.[26] Nothing like this can be found in any of the

---

26. V. Ciaffi (1967) and J. Adamietz agree in the attempt to turn Petronius' narrative into a composite satiric work. Ciaffi, vii-xi, who like other critics is unable to accept the enormous length suggested for the *Satyricon* by some of the manuscript evidence, is compelled to imagine (with rather weak arguments) that Petronius' work was not a continuous narrative but rather a collection of individual satires, of which only part of an "Encolpius satire" has come down to us. Adamietz (1987), who is more cautious but also forced to some special pleading, says of the extant parts, "Gliedert man in einem gedanklichen Experiment die kontinuierliche Darstellung Petrons in einzelne mit Titeln versehene thematische Teile, wobei als Modell die Sammlung separater Satiren bei Varro dienen kann, dann wird der innere Zusammenhang mit der satirischen Tradition noch deutlicher" (339). In reality, even if the "titles" were conceived purely as a form of orientation, the list on 339–40 is far from persuasive; it is obviously exceptionally difficult to reduce chapters 6–11 to a satire that could be called *Molestiae amoris* or to find real satiric motifs in other passages of similar narrative tone like 79–82 and 91–99 (*Amor incertus*). For the ship episode and the events at Croton Adamietz makes no attempt to give titles, but notes in general terms and with some embarrassment that these chapters (there are over thirty-five of these, even if 118–24 are excluded) include "several themes." In my opinion one should at most speak of comic treatment of motifs predominantly belonging to the novel. Some of these (such as the section on will hunters) naturally lend themselves excel-

preserved collections of satires. On the other hand it is easy, once we look for a real *structural* constant in the *Satyricon,* to recognize a continuous action constructed of narrative elements from the novel (shipwreck, erotic adventures, intrigues and disguise) which must have been represented in the *Trivialliteratur* of the Greek novel. For instance, confronted by the moment of recognition on board Lichas' ship that recalls both Encolpius' and Giton's earlier relationships with Lichas and his wife (105), any reader is bound to recognize the unity of intrigue and action. I will go further: an unprejudiced reader, who keeps in mind the narrative seriality of novels and the repetitious nature of their themes, will know at the moment of embarkation that a shipwreck is foreshadowed. (Think, for instance of the *omen* of the haircut and the premonitory dream.) It is just this narrative treatment of the material that makes it impossible to interpret the ship episode as a pretext for the insertion of passages which parody different genres (rhetorical harangues, battle descriptions, *pastiches* of legal language, etc.) or excerpts that satirize traditional themes (the vanity of dreams, the luxury of women, etc.).[27]

---

lently to satiric development, but not all are handled by Petronius with satiric wit or style, still less in the style of the Menippean.

27. I do not want to deny the tendency in the *Satyricon* to digression. The "exkursartige Einlagen der Romane" (Adamietz is right, 336–38) are different from the digressions that appeal to Petronius: in the novel they are conceived more for the sake of entertainment and light relief. But one should not overemphasize the "digressivity" of the *Satyricon* in order to devalue (as does Adamietz, 338–39) the role of the intrigue, reducing it to a mere support for the digressive development of satiric motifs. Apart from other factors, the criteria of selection of the medieval epitomators may have exercised a heavy influence on the choice of passages because their nature allowed them to be reduced to *excursus* or they were marked by a particular stylistic vividness (e.g., speeches and poetic insertions); too much has been lost in episodes like that of Quartilla or the *heredipetae* to warrant any verdicts on the continuity of the narrative action. It may be a methodological error to set up a critical discourse which seeks to lay down a temporal order or to offer a quantitative assessment of the importance of various ingredients; in this respect the path that has been followed is doomed to leave us eternally dissatisfied. Precedents, which are

Let us return to the point where we left Menippean satire. Which of its features—essential features—survive and can be recognized in the *Satyricon?* In the end, only those which have always led to the assertion of its importance: prosimetrum and parody. I believe there are good reasons to declare that neither prosimetrum nor parody are in fact exclusively Menippean elements. Ancient literature provides us with clear evidence that such elements can function, admittedly with different purposes, in genres other than the Menippean satire.

It is well known by now that papyrus discoveries have restored fragments of a popular narrative, which we may or may not choose to call a novel, relatively low in style and composed in prosimetric form. This is the tradition of the comic novel represented above all by the so-called Romance of Iolaus.[28] We should bear in mind that it is only with the publication of this papyrus fragment that scholars have been even able to conceive of a "Greek *Satyricon.*"[29] In it we are told the story of a man

---

taken into account only because they exist and have a tradition, are confused with "formative models," which are something completely different since they determine the work and its significance. Many previous experiences function only as thematic "reservoirs" to furnish arguments for many different genres; perhaps this is why the arguments of satire are so close to certain kinds of rhetoric, as for example when there is criticism of the decadence of oratory or art or poetry. Petronius does not create direct satire from these arguments, but rather lets the characters of his story express these commonplace themes *with their own voice,* not in satiric terms but with speeches apparently composed like the most canonical declamations or scholastic lectures. All of this occurs without the internal leaps, more or less burlesque quotations, etc., which characterize discussions on any theme in Menippean satire.

28. *POxy* 3010. See the important study of A. Barchiesi, "Tracce di narrativa greca e romanzo latino: Una rassegna," 219–36, esp. 227–30. It is no accident that an authority on Menippean satire, R. Astbury, in "Petronius, *POxy.*3010 and Menippean Satire," *CP* 72 (1977) 22–31, was the first scholar to oppose, if largely in formal terms, Menippean prosimetrum and narrative prosimetrum, and to challenge the privileged relationship of Petronius with the Menippean tradition.

29. Cf. P. Parsons, "A Greek *Satyricon?*" *BICS* 18 (1971) 53–68: also *The Oxyrhyncus Papyri,* vol. XLII (London, 1974) 34–41. For an edition with commentary of the papyrus of Iolaus (and of the Tinuphis fragment, on which

with the same name as Heracles' traveling companion, Iolaus. A friend who wants to help him gets initiated into the mysteries of Cybele and loses his manhood in order to become the priest of the goddess. So he becomes a Gallus (although in fact we don't know if he has really carried out the dreadful sacrifice: hence the possibility of future trickery, worthy of a mime or *fabula Milesia*). He comes back to his friend Iolaus and addresses him with a speech in verse (about twenty Sotadeans) in which he boasts of his new expertise as an initiate in the mysteries. Iolaus expresses satisfaction with the revelations which may be helpful to him. The scene ends with the quotation of a verse about friendship from the *Orestes* of Euripides.

I admit that what we have preserved of this text is not enough to allow far-reaching conclusions, but it can hardly be pure coincidence that a casual find has transmitted to us a passage in prose with an insertion in Sotadeans (an uncommon verse-form, used twice by Petronius in the surviving extracts). From a thematic point of view, it is interesting that the ambiguous characters who appear in this passage seem to be occupied in staging a disguise. You may object: "How can we be sure that this is not a Menippean satire rather than a novel?" [30] But this objec-

---

see below, p. 165), see the recently published volume by S. A. Stephens and J. J. Winkler, 358–74 and 400–408. Also, for discussion and bibliography on this kind of literature and its relationship with the *Satyricon,* see the introductions by Stephens and Winkler and also the very recent contributions by Horsfall, 130–32; Relihan, *Ancient Menippean Satire,* 199–202; Holzberg, 62–63; M. Fusillo, "Letteratura di consumo e romanzesca," in *Lo spazio letterario della Grecia antica,* vol. 1, *La produzione e la circolazione del testo,* tomo III: *I Greci e Roma* (Roma, 1994), 261–63. Cf. also above, chapter 1, p. 32, n. 38.

30. A. Stramaglia has answered the important objections in "Prosimetria narrativa e 'romanzo perduto': PTurner 8 (con discussione e riedizione di PSI 151 [Pack² 2624] + PMil Vogliano 260)," *ZPE* 92 (1992) 121–49, esp. 141 and n. 79 (see also n. 77 on the evidence for obscene novels). He talks justifiably of "osmosis" between novel and Menippean. Cf. again Barchiesi, "Tracce di narrativa greca," 231–32, for a shrewd consideration of Astbury's important article (above, n. 28). Petersmann, 393 and n. 21, shows some perplexity in response to Astbury; good observations in Stramaglia pp. 137–38

tion cannot stand in view of the even more recent publication of a new fragment of the same type, the romance of Tinuphis. This is a narrative text containing the tale of the Egyptian *Prophetes* Tinuphis, condemned to death by a Persian king for presumed adultery and then saved at the last minute through a trick.[31] The structure of the narrative is prosimetric: iambic tetrameters in paratragic style alternate with prose. The most recent studies have produced convincing reconstructions of a whole series of thematic motifs and elements of plotting which justify the inclusion of such texts within the generic boundaries of romance.[32] We can still discern the shadowy outline of this genre, or simply this cluster of texts, if we evaluate properly not only the directly attested fragments but also the literary testimony that is already known.

It is not my intention to propose that the *Satyricon* be included here and now in this tradition of the "lost novel," as if it

---

and nn. 49 and 50. Astbury's procedure, in my opinion, is essentially the converse of that used by Adamietz. The sterile game of finding elements that refute any specific hypothesis for classifying the *Satyricon* can also work against proposers of any other hypotheses which are precise and exclusive: we need only trace other elements of contrast with the alternative thesis. This is why I support Stramaglia's formula (despite the reservations of Stephens and Winkler, 365 n. 18); the concept of "osmosis" between novel and Menippean can explain the difficulty of establishing fixed boundaries between different genres, especially in the dangerous territory of *Trivialliteratur*. I am quite sure that the importance of mime in this context cannot be sufficiently emphasized: it seems that the mime was the privileged referent of Petronius (and his readers) among the low genres to which characters and situations of the *Satyricon* can be related once they have been purged of their whims. On the *Satyricon's* relationship with mime and theater in general, see the recently published work of Panayotakis.

31. Editio Princeps and commentary by M. W. Haslam, "Narrative about Tinuphis in prosimetrum," in *Papyri, Greek and Egyptian,* ed. by various hands in honour of Eric Gardner Turner (London, 1981), 35–45 + Plate IV.

32. For a more complete and detailed treatment of the romance of Tinuphis, see Stramaglia; on pp. 138–39 he lists the various examples of prosimetric narrative known to us (with a rich individualized bibliography). In particular, on the romance of Iolaus, one should consult Astbury; his careful criticism of some parallels between Menippean authors and Petronius traced by previous scholars (especially Courtney) deserves support.

were the faithful representative of a genre widespread in Greek cultural contexts in the first century. To abandon the notion of Menippean satire as the formative model of the *Satyricon* in order to embrace the notion of the comic novel (lost, of course!)[33] would be like moving from a lesser to a greater darkness—an unrewarding hazard. All the more so, since it would not be difficult to list the elements which distinguish Petronius' work from these papyrus fragments: not only the different linguistic and literary—in one word, *artistic*—level, but also the traces of an exotic or at least oriental ambiance; the East which provides the fabulous setting for so many adventures of kings, tyrants and priests could hardly have been at home in the *Satyricon*.

I will limit myself rather to noting, quite briefly, that in these two papyri there are traces of parodic treatment in the metrical insertions: at least there is a ludic element in the tone of these verses which could be adapted as well to the Menippean as to the *Satyricon*. It is more important to stress that, on the basis of the few surviving documents, we would be mistaken in identifying every prosimetric creation as evidence for Menippean satire.[34] And we would be equally misled if we claimed to distinguish *a priori* between the prosimetrum of the novel and Menippean prosimetrum, hoping in this fashion once again to

33. The happy definition of the "lost novel" is found in A. Barchiesi, "Il Romanzo," in F. Montanari, ed., *Da Omero agli Alessandrini. Problemi e figure della letteratura greca* (Roma, 1988), 345–48.

34. Cf. Stramaglia, 139 n. 67, with bibliography. Although he rightly stresses the need for caution, Horsfall, 132–33, continues to assume an identification between prosimetrum and Menippean satire in referring to the "prosimetric form of the *Satyricon* Petronius inherits from Menippean satire through Varro," and he gives the impression that the verse insertions in Chariton, the novel of Iolaus and above all that of Tinuphis all belong to the Menippean tradition. I endorse his formulation on p. 133: "To say that the *Satyricon* is 'a Menippean novel,' is only to couple a correct definition of the mode with an equally correct modern definition of the genre. As labelling it is irreproachable, as criticism it is not very helpful!" But if the Menippean is to be understood only as a "mode," I would prefer to call it a "prosimetric novel." The medievalist Peter Dronke, in his study, *Verse with Prose: From Petronius to*

equip ourselves with a guaranteed criterion for classifying the work of Petronius.

It seems to me very interesting that for a narrative like the *Satyricon,* in prosimetric form with a novel-like action and fantasizing characters, parallels can be found (parallels, not necessarily models) which in all probability are completely foreign to the sophisticated texture of the Menippean. It is just as probable that no single definition can be given of the use of prosimetrum. Rather, the mixture of prose and verse is simply a *formal element without a canonical literary function,* and accordingly it does not function in itself as a mark of genre.[35] Petronius has gone to extraordinary lengths to remain elusive, not to be pinned down under a single identifying label. Nothing

---

Dante (Cambridge, Mass., and London, 1994), 9–12 and notes pp. 118–19, takes into account the theories of Bakhtin and Frye on Menippean satire and also the recently discovered papyri of Greek novels, but argues against Astbury's underestimation of the Menippean and Varronian elements in the *Satyricon.* Despite this disagreement, he ends up moving in the same direction as Astbury when he admits, "it now seems virtually certain that Petronius must have had Greek precedents for a prosimetric narrative with satiric or erotic or sensational elements" (119, n. 23). Only a little earlier, however, he had stated, "The intriguing question that has arisen concretely only in the last two decades is whether Petronius was the first to make a certain creative leap, taking *prosimetrum* and Menippean satire in the direction of the novel" (9). This appears to be a concession to Sullivan's view (see n. 23 above). It is just this orientation which leads Dronke to discuss Petronius—briefly but lucidly—in the chapter entitled "Menippean Elements."

35. However, one must not forget that a mixture of prose and poetry could be found in the mime: cf. H. Reich, *Der Mimus* (Berlin, 1903), 569–74; J. R. A. Nicoll, *Masks, Mimes and Miracles* (New York, 1931), 127; S. Santelia, *Charition Liberata (P Oxy. 413)* (Bari, 1991), 75–80 (but see also 81–89). Indeed the Charition mime contains Sotadeans like the Iolaus fragment and is set in the orient with comic priests and kings like the tale of Tinuphis. At the same time we should not underestimate the possibility of *fabulae Milesiae* in prosimetrum or at least with occasional verse insets: see Petersmann, 400 n. 34. Note that, as Bücheler suggests, fragment 1b of Sisenna, *nocte vagatrix,* looks very like a hexametric clausula. Even from the lexical point of view the combination seems to belong to a snatch of verse; it could be the calque of a Greek poetic epithet ($\nu\nu\kappa\tau\iota\pi\lambda\alpha\nu\dot{\eta}\varsigma$ or $\nu\nu\kappa\tau\iota\pi\lambda\dot{\alpha}\nu\eta\tau\sigma\varsigma$ [Opp. *Cyn.* 3.268] or even $\nu\nu\kappa\tau\iota\beta\dot{\alpha}\tau\eta\varsigma$).

would have been more perverse and contradictory for him than to acknowledge himself as Menippean, with all the trappings of Cynicism which the inheritance would have entailed. His work is not a real Menippean satire, not because he has exploited only one aspect of the Menippean but because he did not want it to be one.

Petronius programmatically blurs the Menippean features of his work; he creates expectations and then systematically disappoints them; he eliminates the popular elements and above all the most ostentatiously cynic ones (those that would lead him to take up overt positions); he avoids close parody, uses no proverbs, does not try to lower the speech of lofty characters. (Indeed there are no such characters. From this point of view it would be futile to search in the *Satyricon* for the subversive force of the Menippean.) Prosimetrum he accepts—as a dialectic expressive form. The hybrid nature of the discourse allows him to redistribute in contrasting form the two divergent functions of language: prose and poetry. Thus in a bare and simple narrative Petronius inserts a comment in verse that enriches the narration with satiric or parodic connotations, producing a modulated alternation like a continual counterpoint. The result is a sparkling product that lets us see behind a highly original and indefinable form the bold contamination of different literary experiences—some popular and degraded, others sophisticated and ironic—in a constant switching of stylistic levels and registers. This is a work that aims to be a problematic discourse on literature and literariness, but also a real story rich in action, characters and wit, and it is controlled by a desire to retrace and display the conventions and stereotypes of Hellenistic narrative.

Hidden behind the text—an invisible but weighty presence—is the author who provokes us to reflection but also entertains us, who loves critical irony but equally relishes telling a tale. He wants to narrate and at the same time to play with narrative conventions. Irony measures the distance that separates the degraded characters of the *Satyricon* from the great figures of "high" literature which fill their fantasies. On the other hand, the same irony measures the distance that separates the narrative of the *Satyricon* from the raw material drawn from the "lower" levels of literature.

The hidden author stays completely detached both from the high and from the low levels of the world he represents. He begins with the ironic choice of an urbane diction devoid of obscenity, as if to make us forget that his characters are really forced to live in a sordid reality—which is that of the comic and obscene romance. However, he complicates his ironic game by contriving that these same characters, conditioned and imprisoned by their *scholastic* training, constantly usurp the magniloquent poses of the great epic and tragic heroes. Failed heroes, they would be happy to be treated at least like characters of an idealizing novel, to live a life composed of melodramatic intrigues: but forced as they are into a low and petty way of life, they see their own sublime ambitions fail even as the characters of a novel. Thus the hierarchies of literature—representations, forms, content, levels, registers—are all ironically inverted and overthrown. And from this great irony is born a paradoxical suspicion of a profound seriousness.[36]

36. Cf. the interesting considerations of Holzberg, 61, on the relationship between the origins of the realistic novel and the parody of the idealized novel in modern Europe—a relationship analogous with what is found in Petronius (on his type of realism see the next chapter). As to the "serious-mindedness" of the *Satyricon*, I find myself in partial agreement with the suggestive essay of F. I. Zeitlin, "Petronius as Paradox: Anarchy and Artistic Integrity," *TAPA* 102 (1971) 631–84, who is inclined to recognize a substantial degree of seriousness in the playful irony of Petronius. For Zeitlin, however, Petronius is above all a nihilist (680). We may well allow that the expressive technique of the *Satyricon* is not that of classical writers, and that the structure "rejects the forms of the past" (677), but I believe that the cultural ideology of Petronius remains "classicist." For our author has chosen the indirect strategy of ironic discourse precisely in order to demonstrate his nostalgia for the classics. He has invented a character who, by the inadequacy of his interpretation of the

great models of past literature, shows the extent to which his own contemporary culture has fallen away from that of the classical authors. Yet at the same
time Petronius has made this character ridiculous and unreliable. In this way
the position of the author is developed by working through oppositions, in
that he systematically corrects the faults of the mythomaniac narrator. The
image which the author has in mind is given in negative, as it were, and must
be discovered indirectly. Moreover, Zeitlin, a remarkably sensitive reader, also
notices in Petronius "a poignant regret for what is past and gone" (677). But
is this not perhaps the poignant regret of a "classicist" who contemplates the
great literature of the remote past as having a value now irremediably lost?

CHAPTER SIX

Realism and Irony

To attempt to establish the nature of reality is the task of philosophers—a Sisyphean task that we can be sure will never be completed. But we critics preoccupied with literary texts learned long ago that in literature the Real World is simply a construction composed of signifying elements that "stand in" for things. It is a question of representation and symbols. We have accepted that there is no single model of existence in the world, no way that is "the real one." The world has as many ways of being as the ways in which it can be represented or described. And as far as *we* are concerned, to talk of ways of describing the world does not imply that there is a single object to be described.[1]

When "realist" texts are under discussion, critics often commit the error of believing that a strong degree of resemblance between things and their representation is essential. But the problem of realism in literature is not a problem of resemblance; in fact no degree of resemblance is close enough to establish the relationship between the representation and the "real thing." In debating the issue of literary realism there are two prejudices to combat: the myth of the innocent eye, and the

1. For a useful general introduction to the problem see J. P. Stern, *On Realism* (London and Boston, 1973); see also N. Boyle and M. Swales, edd., *Realism in European Literature: Essays in Honour of J. P. Stern* (Cambridge, 1986).

illusion that absolute facts exist. On these assumptions realistic representation would be a way of reaching the things of this world in their pure state by stripping them systematically of every feature of interpretation. But the innocent eye—so we might say, paraphrasing Kant—is blind, just as the virgin mind is void. Perception of the real world and its interpretation are not two separable activities: within a representation we cannot distinguish "things" (objects just as they are) from the interpretation given of them. You cannot peel away the rind of interpretation to expose the flesh of reality. Furthermore, the more neutral and the more distorting eye both produce artificial gazes, even if their artificiality differs, since neither can provide an image of any thing without interpreting it.

In fact, description is more an act of invention than of copying. Even the author who makes a display of registering things passively is not really passive. When he describes he inevitably introduces preferences, inevitably uses criteria of selection, marks certain connections, analyzes things and organizes them. And while he shapes the world he is in fact producing it. Thus the inventive and characterizing details which Petronius introduces in his descriptions are the privileged signs with which he fits out the image of the real: undifferentiated chaos is tailored, so to speak, to allow a design of the world to emerge. So where does this "resemblance" come in to which critics usually appeal as more valid than other criteria of judgment? Why do critics, in assessing a description as realistic, usually have regard to its fidelity? Resemblance and fidelity to appearances are only the product of deception.[2] I mean that a description seems

---

2. To trick, *fallere*, even seems to be the prerequisite of artistic success: cf. Plin. *nat.* 35.65: *cum ille [Zeuxis] detulisset uvas pictas tanto successu ut in scaenam aves advolarent, ipse [Parrhasius] detulisset linteum pictum ita veritate repraesentata ut Zeuxis alitum iudicio tumens flagitaret tandem remoto linteo ostendi picturam atque intellecto errore concederet palmam ingenuo pudore, quoniam ipse volucres fefellisset, Parrhasius autem se artificem.*

realistic to the extent that it is a successful illusion, one that can induce the reader to suppose it has the characteristics of the thing it represents.[3]

The aesthetics of *mimesis,* in short, cannot help being an aesthetics of deceit. Even Trimalchio finally buys this idea. At 52.1 he parades before Agamemnon his competence as a connoisseur of the arts. Amongst the countless objects he possesses is a silver vessel upon which is represented Cassandra (obviously confused with Medea) killing her own children: *et pueri mortui iacent sic ut vivere putes* ("the dead boys lie there so beautifully they seem alive").[4] The reader laughs at the paradox, but Trimalchio is quite serious (and it is just this that makes us laugh). In fact Petronius here is caricaturing a stereotype of contemporary art criticism, and in his usual fashion pushes to an extreme the implications of the artistic theory of mimesis, almost to the point of subverting it.

But as we know, the problem of realism in figurative art in antiquity ranges well beyond the evaluation of works of painting and sculpture. In a sense it becomes the essential problem of all artistic mimesis, encompassing as well the realism of literary works.[5] In ancient literature, when the aim is to show that something creates a completely realistic impression, the problem is usually approached by resorting to the example of works of sculpture and painting. It is as though, in producing outright deceptions, the art of words suffered from an inferiority complex in relation to the expressive powers of sculpture and painting. The appearance of reality that is the goal of verbal artistry

3. See R. Brinkmann, *Wirklichkeit und Illusion* (Stuttgart, 1966[2]).

4. A certain restoration of the text due to Nicholas Heinsius: the traditional text (*sicuti vere putes*) is unacceptable and, without the point introduced by the minor correction, entirely colorless. Bücheler's apparatus notes the comparison with Ov. *Met.* 10.250 (see below) cited by Jacobs in support of Heinsius' correction.

5. See in general H. Koller, *Die Mimesis in der Antike* (Bern, 1954).

is inadequate. Men want reality itself, and only figurative art, by deceiving the eyes, can compete with nature.

To understand the comic paradox into which Trimalchio falls we need only think of the miracle that befalls Pygmalion in Ovid: the statue modeled by the sculptor becomes the real body of a living creature (*Met.* 10.243–97). In Ovid the stereotype that proclaims the confusion of nature and art is realized. Before Venus miraculously gives life to the molded matter, the quickening of the statue has been foreshadowed by the deception of appearances: (ibid. 250) *Virginis est verae facies, quam vivere credas.* Pygmalion's artistic deception, in fact, is so successful that the ivory of the statue seems alive, just as Medea's little boys, even when represented as dead, seem . . . alive. The stereotype that wants a work of art "full of life" has become so normal that it makes Trimalchio forget that his boys are really corpses. For Propertius too *signa* are *vivida* (2.31.8) or *animosa* (Lysippus' statues, 3.9.9). The statues "breathe" life in *Aeneid* 6.847–48: *spirantia . . . aera / . . . vivos de marmore vultus* (cf. *Georg.* 3.34).[6]

Illusionism is the other face of realism. It is not the quantity of data that determines the more or less realistic nature of a representation, but the greater or lesser ease with which the reader accepts the information and lets himself be deceived. For this purpose the details of representation are no more than signs strategically selected by the author to ensure the image of the world that he wants to suggest. This is how the different "real" worlds are produced: by selection and emphasis of significant features. In short, realistic description depends less on imitation of objects than on the reader's familiarity with the objects described. If representation is a matter of choices on the part of the author, on the reader's part realism is above all a matter of

6. See F. Bömer (Heidelberg, 1980) on Ov. *Met.* 10.250; cf. ibid. 6.104 and Martial 3.41, *inserta phialae Mentoris manu ducta / lacerta vivit et timetur argentum.*

habits. It is linked to the greater acceptability of certain beliefs. And it is not even necessary that these beliefs be universally shared. Indeed, a belief which is precisely limited to a certain group presents itself as realistic in the text because, being partial, it serves to identify that group (in fact it becomes one of the group's defining features).

In the ambiance of the *Cena,* for example, believing in werewolves and witches is realistic for anyone who accepts them into his own interpretative system. The freedmen, of course, find these beliefs completely acceptable. Niceros begins his tale (61.3) by openly declaring that the *scholastici* will not believe him and so will laugh at him (*timeo istos scholasticos ne me rideant*); but then, true to himself and his own beliefs and sure of finding among his audience others inclined to give those beliefs credit, he agrees to tell the story of the *versipellis*. On one side we have the predictable skepticism of the intellectuals, with *their* criteria for evaluating the world, on the other Niceros and his fellow freedmen, ready to believe. Thus in Niceros' tale the assorted idioms, proverbs, colloquialisms, the lively oaths and imprecations, are the validating marks of his world-vision; Petronius picks out certain beliefs and forms of speech and makes them fit such apparently typical carriers.

The realistic effect of the *Cena* derives from the dense weave of the narrative. It is like a carpet: the more knots there are, the sharper the contours of the figures in the design.[7] The realism of the *Satyricon* is of the same sort that we can find in the unicorn or the centaur, whose individual parts are realistic, but not the complete figure. The individual parts are exaggerated, bloated; and yet a total effect of realism is generated by the exaggeration

---

7. Vitality of detail is part of the realistic author's attitude towards life; that attitude should not be subordinate to the conventions of a narrative technique that has time only for major features. It should take shape as an immediate response to the minute stimuli of reality—a form of respect for particulars which refuses to sacrifice them and actually privileges them. Cf. G. Levine, *The Realistic Imagination* (Chicago and London, 1981), 21.

and distortion of the parts. This effect approaches caricature.[8] Obviously Trimalchio believes his friend Niceros and instantly confirms his complete trust with an oath (*"salvo" inquit "tuo sermone" Trimalchio, "si qua fides est, ut mihi pili inhorruerunt"*). He adds immediately (as if by natural association) his own contribution—the story of the witches. Here we have the same narrative style, the same taste in expression, the same superstitious tendency to swear, and the same final reaction—of alarm and amazement—from the others.

What we must notice is that during the dinner there is a symbolic exchange between the *scholastici* and the freedmen: the former get they food they want, but have to accept an alien symbolic code. The intellectuals, with some dissimulation, accept the enforced relationship imposed by the others. For the *scholastici*, the symbolic code *par excellence* is culture and, in particular, literature; for the freedmen it is rather the ownership of villas, gold and silver, drinking rare wines and eating exotic foods. Thus food, sex and money emerge as symbolic systems. It becomes obvious that the effect of realism is created by the vigor with which certain codes are given status.

Auerbach maintains in his splendid study[9] that the concept of *mimesis* is fluid, but he seems to me to be governed by a relatively unsophisticated vision: for him, changes of style are changes of *Weltanschauung*. I do not believe that one can pre-

---

8. In the *Satyricon* the realistic impulse is mainly located in the strong handling of characters. Within Petronius' narrative strategy, the plot is a secondary component of the story, while the text teems with a mass of original figures and lively portraits of the vicious and the grotesque. In the parodic game which links the *Satyricon* to the Greek romance, the plot is only a guideline for conventional misadventures against which the narrated action is (parodically) constructed. Thus the plot is turned into a means for introducing a wide variety of characters of satiric inspiration. This view is in accordance with that of Levine, 146–151, who notes that in a realistic narration the plot is often downgraded in relation to the vivid representation of characters.

9. E. Auerbach, *Mimesis: Dargestellte Wirklichkeit in der abendländischen Literatur* (Bern, 1967[4]) (= *Mimesis: The Representation of Reality in Western Literature*, trans. W. Trask [Garden City, 1957]).

sume a direct relationship between style and society (or rather, between stylistic indicators and changes of *Weltanschauung*): the relationship is not direct because inherent in symbolic systems (especially systems of language) are also different cultural codes, which act like different conditioning forces. Let me explain myself more clearly. All naive concepts of realism imply belief in a unique reciprocal correspondence between life and literature (if you like, literature as a looking-glass). Auerbach too conceives realism in terms of reciprocal correspondence: to changes of style, as we said, different *Weltanschauungen* correspond. But if we reject this naive, one-on-one reciprocal correspondence, the principle of realism itself vanishes: that is, no reflection of social life is left in the text.[10] Thus Petronius seems rather to be an author who creates embodiments of every possible thing, blends them all together and heaps them up. Thus realism is better reformulated as a level of "specific individualization": certain apparently typical features are associated as fitting certain groups. We have the pleasure of recognizing common features in characters who constitute a class.[11]

Realism presupposes in fact that behind the language representing things one can find the things themselves, and so one expects that things will be distinct and distinguishable from language. As if one could shed language the way one sheds one's own skin.[12] (In saying this I would not want to argue for the opposite extreme, that instead everything can be reduced to language, to literature: literature is only one of the ways of controlling human life.) It seems to me that Petronian realism, if we want to call it realism, is the capacity to transpose into the text different symbolic systems and different spheres and experi-

10. See G. Gebauer and Chr. Wulf, *Mimesis: Kultur, Kunst, Gesellschaft, Rowohlts Enzyklopädie* (Reinbek bei Hamburg, 1992) (= *Mimesis: Culture, Art, Society,* trans. D. Reneau [Berkeley, 1995]).

11. Cf. Knight, 346–49.

12. For some interesting general considerations see H. Feldmann, *Mimesis und Wirklichkeit* (Munich, 1988).

ences of life, and to do so with an empathy that excludes both sympathy and the aggressivity of satire. He represents things, so to speak, from *inside* various partial spheres of life. And this explains why Petronian realism offers a collection of vignettes but does not aspire to become a totality.

The imperturbability of the author arises precisely from the empathy of this kind of realism; this too explains his apparent lack of participation in the narrative and in the descriptions which he creates. His ironic detachment is even intensified by it. Petronius' ability to incorporate alien elements, to enter into the mentality of the *scholastici* and the freedmen, of Quartilla, Circe, Oenothea, is also a kind of realism. It is his purpose to play modulations on the narrative while standing behind the scene. The variations derived from it are simply products of his ability to assume the codes of different perspectives. Thus Petronius brings together a series of experiences and combines in his text (in the narrative form of a novel) aspects that previously belonged to satire and the critical thinking of moral diatribe. At the same time there is no authorial reaction to his material, none of the shocked aggressivity typical of moral satire. There are indeed some reactions to events in his text, but these belong to the narrator, discredited and untrustworthy as he is: the hidden author is free of liability. While the author allows himself the privilege of detachment and irony, he assumes a position of objectivity; he leaves subjectivity (in an exaggerated and absurd form) to his narrator Encolpius.

We will see below that it is precisely the uncontrolled subjectivity of the narrator that provides the negative to which the positive value of realism is opposed. It is positive inasmuch as it can deflate false pretenses and restore matters to the proper limits of their nature.[13] It is as though Encolpius' entire narrative is

13. I agree with the position of Levine, 5ff., who considers realism to be a method of discovery rather than the representation of predetermined realities.

misguided because he is unable to acknowledge reality. So reality does not exist in its own right; it exists only as the opposite of a mistaken interpretation of things. It is as though reality was not envisaged as an ingredient of the text and has not been invited to share in its construction, but even uninvited it forces the will of the narrator-protagonist and bursts into the text of the *Satyricon* crying out "I am stronger." The ironic author lets it be, content to see his narrator checkmated, and acquiesces in the aggressivity of things.

It is difficult to talk of realism in literature.[14] Realism is a category covered with incrustations, applied to matters that have too little in common.[15] For the *Satyricon* it is much more

---

The overriding aim of the realistic author is to explore reality by resisting inherited narrative conventions. This is the reason for his semi-aware attention to language. In this sense Petronius realizes that his protagonist-narrator is unable to perceive the world around him without strong subjective distortion; the author displays this distortion as a discrepancy between illusion and reality.

14. Cf. W. Preisendanz, *Wege des Realismus* (München, 1977). The most exhaustive discussion known to me on the many problems related to realism in literature is found in D. Villanueva, *Teorías del Realismo Literario* (Madrid, 1992), with a good bibliography. See also "Realism: A Symposium," in *Monatshefte für deutschen Unterricht* (1967), 97–130; "Le discours réaliste," special issue of *Poétique* 16 (1973); "The Construction of Reality in Fiction," special issue of *Poetics Today* 5.2 (1984).

15. See H. Meili Steele, *Realism and the Drama of Reference* (London, 1988), 4: "Realism is a notoriously slippery term that has been used in so many contexts that its meaning threatens to disappear." The many valences of the term "realism" are one reason for avoiding its use. Given the many meanings it has acquired in literary history, the only remedy may be to use it exclusively to mean the use of language to get *beyond language* so as to discover some non-verbal truth lying outside language. Conventions suffocate literature, threatening to transform it into a series of set schemes obeying a mummified rhetoric. The search for a world beyond words is deeply moral, since it recognizes the need to reorganize experience by looking for new, unconventional parameters. Petronius' parodic play with the pathetic stereotypes of great literature—after they have fallen into the incongruous hands of the *scholastici*—is not only a way of rejecting the sentimental and the sensational, it is also an implicit appeal to find a new status and a new authenticity for literature itself.

profitable to speak of "materialist elements." Literature, as we said before, does not generate reality, only the impression or effects of reality: so we have to ask ourselves what function these deliberate effects have on the reader of the text. However, I would not want food, sex, and money to be understood only as the harsh retorts of reality to the banal reveries of the *scholastici*: this would mean that the *Cena* was a slice of realism in a text that is not all that realistic. The truth is rather that the entire text of the *Satyricon* is less concerned with the representation of reality than with its misinterpretations.

If Encolpius' visions are literary phantasms, the visions of Trimalchio and his companions are money and food. As the grand melodramatic scenarios of literature are the forms of Encolpius' consciousness, so food and money are the forms in which the freedmen *display their natures*. Without money and the great surfeit of food, Trimalchio and the freedmen would be nothing, just as Encolpius would have no identity without literature. Food and money on the one hand, and literature on the other, are like a "cloak of existence" which they wrap around themselves. To the same extent that literature is a substitute for real life, so food and money are a mode of existence for the freedmen. All of them alike, the *scholastici* with literature, the freedmen with food and money, are trying to give themselves substance, in the sense of "a place to stand." In this sense we understand that the triumph of food and money is not a victory of realism, but the victory of elemental forces over those who have no moral consistency.

It is enough to recall here the passage in 1.2 where it is stated that the young men who enter the forum (the arena of real life) are, as it were, transported *in alium orbem terrarum*. This means that the *scholastici* live literally in another world. The reality in the controversies which they practice formulating is not external, objective reality; there is no adjustment of their intellect to reality, only of reality to their intellect. The real could not be more fossilized than this. In short we have a symmetrical inversion of mimesis: on one side life, rather than imitating the great paradigms of art, merely apes them; on the other side there is the symmetrical inversion of those who confuse the totality of the real with food, money and sex. Ultimately, the portrait of reality is achieved by the demolition of these opposites. Petronius' ironic aggression oscillates between two poles and makes them converge. So the hidden author works and can keep himself hidden, making no direct appearance.

Scholastici and freedmen (but also Quartilla, Oenothea and others like them) are the representatives of two *demi-mondes*. I would like to explain this by the analogy of the Magdeburg experiment, in which two hemispheres sealed by a vacuum could not be pulled apart even by two strong cart-horses. So the two half-worlds, that of the *scholastici* and that of the freedmen, are emptied by Petronius of all social complexity and remain absolutely solid, since one is perfectly complementary to the other. I mean that reality is not the externally real, composed of infinite complexities, but rather a world produced by the adhesion of two half-worlds.

But the fundamental question we must ask ourselves is this: "Why does the low and vulgar element get the upper hand?" Sex, money and food share a common feature, the notion of devouring, of sheer greed. Not sex, but the manic frenzy of Quartilla; not food, but unrestrained guzzling; not wealth, but the overflowing riches of the freedmen. There is here a hyperbolic voracity, an idea of superfluity; and this voracity becomes a way of life and produces a paradox. The culture of the *scholastici* crams itself with sex and food, while those who have already every kind of material wealth turn their voracity on culture. The overconsumption of literature cannot support itself and prefers to fawn on the powerful, while men with the wherewithal use literature as decoration.

However, both groups are desperate to give themselves

"more substance" through the things they lack: the *scholastici* through the luster shed by wealth on the satisfaction of two basic instincts, and the freedmen through the glamour that a dusting of culture can provide. What we must notice is that literature is used to ennoble each of the two groups: one group lives it as a paradigm, the other uses it as a side-dish, or a garnish, for their meals. But at bottom there is no real opposition between the world of appearances (of the *scholastici*) and the world of reality (sex, food and money). The more materialist of the two worlds is no less fantastic than the other, and conversely, that which is more prone to fantasy is no less materialist. So the fact remains that literature is the central theme of the *Satyricon*.

It is not false to say, as Auerbach does, that realism in ancient literature is inevitably comic, but it is a bit simplistic. In the *Satyricon* there is an entire *à la carte* of perspectives. There is the tragic aspect of the comic and the comic aspect of the tragic. Auerbach's idea remains a little marginal to the text of Petronius; the *scholastici* and the freedmen may be vulgar, but they still have ideals. It is by means of literature that they reveal their identity, or, better, give themselves a material substantiality. Moreover, we must not forget that Auerbach's critical perspective is conditioned by his having taken his sample from the *Cena,* a part in which the expressive and stylistic orchestration of the narrative is distinct from the rest of the work.[16]

This is clear enough if we simply note that the narrative time of the *Cena* is significantly different compared with the treatment of time in the preceding and following episodes, for example with the events at Croton. Here the narration seems to be

16. Here too one recognizes a disadvantage of the stylistic method applied by Auerbach in his magisterial lectures on *mimesis:* the technique of "samples of style" inevitably presupposes an essential structural homogeneity in the texts examined, with the danger of extending, by generalization, to the entire text traits of style confined to individual sections. Indeed Auerbach himself

conducted in "real time," while elsewhere (even making allowance for the cuts of the epitomator) it seems to undergo *ac-
celerandi* and *ritardandi,* it contracts and expands according to
the effects desired. In the narrative of the *Cena* there is a kind of
isochrony between the time of the story (the events that occur in
it) and the time of the discourse (the events as they are told). But
the time of the discourse is slowed down through the effect of a
textual strategy; thus a slower pace is imposed on the reader. In
short, even in this case realism is shown to be the fruit of a con-
straint imposed on the reader who—through the eyes of Encolpius as narrator—is obliged to follow step by step the narrated
occurrences as if he were himself present and attending the
freedmen's dinner. On the other hand, the treatment of narrative time also serves to represent indirectly the way in which
things are perceived by the narrating I: if Encolpius tells us
about the dinner step by step and in detail, it is because he himself is still impressed by it.

In short, in the *Satyricon* things do not reach us directly but
are filtered through the narrator. In this way, reality, or better
realism as a narrative form founded on the representation of
reality, becomes a tool of the author's deflating irony.[17] Is the
perspective of Encolpius illusory and fallacious? Well then, to
put him in check it will be enough if the hidden author gives
clear evidence of the way things are. Realism becomes the de-
mystifying counterpoint, the corrective which restores the fan-

---

was fully aware of this risk and granted validity to his own analyses only
within the samples of the texts he was examining. This limit is intrinsic to the
methods of *Geistesgeschichte* and especially of stylistic criticism; even the
"Zirkel im Verstehen" of Leo Spitzer could not entirely escape this hazard.

17. H. Levin, *The Gates of Horn* (New York, 1963), 43–48, demonstrates
how close realism can be to parody. By attacking literary illusions Petronius
was able to capture and transmit an illusion of reality. He achieved realism
by challenging the conventions that gave literature its often unreal air. He
was capable of satirizing an institution simply by deriding a convention: he
used fiction to break down fictitious barriers and wrote a romance to end all
romances.

tasies of the narrator to the proper measure of things. The truth is that Encolpius does not know how to measure himself against objective reality: if he calls *naturae veritas* into the arena it is only to produce a banal aesthetic judgment.

Let us reconsider the passage of the *Satyricon* (already partially examined above)[18] in which Encolpius goes to visit a picture gallery full of marvelous paintings (chapter 83). He is spellbound by the suggestive power of the representations. They are all love-scenes from mythology. He sees Ganymede, Hylas, Hyacinth, all boys snatched away from a lover, as he himself was robbed of his beloved Giton by Ascyltus. He identifies with them and is transported by emotion. He claims that he has been struck by the faithful representation of the characters and their sentiments: (83.1–2) *cum ipsius naturae veritate certantia* and then *ad similitudinem praecisae ut crederes etiam animorum esse picturam*. But in fact he uses the objective realism of the representations only to abandon himself to his subjectivism as a lover in torment. So he falls victim to his own exalted projections; he confuses his own situation with that of the myth and transforms reality into fantasies. Reality will get its revenge on him shortly, when the old poet Eumolpus brings Encolpius down to earth by telling him the story (based on crude lust) of the Pergamene boy and, in so doing, demystifies the inflated amorous pathos of the narrator-protagonist.

For Encolpius' scholastic culture, the whole corpus of myth is simply a series of pathetic topoi, literary structures ready for dramatic recycling. Encolpius' perceptive framework, as we saw, is an anthologized literature, made up of exaggerated postures and gestures. In him the great models of literature are trivialized and made spectacular. This is the same process—of anthologizing, banalizing and dramatizing—which created pantomime at Rome, the theatrical form destined to dominate

18. In the first and second chapters.

the culture of the empire. Pantomime, which brought on stage the grand moments of mythology, was destined for a quite extraordinary popular success.

As a means of mass communication, but also as a popular and vulgarized text,[19] pantomime presented itself as the reduction or adaptation of the masterpieces of mythic poetry (epic, tragedy, choral lyric). Just recall that most of Virgil, not just the *Bucolics* but the *Aeneid* too, was immediately subjected to the theatrical transformation of pantomime.[20] Macrobius reminds us that the story of Dido in love was included not only in the figurative programs of painters and sculptors,[21] but was a favorite theme of the pantomime dancers (*Saturnalia* 5.17.5: *histrionum perpetuis et gestibus et cantibus celebretur*).[22] It is unlikely that Ovid's *Heroides* were really staged to the accompaniment of music and dancing,[23] but at base there is a similarity of taste between the melodramatic character of the Ovidian

19. The discussion of G. F. Gianotti, "Sulle tracce della pantomima tragica: Alcesti tra i danzatori?" *Dioniso* 61 (1991) 121–49, esp. 147–49, rightly sees the pantomime as the last chapter in the *Rezeptionsgeschichte* of ancient drama, because "lo spettacolo dei mimi e dei pantomimi raggiunge un pubblico vastissimo e continua a diffondere ... mitologia e tradizione." In this connection it is worth noting that when Lucian defends the pantomime (*De salt.* 35–67), he asserts that an actor should know the whole of world history, from chaos to Cleopatra, after which he briefly mentions an interminable series of myths. A selected bibliography on pantomime is found in Gianotti, 126, and in M. Bonaria, in F. Della Corte, ed., *Dizionario degli scrittori greci e latini* (Settimo Milanese, 1988), II, 1365f., s.v. Mimografi.

20. Donat. *Vita Verg.* 26; Servius *ad ecl.* 6.11; cf. Gianotti, 123 (with bibliography).

21. See F. Canciani, *Enciclopedia Virgiliana*, (Roma, 1984–1991), II, s.v. *Didone*, (*Iconografia*) 57.

22. Lucian (*De salt.* 46) notes that the Trojan cycle offers abundant material for the pantomime repertory, from the rape of Helen through the vicissitudes of the *Nostoi*, "down to the wanderings of Aeneas and the love of Dido."

23. Contrast the view of M. P. Cunningham, "The Novelty of Ovid's Heroides," *CP* 44 (1949) 100–106. (But the many explicit acknowledgments that the heroines are engaged in the act of writing seem to militate against their roles being dramatized and danced.)

letters and the strong pathos of the pantomime presentations of the imperial age.[24] Even the grander poets like Lucan and Statius were prepared to write libretti for the *fabulae salticae*— a mark of the powerful sway exercised on the public by this type of show.

Rapiebant me spectacula theatrica plena imaginibus miseriarum mearum et fomitibus ignis mei ("I was carried away by the theatrical spectacles in which I saw likenesses of my own torment and found fuel for the passion of my heart"). These words sound as though they could have been spoken by Encolpius, the mythomaniac *scholasticus* always ready to confuse the pathos of myth with the events of real life. But they come from a genuine autobiography: they occur in the memoirs of Augustine (*Confessions* 3.2.2). Years before, as a young *scholasticus,* he had discovered in the pantomimes the same great literary models that were taught to him at school, but in a more vivid form because they were enhanced by the melodramatic *mise en scène.* He records that he himself actually entered a competition to compose libretti for pantomime (*Conf.* 4.2.3) because he was so susceptible to the attraction of this kind of show. It is probable that in the culture of Encolpius also, pantomime was a form of literary experience particularly capable of producing a strong and pathetic identification since it too offered a degraded and banalized *tragôidia,* just like the contemporary novels of love and adventure. In its mythomaniac excesses, the character of Encolpius is to some extent the embodiment of current imperial culture.[25]

24. Dio Chrysostom in his *Trojan Oration* (*Or.* 11.7–9) polemicizes against the fashion for pantomime, denouncing the bad taste of the spectators, who rave in the theater about the representation of the great myths of the literary tradition and award prizes to "the man who is able to interpret the stories most pathetically (οἰκτρότατα) in verse and music."

25. As early as the Augustan age the popularity and success of pantomime was seen to be a corruption of the *grande ingenium* (that is, of the literary conquests which the generation of Virgil and Horace had achieved). Cf. Sen. *Suas.*

In any discussion of Petronian realism one passage of the *Satyricon* takes pride of place, and now we must confront it. This is the eight-line poem of 132.15.

> quid me constricta spectatis fronte Catones
>   damnatisque novae simplicitatis opus?
> sermonis puri non tristis gratia ridet,
>   quodque facit populus, candida lingua refert.
> nam quis concubitus, Veneris quis gaudia nescit?
>   quis vetat in tepido membra calere toro?
> ipse pater veri doctos Epicurus amare
>   iussit et hoc vitam dixit habere τέλος.

("Why do you Catos look at me with furrowed brow and condemn this work of fresh simplicity? The joy, not severe, of innocent discourse smiles, and whatever the common people do my honest tongue relates. For who does not know intercourse, who does not know the joys of Venus? Who forbids us to heat our limbs in a warm bed? Epicurus himself, father of truth, bade his pupils love and told them this was the purpose of life.")

For the most part scholars have preferred to see in these verses a direct intervention of Petronius, the author, who for once has chosen to come out of hiding into the open, to talk to his reader face to face. And they argue that he uses the first person here for nothing less than a vindication of literary realism.[26] So why weary oneself with interpretation, since the realism of the *Satyricon* is apparently given a direct theoretical analysis by

---

2.19: *Abronium Silonem, patrem huius Silonis, qui pantomimis fabulas scripsit et ingenium grande non tantum deseruit sed polluit.*

26. This was the position of Collignon (cf. 53: "il semble même qu'à un moment donné, Pétrone s'applique ouvertement à mettre son récit sous le patronage d'Épicure. Au chapitre 132 se lit une pièce de quatre distiques, où l'on croit entendre l'auteur lui-même s'addressant à ses lecteurs et en plus cette fois par la bouche d'un de ses personnages"), and it has enjoyed much favor; see, for example, the chapter "The Realism of Petronius" in Sullivan, 98–102 (132.15 is "an aside of the author to the audience, explaining part of his

Petronius himself? In fact the matter is not so simple. 132.15 is certainly an explicit metaliterary declaration, a programmatic manifesto of realism, if you like. But the speaker is not the author. The speaker in 132.15 is none other than Encolpius, the mythomaniac narrator. Why should the hidden author throw off his mask here, and *here alone?* Why in such a clumsy and intrinsically improbable way, and using such an Encolpian style of reasoning?

Let us quickly recall the context. In 132.9–11 Encolpius has pronounced an indignant speech against his offending member (*mentula*), which has just recently let him down in his second assignation with Circe; this is a melodramatic tirade typical of this narrator's mythomania. Then follows, by this mechanism of "rise and fall" of which I have already spoken at length, the apparent "awakening" of the narrating character. The reality of the situation seems to be taking its revenge: "But what am I doing? Talking to my prick? (*mentula*)" (132.12). *Paenitentiam agere sermonis mei coepi secretoque rubore perfundi, quod*

---

intentions and principles in a defense of the subjects of the *Satyricon* and his literary treatment of them"). See too, among others, H. Stubbe, *Die Verseinlagen im Petron, Philologus Suppl.* 25.2 (Leipzig, 1933), 152: O. Raith, *Petronius. Ein Epikureer,* 44 and "*Veri doctus Epicurus,*" WS 4 (1970) 138–51; M. Coccia, "*Novae Simplicitatis Opus* (Petronio 132.15.2)," in *Studi di poesia Latina in onore di A. Traglia* (Roma, 1979), 789–99: P. Soverini in *ANRW* II 32.3. (1985) 1772–79. E. Courtney, *The Poems of Petronius, American Classical Studies* 25 (Atlanta, 1991), 13, is more doubtful. While he thinks it possible to read these verses as a programmatic vindication by the author, he allows that it could be the narrator Encolpius who speaks these lines. The sententious phrase, *nihil est hominum inepta persuasione falsius nec ficta severitate ineptius* ("nothing is more deceptive than men's foolish conviction, nor more foolish than their false severity"), that follows the group of verses in our excerpts, could betray the author's preoccupation, as Courtney shrewdly notes, but in truth (even without taking the poor state of the text into account), it is impossible to deduce from the content of these verses who is responsible for their utterance. In fact the extreme sententiousness of the language suggests a return to the ironic author's mockery of the narrator Encolpius' untimely pretenses, since the scholastic protagonist is always ready to put on a pose of magniloquent authority.

*oblitus verecundiae meae cum ea parte corporis verba contu-
lerim* ("I began to regret talking like this and I blushed privately
that I had abandoned my sense of shame and bandied words
with a part of the body that more dignified people do not even
think about"). But he quickly finds a self-justification: Isn't this
how heroes behave when they are suffering in some part of their
body? Doesn't Ulysses scold his own heart? Don't tragic actors
accuse their own eyes (132.12–14)? Here the verses of 132.15
are inserted, beginning with an appeal to the Catos among his
readers, who would condemn a *novae simplicitatis opus.*

Already at this juncture we are no longer dealing only
with the declamation against his *mentula.* From the specific
provocation Encolpius passes to more general considerations:
(132.15.3–4) *sermonis puri non tristis gratia ridet, / quodque
facit populus, candida lingua refert.* After justifying his own address to his *mentula,* Encolpius turns to justifying—in the name
of something it would be difficult *not* to call realism—the presence of sex in his creation: *nam quis concubitus, Veneris quis
gaudia nescit? / Quis vetat in tepido membra calere toro? / Ipse
pater veri doctos Epicurus amare*[27] */ iussit et hoc vitam dixit
habere* τέλος (132.15.5–8).

There is a profound incongruity in the thread of his reasoning
which is perfectly appropriate to Encolpius' typical style of argument.[28] In particular vv. 5–8 are not only incongruent with
what immediately precedes them; as has been well observed,[29]
these last two distichs create a more significant incongruity,
which can hardly fail to arouse doubt in any reader who wants

27. *Amare* is the brilliant correction of Canterus for the transmitted *in
arte.*

28. The logical gap between the first two distichs and the last is obvious,
but this need not be a motive to postulate (with R. Beck) a lacuna between v. 4
and v. 5. Beck in fact has rightly insisted on the need to consider the excerpt in
context: "Some Observations" 50–54.

29. By C. Gill, "The Sexual Episodes in the *Satyricon,*" CP 68 (1973)
183–85.

to take these lines as a serious poetic manifesto of the author Petronius himself. Could any situation, in fact, be more inopportune for the rhetorical challenge, "Who does not know mating and the joys of Venus?" than a passage in which the subject is the impotence of Encolpius, his sexual collapse, his failure to know these embraces, not to mention "mating and the joys of Venus"? [30] Then again: could the author ever accept as his own the crude and vulgar definition which turns Epicurus into the eulogist of the "joy of sex" as the sole purpose of life? [31] Such a definition of Epicurean doctrine could only belong to the shallow scholastic culture of Encolpius. [32]

So even in this passage, as in the whole *Satyricon*, we feel behind the back of the mythomaniac narrator the ironic presence of the hidden author, who allows him to compose a pretentious declaration of his poetics as if he were a committed writer. Encolpius—this discredited narrator usurping the professional trappings of a critic—utters verses as a commentary on his sordid autobiography and he even employs the sacred terminology of literary criticism: *novae simplicitatis opus, sermonis puri, non tristis gratia, candida lingua*. A real treatise of literary criticism, to be sure!

Let us go back to considering 132.15 as a programmatic declaration of realism. How ironic is it? What is the hidden author trying to convey through it? It has been justly observed that the vindication of realism in 132.15 echoes the programmatic declarations of other writers of the silver age who stress their deci-

---

30. See also Slater, *Reading Petronius*, 129.

31. See above chapter 1, n. 24.

32. There are clear traces of a similar distortion of Epicurean doctrine in the repertory of rhetorical training; for a particular instance, cf. P. Kragelund, "Epicurus, Pseudo-Quintilian and the Rhetor at Trajan's forum," *C&M* 42 (1991) 259–75. In the same way Epicurean-Lucretian *voluptas* is reduced to sexual pleasure in the half-serious history of human civilization offered by Ovid in *Ars* 2.477f. E. Courtney, *The Poems of Petronius*, 35, notes that Epicurus wrote a Περὶ τέλους: Encolpius' words might be a crude and garbled memory of this work.

sion to deal with every possible aspect of human life (e.g., Juvenal 1.85f.).[33] Their aim is to describe reality (precisely *quod...facit populus*) rather than repeat the formulae of literary tradition (Mart. 10.4.7–10, discussed below).[34] To describe reality—that is the artistic goal of this kind of literature. But to justify his address to his *mentula,* Encolpius does not appeal to reality as much as to literature (to Homer and the tragedians), or rather he mixes and juxtaposes the plane of literature with that of "reality" (of everyday life, of sick men who quarrel with their defective organs). For Encolpius reality and literature are thoroughly confused.

In fact Encolpius has done precisely the opposite of what someone like Martial set as his goal: he has used literary formulae in life. There can be no realism in this, when reality is literature, when reality is trapped in literary formulations. It is realism to describe a sexual failure (with all the limitations of the concept of realism that we have discussed). But it is not realism to describe a sexual failure as an epic or tragic event. And it is paradoxical for the speaker to assert the realism of his own composition when he has been so completely detached by his mythomania from *quod facit populus*. Think, for instance, of Martial's famous lines (10.4.7–10), *quid te vana iuvant miserae ludibria chartae? / Hoc lege, quod possit dicere vita "meum est." / Non hic Centauros, non Gorgonas Harpyiasque / invenies: hominem pagina nostra sapit* ("What pleasure do you find in the empty follies of a wretched piece of paper? Read this, of which life can say: 'It's mine.' You won't find Centaurs here or Gorgons or Harpies: my page smacks of humanity"). Encolpius is certainly talking about real life, but about a life that is filtered—in its living, long before it is filtered in his narration— through the *miserae ludibria chartae*. This simply reinforces our

33. *Quidquid agunt homines, votum timor ira voluptas / gaudia discursus, nostri farrago libelli est.*
34. Cf. Gill, 183.

estimation of the hidden author himself as a "realist," in the sense that he represents with realism an anti-realistic narrator. But realism, for the hidden author, is a function of his irony.

On the other hand, how can one take seriously a declaration of realism expressed at this moment in the text, when the whole episode of supposed "sexual realism" begins with an encounter, at the metaliterary level, between a Circe and a character who, with natural spontaneity, has decided to call himself, adopting one of Odysseus' epithets, Polyaenus? And, it should be noted, a character who narrates an *opus* which is supposed to be characterized by *simplicitas* (yes, *nova*, of course, but a *simplicitas* so new that it is in fact extremely complicated). Moreover, the whole affair takes place in a city created and composed out of *literature*. For Croton is a hyper-realistic city, in the sense that it is not just a corrupt city but rather the corruption of a city. Better: Croton is the rhetorical topos of the "corrupt city," as it was codified in moral and satirical writing—a rhetorical topos that has gone and turned itself into narrative reality. That is why Croton is a hyper-realistic city, because it is produced by the literary illusion of reality; it arises not directly from reality, but from an *idea* of realism.[35] A realism of this sort, a realism of the second degree, like the kind that arises from the realistic literature of satire—how can this still be realism?

The reader anticipated by the text of the *Satyricon* is not a Cato, ready to furrow his brow before the narrative of an action. Only Encolpius can imagine him like this. The reader-as-Cato is only a projection of the mythomaniac narrator. But the author's strategy aims at a reader who relishes with irony the contrast between the wretched factuality of events and the exaggerated reelaborations of the narrating character. What counts in the excerpt of 132.15 is that the actual address made by Encolpius to the reader is no different from the address he

---

35. See the last pages of chapter 4, above.

has just directed at his *mentula*. Among the narrator's fantasies there was a *mentula* seen as a wilting cabbage stalk, but
also as a reluctant and disdainful Dido, or a dying Euryalus
(132.8.1–3: *ter corripui terribilem manu bipennem, / ter lan-
guidior coliculi repente thyrso / ferrum timui,* "three times I
snatched the dreadful axe in hand, three times more drooping
than a cabbage stalk, I feared the steel," and 11: *illa solo fixos
oculos aversa tenebat / nec magis incepto vultum sermone
movetur / quam lentae salices lassove papavera collo,* "She
turned away keeping her eyes fixed on the ground, and is no
more moved in expression by the speech I had begun than sup-
ple willows or the poppy's weary neck").[36] Finally, the whole sequence is interpreted as the vengeance of the god Priapus. Thus
a realistic erotic failure is distorted in an absolutely *un*realistic
fashion. The event is realistic, but the narrative is anti-realistic,
indeed this is its only narrative function. What interests the
ironic reader is the ways in which the real can be transformed.

So the reader-as-Cato is not the reader desired by Petronius
(the hidden author) but rather the one imagined by Encolpius
(the mythomaniac narrator). This reader is the product of the
narrow culture of the *scholasticus* protagonist, and is a severe
and rigidly moralistic reader. The schools had taught him again
and again that Cato, indeed *both* Catos (*Catones* in v. 1), repre-

36. In this collage of Virgilian verses the *mentula* stays silent, insensible to
Encolpius' reproaches. After the verses from *Aen.* 6.469–70 the reader expects the Virgilian citation to continue with 471 (Dido stiffens like a lofty
crag): *quam si dura silex aut stet Marpesia cautes,* but the text of the *Satyricon*
jokingly frustrates the reader's expectations: it is not the hardness of the
"rock" but the softness of the "poppy stalk" (cf. P. Fedeli, "Le intersezioni dei
generi e dei modelli," in G. Cavallo, P. Fedeli and A. Giardina, edd., *Lo spazio
letterario di Roma antica* [Roma, 1989], I, 394–96). Furthermore, it is very
appropriate that the *mentula* here is identified with the shade of the departed
Dido, since it was just the failure of his *mentula* that had taken Encolpius to
the shades (see, a little earlier in the text, 132.10: *hoc de te merui ut me in
caelum positum ad inferos traheres?*). Thus Encolpius' recovery in 140.12 will
be presented as a return from the other world.

sented the *exemplum* par excellence of Roman virtue. The Censor and the suicide of Utica were permanent residents of the rhetorical imagination, paradigms of every declamatory tirade in defense of morality. Seneca the philosopher could recommend to Lucilius (*Ep. Mor.* 104.21), *ad meliores transi: cum Catonibus vive!* Encolpius lets himself become obsessed with these two severe phantoms, complete with furrowed brow, who appeared before him just to censure his licentiousness. In Phaedrus, the apostrophe to Cato had still the air of a typical gesture in defense of his own literary work (4.7.21–22: *Quid ergo possum facere tibi, lector Cato, / si nec fabellae te iuvant nec fabulae?* "What can I do for you then, my reader, Cato, if neither fables nor plays give you pleasure?"); in Martial, Cato will be an almost obligatory topos to introduce his lascivious epigrams (Book 1 Praeface[37]). This bugbear is turned by the exalted scholastic fantasy of Encolpius into a real apparition, spectral and menacing: (132.15.1) *quid me constricta spectatis fronte Catones?*

The reader to whom Encolpius addresses this apostrophe in 132.15, the reader-as-Cato who is expected to be shocked by the realism of the narrative, in truth does not exist, or rather exists only in Encolpius' head. Naturally, there do exist concrete readers who offer misconceived (i.e. moralizing) interpretations of the text, but these interpretations are misconceived precisely because they try to correspond to the grandiose delusions of a person like Encolpius. The hidden author is smiling at Encolpius, but at the same time at all those who neglect the ironic strategy of the *Satyricon* and confuse the author with his discredited narrator, the *scholasticus*. All Petronius' Cato-readers, now and in the future, deserve no other interlocutor than Encolpius.

37. On this topos see M. Citroni, ed., *M. Valerii Martialis Epigrammaton Liber Primus* (Firenze, 1975), 3–12.

Abbreviations

Enn.		Ennius	See editions: Joc., V.²
Eur.	*Phoen.*	Euripides	*Phoenissae*
Hel.		Heliodorus	*An Ethiopian Story*
Hippocr.	*De Victu*	Hippocrates	*De Victu*
Hor.	*Ars*	Horace	*Ars Poetica*
	Epist.		*Epistles*
	Sat.		*Satires (Sermones)*
Juv.	*Sat.*	Juvenal	*Saturae*
Liv.		Livy	*Ab Urbe Condita*
Luc.	*De Saltat.*	Lucian	*De Saltatione*
	Icaromenipp.		*Icaromenippus*
Lucil.		Lucilius	
Lucr.		Lucretius	*De Rerum Natura*
Mart.		Martial	*Epigrammata*
Ov.	*Am.*	Ovid	*Amores*
	Ars		*Ars Amatoria*
	Ex Ponto		*Epistulae Ex Ponto*
	Tr.		*Tristia*
Pac.		Pacuvius	See editions: R.
Panyass.	*Heraclea*	Panyassis	*Heraclea*
Pers.	*Sat.*	Persius	*Saturae*
Petr.	*Sat.*	Petronius	*Satyricon*
Plaut.	*Cist.*	Plautus	*Cistellaria*
Plin.	*Nat.*	Pliny (the Elder)	*Naturalis Historia*
Plin.	*Epist.*	Pliny (the Younger)	*Epistulae*
Plut.	*Ant.*	Plutarch	*Antonius*
	Mor.		*Moralia*
	Rom.		*Romulus*
Polyb.		Polybius	*Histories*
Porph.		Pomponius Porphyrio	*Commentarii in Horatium*
Priap.		*Priapea*	
Prop.		Propertius	*Elegies*
Ps.-Long.	*Subl.*	Pseudo-Longinus	*On the Sublime*

Ps.-Quint.	*Decl.*	Pseudo-Quintilian	*Declamationes Maiores*
Quint.	*Inst.*	Quintilian	*Institutio Oratoria*
Sen.	*Contr. Suas.*	Seneca (the Elder)	*Controversiae Suasoriae*
Sen.	*Ben.* *Epist.* *Nat. Quaest.*	Seneca (the Younger)	*De Beneficiis* *Epistulae Morales* *Naturales Quaestiones*
Serv. Dan.	*Aen.*	Servius	*Scholia Danielis in Aeneidem*
Tac.	*Dial.*	Tacitus	*Dialogus de Oratoribus*
Varro	*Sat. Men.*	Varro	See editions: Büch.
Virg.	*Aen.* *Cat.*	Virgil	*Aeneid* *Catalepton*
Xenoph.	*Mem.*	Xenophon	*Memorabilia*
Xenoph.		Xenophon of Ephesus	*An Ephesian Tale*

Editors whose readings are discussed in the notes

Bücheler	F. Bücheler, *Petronii Arbitri Satirarum Reliquiae.* Apud Weidmannos, Berlin, 1862 (editio maior)
Burman	P. Burman, *Titi Petronii Arbitri Satyricon Quae Supersunt,* revised by J. J. Reiske. Janson-Waesbergii, Amsterdam, 1743[2] (Utrecht, 1709[1])
Díaz y Díaz	M. C. Díaz y Díaz, *Petronio Arbitro: El Satiricón.* Ediciones Alma Mater, Barcelona, 1968–1969 (2 vols)
Ernout	A. Ernout, *Pétrone: Le Satiricon.* Les Belles Lettres, Paris, 1922 (and many subsequent editions)
Fraenkel	conjectures proposed by E. Fraenkel and reported in Müller[1] and subsequent editions

Müller[1]   K. Müller, *Petronii Arbitri Satyricon*. Ernst Hei-
                   meran Verlag, München, 1961
Müller[2]   K. Müller, *Petronius: Satyrica (Schelmengeschich-
                   ten)*, Lateinisch-Deutsch von K. Müller und W.
                   Ehlers. Ernst Heimeran Verlag, München, 1965
Müller[3]   K. Müller, *Petronius: Satyrica*, Lateinisch-Deutsch
                   von K. Müller und W. Ehlers. Artemis Verlag,
                   München, 1983
Müller[4]   K. Müller, *Petronius: Satyricon Reliquiae*. Teub-
                   ner, Stutgardiae et Lipsiae, 1995
Pithou   P. Pithou, *Petronii Arbitri Satyricon*. Paris, 1587

Journals and Works of Reference

A&A   *Antike und Abendland*
AJA   *American Journal of Archaeology*
AJP   *American Journal of Philology*
ANRW   *Aufstieg und Niedergang der römischen
                           Welt*
W. H. Roscher, *Ausf.*   W. H. Roscher, *Ausführliches Lexikon der
  Lex. d. griech. u.   griechischen und römischen Mythologie*
  röm. Myth.
Boll. Ist. Fil. Gr.   *Bollettino dell'Istituto di Filologia Greca
  Univ. Padova*   dell'Università di Padova*
CB   *The Classical Bulletin*
CPh   *Classical Philology*
CQ   *Classical Quarterly*
Inschr. von Priene   *Die Inschriften von Priene*
LIMC   *Lexicon Iconographicum Mythologiae
                           Classicae*
MD   *Materiali e discussioni per l'analisi dei testi
                           classici*
Meded. Rome   *Mededelingen van het Nederlandsch his-
                           torisch Instituut te Rome*
MH   *Museum Helveticum*

QUCC	*Quaderni urbinati di cultura classica*
RE	Pauly, Wissowa, and Kroll, *Real-Encyclopädie der klassischen Altertumswissenschaft*
Reallex. f. Ant. u. Christ.	*Reallexikon für Antike und Christentum*
REL	*Revue des études latines*
RFIC	*Rivista di filologia e di istruzione classica*
RhM	*Rheinisches Museum*
SIFC	*Studi italiani di filologia classica*
TAPA	*Transactions and Proceedings of the American Philological Society*
WSt	*Wiener Studien*
Büch.	F. Bücheler and Heraeus, *Petronii Sat.*, 1922.
CIL	*Corpus Inscriptionum Latinarum*
Joc.	H. D. Jocelyn, *The Tragedies of Ennius*, 1967.
POxy	*Oxyrhynchus Papyri*
R.	O. Ribbeck, *Scaenicae Romanorum Poesis Fragmenta, Tragicorum Romanorum Fragmenta*. R.^{2} = 1871, R.^{3} = 1897
V.^{2}	I. Vahlen, *Ennianae Poesis Reliquiae*,^{2} 1903.

Bibliography

Abbott, F. F. "The Origin of the Realistic Romance among the Romans." *CP* 6 (1911) 257–70.

Adamietz, J. "Zum Literarischen Charakter von Petrons 'Satyrica,'" *RhM* 130 (1987) 329–46.

———. "Circe in den Satyrica Petrons und das Wesen dieses Werkes." *Hermes* 123 (1995) 320–34.

Alfonsi, L. "Petronio e i Teodorei." *RFIC* 76 (1948) 46–53.

Ampolo, C. Comm. *Plutarco Teseo e Romolo*. Milano, 1988.

Anderson, W. S. *Essays on Roman Satire*. Princeton, 1982.

Astbury, R. "Petronius, P.OXY.3010 and Menippean Satire." *CP* 72 (1977) 22–31.

Auerbach, E. *Mimesis: Dargestellte Wirklichkeit in der abendländlischen Literatur*. Bern, 1967⁴. (= *Mimesis: The Representation of Reality in Western Literature*. Trans. W. Trask. Garden City, 1957.)

Austin, R. G. *P. Vergili Maronis Aeneidos Liber Primus*. Oxford, 1971.

Avery, W. T. "*Cena Trimalchionis* 35.7: *hoc est ius cenae*." *CP* 55 (1960) 115–18.

Bakhtin, M. *Rabelais and his World*. Trans. H. Iswolsky. Bloomington, Indiana, 1984.

———. *Esthétique et Théorie du Roman*. Trans. D. Olivier. Paris, 1987.

Barchiesi, A. "Il Nome di Lica e la poetica dei nomi in Petronio." *MD* 12 (1984) 169–75.

———. "Tracce di narrativa greca e romanzo latino: Una rassegna." In *Semiotica della novella latina,* "Atti del Seminario interdisciplinare 'La novella latina,' Perugia 11–13 aprile 1985." Roma, 1986, 219–36.

———. "L'incesto e il regno." In A. Barchiesi, ed., Seneca, *Le Fenicie.* Venezia, 1988.

———. "Il Romanzo." In F. Montanari, ed., *Da Omero agli Alessandrini. Problemi e figure della letteratura greca.* Roma, 1988.

Bartoňková, D. "*Prosimetrum:* The Mixed Style in Ancient Literature." *Eirene* 14 (1976) 65–92.

Bartsch, S. *Decoding the Ancient Novel: The Reader and the Role of Description in Heliodorus and Achilles Tatius.* Princeton, 1989.

———. *Actors in the Audience: Theatricality and Doublespeak from Nero to Hadrian.* Cambridge, Mass., 1994.

Beck, R. "Some Observations on the Narrative Technique of Petronius." *Phoenix* 27 (1973) 42–61.

———. "Encolpius at the *Cena.*" *Phoenix* 29 (1975) 271–83.

———. "The *Satyricon:* Satire, Narrator and Antecedents." *MH* 39 (1982) 206–14.

Bernardini, P. A., and A. Veneri, "Il Gorgia di Platone nel giudizio di Gorgia e l''aureo' Gorgia nel giudizio di Platone (*Athen.* 11, 505d-e)." *QUCC* 7 (1981) 149–60.

Bessone, F. "Discorsi dei liberti e parodia del 'Simposio' platonico nella 'Cena Trimalchionis.'" *MD* 30 (1993) 63–86.

Bianchi, L. "A proposito del giudizio di Platone su Gorgia." *Maia* 6 (1953) 271–82.

Billault, A. *La création romanesque dans la littérature grecque à l'époque impériale.* Paris, 1991.

Bömer, F. Ovidius *Die Fasten,* I-II. Heidelberg, 1957–1958.

Bonner, S. F. *Roman Declamation in the Late Republic and Early Empire.* Liverpool, 1949.

———. *Education in Ancient Rome.* Berkeley, 1977.

Bowersock, G. W. *Fiction as History: Nero to Julian. Sather Classical Lectures.* Vol. 58. Berkeley, 1994.

Bowie, E. L. "The Readership of Greek Novels in the Ancient World." In J. Tatum, ed., *The Search for the Ancient Novel.* Baltimore and London, 1994.

———, and S. J. Harrison. "The Romance of the Novel." *JRS* 83 (1993) 159–78.

Boyle, N., and M. Swales, edd. *Realism in European Literature: Essays in Honour of J. P. Stern.* Cambridge, 1986.

Bramble, J. C. *Persius and the Programatic Satire: A Study in Form and Imagery.* Cambridge, 1974.

Branham, R. B. "Introducing a Sophist: Lucian's Prologues." *TAPA* 115 (1985) 237–43.

Brink, C. O. *Horace on Poetry: The "Ars Poetica".* Cambridge, 1971.

Brinkmann, R. *Wirklichkeit und Illusion.* Stuttgart, 1966².

Bücheler, F. *Kleine Schriften.* Leipzig, 1915 (= Osnabrück, 1965).

Buchheit, V. *Studien zum Corpus Priapeorum.* München, 1962.

Burkert, W. *Griechische Religion der archaischen und klassischen Epoche.* Stuttgart, Berlin, Köln and Mainz, 1977.

Cameron, A. M. "Petronius and Plato." *CQ* 19 (1969) 367–70.

———. "Myth and Meaning in Petronius: Some Modern Comparisons." *Latomus* 29 (1970) 397–425.

Canciani, F. s.v. *Didone (Iconografia),* in II. *Enciclopedia Virgiliana,* 1985. Roma.

Cataudella, Q. *Utriusque linguae. Studi e ricerche di letteratura greca e latina.* Messina and Firenze, 1974.

Cavenaile, R. *Corpus Papyrorum Latinarum.* Wiesbaden, 1958.

Cèbe, J.-P. *Varron, Satires Ménippées.* Vol. 2. Rome, 1974.

Champlin, E. J. *Final Judgment: Duty and Emotion in Roman Wills 200 B.C.–A.D 250.* Berkeley, 1991.

Ciaffi, V. *La Struttura del Satyricon.* Torino, 1955.

———, trans. *Petronio. Satyricon.* With Introduction by V. Ciaffi. Torino, 1967.

Ciani, M. G. "La Consolatio nei tragici greci. Elementi di un topos." *Boll. Ist. Fil. Gr. Univ. Padova* 2 (1975) 89–129.

Citroni, M., ed., comm. *M. Valerii Martialis Epigrammaton Liber Primus.* Firenze, 1975.

Citroni Marchetti, S. *Plinio il Vecchio e la tradizione del moralismo romano.* Pisa, 1991.

Cizek, E. "Á propos des premiers chapitres du *Satyricon.*" *Latomus* 34 (1975) 197–202.

Coccia, M. "*Novae Simplicitatis Opus* (Petronio 132.15.2)." In *Studi di poesia Latina in onore di A. Traglia.* Roma, 1979.

———. "Cena di Nasidieno e cena di Trimalchione." In R. Uglione, ed., *Atti del convegno nazionale di studi su Orazio.* Torino, 1993.

Coffey, M. *Roman Satire.* London, 1976.

Collignon, A. *Étude sur Pétrone.* Paris, 1892.

Comparetti, D. *Virgilio nel Medioevo.* Firenze, 1937 (reprint of 1896²).

Conomis, N. C. "Graeco-Latina in Charisius," *Glotta* 46 (1968) 156–84.

"The Construction of Reality in Fiction." Special issue of *Poetics Today* 5.2 (1984).

Conte, G. B. *The Rhetoric of Imitation.* Ithaca and London, 1986.

———. "Petronius, Sat. 141.4," *CQ* 37 (1987) 529–532.

———. "Petronio, Sat. 141: Una congettura e un' interpretazione." *RFIC* 120 (1992) 300–12.

———. *Genres and Readers.* Baltimore, 1993.

Cosci, P. "Per una ricostruzione della scena iniziale del Satyricon." *MD* 1 (1978) 201–207.

Courtney, E. "Parody and Literary Allusion in Menippean Satire." *Philologus* 106 (1962) 86–100.

———. *A Commentary on the Satires of Juvenal.* London, 1980.

———. *The Poems of Petronius.* American Classical Studies 25. Atlanta, 1991.

Crosset, J. M., and J. A. Arieti. *The Dating of Longinus.* University Park, 1975.

Cunningham, M. P. "The Novelty of Ovid's *Heroides.*" *CP* 44 (1949) 100–106.

Curtius, E. R. *Europäische Literatur und lateinisches Mittelalter.* Bern, 1954².

Della Corte, F., ed. *Enciclopedia Virgiliana.* Roma, 1984.

———, ed. *Dizionario degli scrittori greci e latini.* Settimo Milanese, 1988.

Denniston, J. D., ed. and comm. *Euripides Electra.* Oxford, 1939.

de Vreese, J. G. V. M. *Petron 39 und die Astrologie.* Amsterdam, 1927.

"Le discours réaliste." Special issue of *Poétique* 16 (1973).

Dodds, E. R. *Pagan and Christian in an Age of Anxiety.* Cambridge, 1965.

Dohm, H. *Mageiros. Die Rolle des Kochs in der griechisch-römischen Komödie.* München, 1964.

Dronke, P. *Verse with Prose: From Petronius to Dante.* Cambridge, Mass., and London, 1994.

Dupont, F. *Le plaisir et la loi: Du Banquet de Platon au Satyricon.* Paris, 1977.

Eden, P. T. *Seneca: Apocolocyntosis.* Cambridge, 1984.

Edwards, C. *The Politics of Immorality in Ancient Rome.* Cambridge, 1993.

Fairweather, J. *Seneca the Elder.* Cambridge, 1981.

Fantham, E. "Imitation and Decline." *CPh* 73 (1978) 102–16.

Fedeli, P. "La Matrona di Efeso: Strutture narrative e tecnica dell'inversione." In *Semiotica della novella latina. Atti del seminario interdisciplinare "La novella latina."* Roma, 1986.

———. "Le intersezioni dei generi e dei modelli." In G. Cavallo, P. Fedeli and A. Giardina, edd., *Lo spazio letterario di Roma antica.* Roma, 1989.

Feldmann, H. *Mimesis und Wirklichkeit.* Munich, 1988.

Ferrero, L. *Storia del Pitagorismo nel mondo romano (dalle origini alle fine della Repubblica).* Torino, 1955.

Fowler, D. P. "Even Better than the Real Thing: A Tale of two cities." Forthcoming in J. Elsner, ed., *Art and Text in the Roman World.* Cambridge.

Friedländer, L. *Darstellungen aus der Sittengeschichte Roms in der Zeit von August bis zum Ausgang der Antonine.* Vol. II. Leipzig, 1872–1873³.

———. *Petronii Cena Trimalchionis, mit deutschen Uebersetzung und erklaerenden Anmerkungen.* Leipzig, 1906² (Repr. Amsterdam, 1960).

Friedländer, P. *Johannes von Gaza und Paulus Silentiarius, Kunstbeschreibungen Iustinianischer Zeit.* Leipzig and Berlin, 1912.

Fry, P. H. *The Reach of Criticism: Method and Perception in Literary Theory.* New Haven and London, 1983.

Fuchs, H. "Zum Petrontext." *Philologus* 93 (1938) 157–75.

Fusillo, M. *Il romanzo greco: Polifonia ed eros.* Venezia, 1989.

———. "La citazione menippea (sondaggi su Luciano)." In A. de Vivo and L. Spina, edd., *Come dice il poeta. Percorsi greci e latini di parole poetiche.* Napoli, 1992.

———. "Letteratura di consumo e romanzesca." In *Lo spazio letterario della Grecia antica.* Vol. 1, *La produzione e la circolazione del testo,* Tomo III: *I Greci e Roma.* Roma, 1994.

Gabba, E. *Dionysios and the History of Archaic Rome. Sather Classical Lectures.* Vol. 56. Berkeley, 1991.

Galli, L. "Petronio e il romanzo greco." Dissertation, Pisa, 1992.

Gebauer, G., and Chr. Wulf. *Mimesis: Kultur, Kunst, Gesellschaft. Rowohlts Enzyklopädie.* Reinbek bei Hamburg, 1992. (= *Mimesis: Culture, Art, Society.* Trans. D. Reneau. Berkeley, 1995.)

Genette, G. *Nouveau Discours du Récit.* Paris, 1983.

George, P. A. "Style and Character in the *Satyricon.*" *Arion* 5 (1966) 336–58.

Giancotti, F. *Mimo e gnome. Studio su Decimo Laberio e Publilio Siro.* Messina and Firenze, 1967.

Gianotti, G. F. "Sulle tracce della pantomima tragica: Alcesti tra i danzatori?" *Dioniso* 61 (1991) 121–49.

Gigon, O. *Kommentar zum 2. Buch von Xenoph. Mem.* Basel, 1956.

———, ed. *Aristotelis Opera,* III, *librorum deperditorum frr.* Berlin and New York, 1987.

Gill, C. "The Sexual Episodes in the *Satyricon.*" *CP* 68 (1973) 183–85.

Goldhill, S. "The Naive and Knowing Eye: Ecphrasis and the Culture of Viewing in the Hellenistic World." In S. Goldhill and R. Osborne, edd., *Art and Text in Ancient Greek Culture.* Cambridge, 1994.

Goldknopf, D. "The Confessional Increment: A New Look at the I-Narrator." *Journal of Aesthetics and Art Criticism* 28 (1969) 13–21.

Goold, G. P. "A Greek Professorial Circle at Rome." *TAPA* 92 (1961) 168–92.

Gowers, E. *The Loaded Table*. Oxford, 1993.

Grondona, M. *La religione e la superstizione nella Cena Trimalchionis. Collection Latomus* 171. Brussels, 1980.

Gudeman, A., ed. *P. Cornelii Taciti Dialogus de Oratoribus*. Leipzig and Berlin, 1914².

Gwynn, A. *Roman Education from Cicero to Quintilian*. Oxford, 1926.

Hägg, T. *The Novel in Antiquity*. Oxford, 1983.

Harrison, E. L. "Was Gorgias a Sophist?" *Phoenix* 18 (1964) 183–92.

Haslam, M. W., ed. and comm. "Narrative about Tinuphis in prosimetrum." In *Papyri, Greek and Egyptian*, ed. by various hands in honour of Eric Gardner Turner. London, 1981.

Hauler, E. "Die in Ciceros Galliana erwähnten convivia poetarum ac philosophorum und ihr Verfasser." *WSt* 27 (1905) 95–105.

Heinze, R. "Petron und der griechische Roman." *Hermes* 34 (1899) 494–519. Reprinted in *Vom Geist des Römertums*. Stuttgart, 1960³.

Helm, R. *Lucian und Menipp*. Leipzig, 1906.

Herter, H. *De Priapo*. Giessen, 1932.

Holzberg, N. *The Ancient Novel*. Trans. C. Jackson-Holzberg. London and New York, 1995.

Horsfall, N. "'Generic Composition' and Petronius' *Satyricon*." *Scripta Classica Israelica* 11 (1991–1992) 122–38.

Huber, G. *Das Motiv der "Witwe von Ephesus" in lateinischen Texten der Antike und des Mittelalters. Mannheimer Beiträge zur Sprach- und Literaturwissenschaft* 18. Tübingen, 1990.

Hunter, R. L. *A Study of "Daphnis and Chloe"*. Cambridge, 1983.

Immisch, O. *Horazens Epistel über die Dichtkunst. Philologus Suppl.* 24.3 (1932) 136–37.

Jeanneret, M. *Les Mets et les Mots*. Paris, 1987.

Jocelyn, H. D. "Ennius as a Dramatic Poet." In *Ennius, Entretiens Hardt*. Vol. 17. Vandoeuvres and Genève, 1972.

Johann, H. T. *Trauer und Trost*. Munich, 1968.

Jones, F. "The Narrator and Narrative of the *Satyrica*." *Latomus* 46 (1987) 810–19.

Kassel, R. *Untersuchungen zur Griechischen und Römischen Konsolationsliteratur*. Munich, 1958.

Kennedy, G. A. *The Art of Rhetoric in the Roman World*. Princeton, 1972.

————. "Encolpius and Agamemnon in Petronius." *AJP* 99 (1978) 171–78.

Kissel, W. "Petrons Critik der Rhetorik (*Sat.* 1–5)." *RhM* 121 (1978) 311–28,.

————, ed., comm. and trans. A. Persius Flaccus *Satiren*. Heidelberg, 1990.

Klauser, Th., ed. *Reallexicon für Antike und Christentum*. Vol. 6. Stuttgart, 1964.

Klebs, E. "Zur Composition von Petronius' Satirae." *Philologus* 47 (1889) 623–35.

Knight, C. A. "Listening to Encolpius: Modes of Confusion in the *Satyricon*." *University of Toronto Quarterly* 58 (1988–1989) 335–54.

Kokolakis, M. *The Dramatic Simile of Life*. Athens, 1960.

Koller, H. *Die Mimesis in der Antike*. Bern, 1954.

Konstan, D. *Sexual Symmetry: Love in the Ancient Novel and Related Genres*. Princeton, 1993.

Korus, K. "Wokoł Teorii Satyry Menippejskiej." *Eos* 78 (1990) 119–31.

Kragelund, P. "Epicurus, Pseudo-Quintilian and the Rhetor at Trajan's forum." *C&M* 42 (1991) 259–75.

Krischer, T. "Der logischen Formen der Priamel." *Grazer Beiträge* 2 (1974) 79–91.

Labate, M. *Orazio: Satire*. Milano, 1981.

————. "Di nuovo sulla poetica dei nomi in Petronio: Corax 'il delatore'?" *MD* 16 (1986) 135–46.

————. "Il Cadavere di Lica. Modelli letterari e istanza narrativa nel Satyricon di Petronio." *Taccuini* 8 (1988) 83–89.

————. "Note petroniane." *MD* 25 (1990) 181–91.

————. "Eumolpo e gli altri, ovvero lo spazio della poesia." *MD* 34 (1995) 153–75.

————. "Petronio, *Satyricon* 80–81." *MD* 34 (1995) 165–75.

La Penna A. "*Me, me adsum qui feci, in me convertite ferrum . . . !* Per la storia di una scena tipica dell'epos e della tragedia." *Maia* 46 (1994) 123–34.

Létoublon, F. *Les lieux communs du roman: Stéréotypes grecs d'aventure et d'amour.* Leiden, 1993.

Levin, H. *The Gates of Horn.* New York, 1963.

Levine, G. *The Realistic Imagination.* Chicago and London, 1981.

Lintvelt, J. *Essai de Typologie Narrative: Le "Point of View", théorie et analyse.* Paris, 1981.

Lullies, R. *Die Typen der Griechen.* Königsberg, 1931.

Maltby, R. *A Lexicon of Ancient Latin Etymologies.* Leeds, 1991.

Marini, N. "Δρᾶμα: Possibile denominazione per il romanzo greco d'amore." *SIFC* ser. 3.9 (1991) 232–43.

Marrou, H. I. *Histoire de l'éducation dans l'antiquité.* Paris, 1965⁶.

Martin, J. *Symposion. Geschichte einer literarischen Form.* Paderborn, 1931.

Massaro, M. "La redazione fedriana della 'Matrona di Efeso,'" In *Atti del convegno internazionale "Letterature classiche e narratologia." Materiali e contributi per la storia della narrativa greco-latina* 3 (1981) 217–37.

Mayer, R., ed. *Horace: Epistles Book I.* Cambridge, 1994.

Mazon, A., P. Chantraine and P. Collart. *Introduction à l'Iliade.* Paris, 1948.

Meili Steele, H. *Realism and the Drama of Reference.* London, 1988.

Michel, A. "Rhétorique et poétique: La théorie du sublime de Platon aux modernes." *REL* 54 (1976) 278–307.

Montanari, F. "Gli 'Homerica' su papiro: Per una distinzione di generi." In *Ricerche di Filologia Classica II: Filologia e critica letteraria della grecità.* Pisa, 1984.

————. "Filologia omerica antica nei papiri." In *Proceedings of the*

XVIII International Congress of Papyrology, Athens 25–31 Mai 1986. Athens, 1988.

Morford, M. P. O. *The Poet Lucan: Studies in Rhetorical Epic*. Oxford, 1967.

Morgan, J. R. "The Greek Novel: Towards a Sociology of Production and Reception." In A. Powell, ed., *The Greek World*. London, 1995.

Müller, C. W. "Die Witwe von Ephesus: Petrons Novelle und die 'Milesiaka' des Aristeides." *A&A* 26 (1980) 103–21.

———. "Der griechische Roman." In E. Vogt, ed., *Neues Handbuch der Literaturwissenschaft*. Vol. 2: *Griechische Literatur*. Wiesbaden, 1981.

Nicoll, J. R. A. *Masks, Mimes and Miracles*. New York, 1931.

Norden, E. P. *Vergilius Maro Aeneis Buch VI*. Leipzig and Berlin, 1957[4].

Oldfather, C. H. *The Greek Literary Texts from Graeco-Roman Egypt*. Madison, 1923.

Otto, A. *Sprichwörter und Sprichwörtlichen Redensarten der Römer*. Leipzig, 1890 (= Hildesheim, 1962).

Pack, R. A. *The Greek and Latin Texts from Graeco-Roman Egypt*. Ann Arbor, 1965[2].

Palm, J. "Bemerkungen zur Ekphrase in der griechischen Literatur." *Kungliga Humanistiska Vetenskapssamfundet i Uppsala* (1965–1966) 108–211.

Panayotakis, C. *Theatrum Arbitri: Theatrical Elements in the Satyrica of Petronius*. Leiden, New York and Köln, 1995.

Parsons, P. "A Greek *Satyricon?*" *BICS* 18 (1971) 53–68.

Pease, A. S. *Aeneidos Liber Quartus*. Cambridge, Mass., 1935.

———. *M. Tulli Ciceronis De natura deorum*. Vols. 1–2. Cambridge, Mass., 1955, 1958 (= New York, 1979).

Pecere, O. *Petronio: La novella della Matrona di Efeso*. Padua, 1975.

Perry, B. E. *The Ancient Romances. Sather Classical Lectures*. Vol. 37. Berkeley, 1967.

Petersmann, H. "Petrons 'Satyrica,'" In J. Adamietz, ed., *Die römische Satire*. Darmstadt, 1986.

Preisendanz, W. *Wege des Realismus*. München, 1977.

Preston, K. "Some Sources of Comic Effect in Petronius." *CPh* 10 (1915) 260–69.

Priuli, S. *Ascyltus. Note di onomastica Petroniana.* Brussels, 1975.

Raffaelli, L. M. "Repertorio dei papiri contenenti 'Scholia minora in Homerum.'" In *Ricerche di Filologia Classica II: Filologia e critica letteraria della grecità.* Pisa, 1984.

Raith, O. *Petronius. Ein Epicureer.* Nürnberg, 1963.

———. "*Veri doctus Epicurus.*" *WS* 3 (1970) 138–51.

Rankin, H. "'Eating People is Right': Petronius 141 and a TOPOS." *Hermes* 97 (1969) 381–84. Reprinted in H. Rankin, *Petronius, the Artist: Essays on the Satyricon and its Author.* The Hague, 1971.

"Realism: A Symposium" In *Monathefte für Deutschen Unterricht* (1967), 97–130.

Reardon, B. P. *Courants littéraires grecs des IIe et IIIe siècles après J.-C.* Paris, 1971.

———. *The Form of Greek Romance.* Princeton, 1991.

———, ed. *Collected Ancient Greek Novels.* Berkeley, 1989.

Reeve, M. D. "Hiatus in the Greek Novelists." *CQ* 21 (1971) 514–39.

Reich, H. *Der Mimus.* Berlin, 1903.

Relihan, J. C. *A History of Menippean Satire to A.D. 524.* (Dissertation, University of Wisconsin, Madison, 1985) Ann Arbor, 1989.

Relihan, J. C. *Ancient Menippean Satire.* Baltimore and London, 1993.

Révay, J. "Horaz und Petron." *CP* 17 (1922) 202–12.

Ribbeck, O., ed. *Scaenicae Romanorum Poesis Fragmenta*, Vol. I, *Tragicorum Fragmenta.* Leipzig, 1897³.

Richardson, N. J. "Recognition Scenes in the *Odyssey* and Ancient Literary Criticism." *Papers of the Liverpool Latin Seminar* 4 (1983) 219–35.

Riikonen, H. K. *Menippean Satire as a Literary Genre, with special reference to Seneca's Apocolocyntosis. Commentationes Humanarum Litterarum* 83. Helsinki, 1987.

Rohde, E. *Der griechische Roman und seine Vorläufer.* Leipzig, 1876, 1914³.

Roscher, W. H. *Ausführliches Lexicon der griechischen und römischen Mythologie.* Leipzig, 1886–1890 (= Hildesheim and New York, 1978).

Rudd, N. *The Satires of Horace.* Cambridge, 1966.

Russell, D. A. "Greek Criticism of the Empire." In G. A. Kennedy, ed., *The Cambridge History of Literary Criticism,* I, *Classical Criticism.* Cambridge, 1989.

———, ed. *"Longinus" On the Sublime.* Oxford, 1964.

———. *Criticism in Antiquity.* London, 1981.

Russo, C. F., ed. *L. Annaei Senecae Divi Claudii Apokolokyntosis.* Firenze, 1985⁶.

Sandy, G. N. "Publilius Syrus and *Satyricon* 55.5–6." *RhM* 119 (1976) 286–87.

———. "New Pages of Greek Fiction." In J. R. Morgan and R. Stoneman, edd., *Greek Fiction: The Greek Novel in Context.* London, 1994.

Santelia, S. *Charition Liberata (P Oxy. 413).* Bari, 1991.

Schauenburg, K. "Hermes Ithyphallikos." *Meded. Rome* 44–45 (1983) 45–53.

Schissel von Fleschenberg, O. "Die Technik des Bildeinsatzes." *Philologus* 72 (1913) 83–114.

Schmeling, G. *"Quid attinet veritatem per interpretem quarere? Interpretes* and the *Satyricon." Ramus* 23 (1994) 144–68.

———. "Confessor Gloriosus: A Role of Encolpius in the *Satyrica." Würzbürger Jahrbücher für die Altertumswissenschaft,* N.F. 20 (1994/1995) 207–24.

Schöll, Fr., ed. *M. Tulli Ciceronis scripta quae manserunt omnia,* Vol. VIII, *Orationes in M. Antonium Philippicae.* Leipzig, 1918.

Schuppe, E. *RE* 19.2, 1561–2, s.v. φαικάσιον.

Scobie, A. *Aspects of the Ancient Romance and its Heritage. Essays on Apuleius, Petronius and the Greek Romance.* Meisenheim am Glan, 1969.

———. *More Essays on the Ancient Romance and its Heritage.* Meisenheim am Glan, 1973.

Shackleton Bailey, D. R., ed. *Cicero Epistulae ad familiares.* Cambridge, 1977.

Shero, L. R. "The Cena in Roman Satire." *CP* 18 (1923) 134–39.

Shey, H. J. "Petronius and Plato's Gorgias." *CB* 47 (1971) 81–84.

Slater, N. W. *Reading Petronius*. Baltimore and London, 1990.

Solmsen, F. *Electra and Orestes: Three Recognitions in Greek Tragedy. Med. d. Konink. Nederl. Akad. van Wet., Afd. Letterk.* 30.2. Amsterdam, 1967. (= F. Solmsen. *Kleine Schriften.* Vol. 3, 32–63. Hildesheim, Zürich, and New York, 1982.)

Soverini, P. "Il Problema delle teorie retoriche e poetiche di Petronio." In *ANRW* 2.32.3 (1985) 1772–79.

Stagni, E. "Petronio, *Satyricon* 94, 11." *MD* 20–21 (1988) 317–21.

Stanzel, F. K. *Theorie des Erzählens.* Göttingen, 1982.

Stark, I. "Strukturen des griechischen Abenteuer- und Liebesromans." In H. Kuch, ed., *Der Antike Roman: Untersuchungen zur literarischen Kommunikations und Gattungsgeschichte.* Berlin, 1989.

Stephens, S. A. "Who Read the Ancient Novel?" In J. Tatum, ed., *The Search for the Ancient Novel.* Baltimore and London, 1994.

———, and J. J. Winkler. *Ancient Greek Novels: The Fragments.* Princeton, 1995.

Stern, J. P. *On Realism.* London and Boston, 1973.

Stramaglia, A. "Prosimetria narrativa e 'romanzo perduto': PTurner 8 (con discussione e riedizione di PSI 151 [Pack² 2624] + PMil Vogliano 260)." *ZPE* 92 (1992) 121–49.

Stubbe, H. *Die Verseinlagen im Petron. Philologus Suppl.* 25.2. Leipzig, 1933.

Sullivan, J. P. *The Satyricon of Petronius: A Literary Study.* London, 1968.

———. ed. *Critical Essays on Roman Literature: Satire.* London, 1963.

Tarrant, R. J., ed. *Seneca Agamemnon.* Cambridge, 1976.

Tracy, V. A. "*Aut captantur aut captant.*" *Latomus* 39 (1980) 399–402.

Trenkner, S. *The Greek Novella in the Classical Period.* Cambridge, 1958.

Treu, K. "Der antike Roman und seine Publicum." In H. Kuch, ed., *Der antike Roman: Untersuchungen zur literarischen Kommunikations und Gattungsgeschichte.* Berlin, 1989.

Van Rooy, C. A. *Studies in Classical Satire and Related Literary The-ory.* Leiden, 1965.

Veyne, P. "Le 'je' dans le *Satyricon.*" *REL* 42 (1964) 303–309.

Villanueva, D. *Teorías del Realismo Literario.* Madrid, 1992.

von Koppenfels, W. "*Mundus alter et idem.* Utopiefiktion und Menippeische Satire." *Poetica* 13 (1981) 16–66.

Walbank, F. W. *A Historical Commentary on Polybius,* I. Oxford, 1957.

Walsh, P. G. *The Roman Novel.* Cambridge, 1970.

Wesseling, B. "The audience of the ancient novel." In *Groningen Colloquia on the Novel.* Vol. 1. Groningen, 1988.

Whitehouse, H. "Shipwreck on the Nile: A Greek Novel on a 'Lost' Roman mosaic?" *AJA* 89 (1985) 129–34.

Winkler, J. J. *Auctor & Actor. A Narratological Reading of Apuleius's The Golden Ass.* Berkeley, 1985.

Winterbottom, M., trans. The Elder Seneca *Declamations.* 2 Vols. *Loeb Classical Library.* Cambridge, Mass., 1974.

————, ed. and comm. *The Minor Declamations Ascribed to Quintilian.* Berlin and New York, 1984.

Woytek, E. "Varro." In J. Adamietz, ed., *Die Römische Satire.* Darmstadt, 1986.

Zalateo, G. "Papiri scolastici." *Aegyptus* 41 (1961) 160–235.

Zeitlin, F. I. "Petronius as Paradox: Anarchy and Artistic Integrity." *TAPA* 102 (1971) 631–84.

————. "Romanus Petronius: A Study of the 'Troiae Halosis' and the 'Bellum Civile'." *Latomus* 30 (1971) 56–82.

General Index

Accius, 40
Achilles, 1–2, 8, 12, 13, 51–52, 86, 99, 102, 150
Achilles Tatius, 18–19
Aeneas, 3–5, 8, 10, 12, 15–18, 39, 49, 51, 86, 94, 102, 150, 155
Aeschylus, 54
Agamemnon; son of Atreus, 1, 52, 127; character in the *Satyricon,* 2n2, 60, 118–120, 126, 132, 138, 173
Ajax, 131
Alcestis, 104
Alcibiades, 121
ambiguity, 23, 46, 68, 117, 135, 141, 146, 148, 164
Amor; see Love
anaphora, 62
Andromache, 104
Anthea, 91
Anthologia Palatina, 65
anthology, 6, 13, 28–29, 50–52, 85, 184
anticlimax, 117
antiphrasis, 34
Apelles, 14
Aphrodite, 101; see also Venus
Apollo, 14, 71
apostrophe, 62, 193–194
aprosdoketon, 94, 155
Apuleius, 101
Argive spectator (in Horace's *Epistles*), 42–43
aristocratic, 31, 70

Aristotle, 7, 53
Arnobius, 98
Ascyltus, 1, 4, 8, 79, 81, 126, 150, 184; significance of name, 39
Asianic, 66
astrology, 122–123
Atellan farce; see farce
Athena, 100; see also Minerva
Attic, 70, 149
auctor absconditus; see author
Auerbach, E., 176–177, 182
Augustan era, 41, 43n8, 50, 186n25
Augustine, 186
author; "hidden author" (*auctor absconditus*), 3, 21–24, 26–27, 29, 37–39, 44, 55, 59, 61, 67, 69, 72–74, 77, 81, 85–86, 90, 92, 101, 105, 107, 115, 117, 124, 138, 157, 169, 178, 181, 183, 188, 190–191, 193–194; supposedly expresses himself through characters, 64, 68, 129n33, 133n39, 187–190; his real voice, 22–23, 31, 65, 84

Bakhtin, M., 143–144, 146
Bal, M., 3
bathos, 9, 11, 14, 21, 100, 105, 113, 117
beauty of the heroine *topos,* 91
Beck, R., 12n12, 26n28
Bellum Civile (poem declaimed in the *Satyricon*), 71, 119, 140n1, 148
Briseis, 1, 8

Index Locorum

Designer: Barbara Jellow
Compositor: G&S Typesetters
Text: 11/14 Sabon
Display: Trump
Printer: Thomson-Shore, Inc.
Binder: Thomson-Shore, Inc.